STEPHEN LORCH

# Off *the* Top *of* My Head

## An Alphabetical Odyssey

D1190346

Printed in the United States of America
First Printing, 2013
ISBN 978-0-9898-8400-6
Library of Congress Control Number: 2013918892
J.W. Lorbek Press, 42 Patten Drive, Little Compton, RI 02837
www.offthetopofmyheadessays.com

# Dedication

The Lorch Mishpocha

*Past*
Karola and Hugo
For their spirit to face and conquer adversity

*Present*
Jane, Benjamin, Elizabeth, Kathryn
Odette, David, and Dennis
For their capacity to enrich everyday

*Future*
Isolde Mae, Lucien David, and those yet to come
For their ability to better the world

# Contents

# Foreword

Steve Lorch and I have been colleagues and friends for more than three decades. We share many common values, interests, perspectives, and even aspirations. As the reader will discover, most of the twenty-six letters in the alphabet (the organizing metaphor for this book) begin with a definition of the chosen word or words with a citation from the *Oxford English Dictionary*. In reading these definitions, it brought back memories of my frequent visits to the library at the University of Chicago to pull one of those heavy, well-worn, thirteen volumes off the shelf to discover the meaning of some word that was of interest.

I remembered turning to the word "symposium" on one occasion since it was part of the title for a new course I was teaching. The OED provided the following definition:

A drinking party, a convivial meeting for drinking, conversation, and intellectual entertainment: properly among the ancient Greeks, hence generally.

This definition was not exactly what I expected to find. A more appropriate definition, perhaps, was one of the historical quotations using this word found in a letter written by Lord Chesterton in 1748:

I take it for granted that ... your *symposium* [is] intended more to promote conversation than drinking.

This sentence could hardly capture any more succinctly the essence of this book! Challenging, engaging, fun, and productive conversations facilitated by Steve Lorch represent so much of what his life has encompassed.

And it was because of such conversations that so many of us who have had the privilege of being with him in many "taverns," metaphorically speaking, that we encouraged him to write about his experiences and philosophies, and to share stories. It took a life-threatening disease to provide the crucible for turning the idea of a book into a tangible product. This event has motivated this book, and more importantly, has led to a successful medical procedure dealing with his melanoma.

The reader, I'm sure, will be somewhat in awe of Steve's insatiable curiosity that is in full bloom within each chapter. Life for him seems to be like going to school every day. He continually learns something new about the world. He learns something new about himself. He continues to evolve his personal philosophy. The sources of his daily learning seem to come from everywhere.

People in his vast personal network have played for him, as he has for them, the roles of teacher, mentor, and long-time friend. They have come from different fields, generations, and locations. They include professors, medical doctors, ministers, rabbis, singers, artists, novelists, psychotherapists, not to mention a pickle vendor, a deaf classmate, an eighth-grade teacher, a radio raconteur, and his imaginary friend "Jack," to name just a few. Life brings many people into one's life; Steve has viewed the people in his life as a source of learning, and he has embraced them fully.

Books represent another powerful source of his learning. I rarely ask Steve the question, "How are you?" but rather I ask, "What have you been reading lately?" There's always some book that he describes with enthusiasm, and that I inevitably buy as a consequence. His recommendations have come from the hard sciences—thermodynamics, information theory, evolutionary biology, and computer science—and/or from the arts, philosophy, fiction, and the like. Similar to my asking Steve, "What are you reading?" these pages provide readers with an eclectic list of book recommendations, annotated with his comments about why each offers something worthwhile. Perhaps this list might even inspire readers to begin a lively virtual book club, hosted by the author of course.

Experiences that Steve has sought out have also been powerful sources for his learning. Taking the subway around New York as a young teenager opened many new worlds of discovery and meaning—museums, the public library, the Metropolitan Opera, wholesale meat markets, etc. He successfully tackled learning how to swim and ride a bicycle, both made extremely difficult due to being born with a physical disability. All of these experiences, which are beautifully described in the book, deepened self-awareness and the ability to listen and guide others in his role as an executive coach and management consultant.

In reading this book, I was reminded of the legendary advertising executive and educator James Webb Young. He was considered an important force behind the creation of the modern advertising industry. At his core, Young was deeply curious and a cross-disciplinary thinker. His short, 64-page book, initially published in 1939, continues to be printed and is a classic on creative thinking. As the first step in the idea-producing process, Young emphasizes the importance of collecting raw materials of two types—materials that are *specific* to a given assignment and those that are *general*. In reflecting on his framework twenty-five years after the book's initial publication, Young concludes:

From my own further experience in advertising, government, and public affairs, I find no essential point that I would modify in the idea-producing process. There is one, however, on which I would put greater emphasis. This is as to the store of *general* materials in the idea-producer's reservoir. I am convinced that you gather this vicarious experience best, not when you are boning up on it for an immediate purpose, but when you are pursuing it as an end in itself.

Young's framework and the perspectives offered in this volume could hardly be more aligned. In the chapter on "Frames," Lorch writes about his general approach when an organization's senior leaders seek his help on some issue:

No matter what the problem or challenge, I am most likely to have the chutzpah to suggest that there is another way to look at the situation, even though I may not at the moment know what it is.... I most often create a fresh perspective that is taken from an entirely different line of endeavor.

Those many connections with people, books, and experiences, earlier described, have provided Steve with an incredibly rich inventory of general materials. They derive from a wide range of academic disciplines. They include material that communicates with all the senses, not just the cognitive. As a result, a spotlight illuminates issues or areas ignored or never seen.

I frequently assign one of the twenty-six essays to a small group of students as the basis for discussion. I ask each person to consider a phrase, a sentence, or an idea that they found particularly meaningful and would like to discuss with the whole group. Some of the topics stimulated by Steve's writing have included:

- How small, seemingly inconsequential experiences often produce the most meaningful insights.

- Why is it that we often do not learn the right lessons from our experiences?

- The limitations of simple cause and effect models.

- What unconscious frames keep us from being open to new experiences?

- How can I live my life to maintain "elements of surprise, delight, and awe?"

- The importance of assessing and changing one's worldview as new experiences enter our lives.

- What keeps us from leading our lives in many more ways than the limited alternatives prescribed by parents, educators, and our culture?

- How could "Zabaglione and Zero" possibly be related to one another?

These discussions invariably continue longer than the allotted time—one idea leading to another in quite unanticipated and exciting ways. We have gone back to the same letter and text for a second time, and even then, there always seems more to discuss.

What do my experiences suggest for how to engage with this book? Clearly, this is not a book to be read linearly from cover to cover in one or two sittings. For me, this book stirs up those memories of days in the library enjoying the sheer physicality of the *Oxford English Dictionary*. Rather than thirteen volumes (plus the supplement), here are twenty-six "little" volumes bound together. I'll keep going back to these little volumes in a quite unpredictable order as my interests, needs, or moods change, read and then re-read some of these essays again and again. No doubt the pages will become somewhat worn.

When all is said and done, I want this book close at hand simply because it keeps me—and many, many others—connected to a truly unique, remarkable, and wonderful human being.

Enjoy.

HARRY L. DAVIS
York Beach, Maine
June 30, 2013

## Acknowledgments

Since these musings encompass a lifetime of experience, it seems fitting to acknowledge almost everyone I have known and write a brief description of their impact on my thinking. Since I can handle only one book at a time, I will forgo that temptation except to say that I have been privileged enough to have had very little differentiation between my personal and professional life. My good fortune of maintaining lifelong friendships and being retained for long-lasting engagements has blessed me with a multitude of intimate, endearing, and enriching friend-ships that have sustained me throughout my life and taught me most of the lessons embodied in these essays.

I am deeply grateful for all the messages of support and encouragement I have received over the years from my readers. I specifically would like to thank the marvelous individuals who have contributed to make this book a reality.

**Physically** I would not be here writing these words if Kel Cohen had not insisted that I consult Elof Eriksson, who performed the radical surgery that saved my life. My indebtedness to both these exemplary physicians goes beyond words.

**Emotionally** I was sustained and supported by my therapist and friend Joan Wheelis who helped guide me through this life-threatening episode and unrelentingly insisted that these essays be written.

**Intellectually** I need to pay homage to my role model and stim-ulating colleague Harry Davis. I now know how hard it is to write twenty-seven thought-provoking articles. I have witnessed Harry work equally as hard for each class presentation he offers. I estimate that number to be 2,700-plus over his fifty-year teach-ing span at the University of Chicago. He is the consummate inspirational teacher and provocateur.

**Spiritually** I have been privileged for the last thirty-five years to listen and learn, first from Beverley Edwards, and then from her successor, Richard DenUyl, in the pulpit at the United Congregational Church of Little Compton. They both are masters at communicating wise, meaningful, and important lessons clearly and concisely.

**Practically**  In my endeavor to match Beverley and Richard's ability to stay on message and to emulate Harry's impact, I have been extremely fortunate to have the editorial oversight of Henry Ehrlich who read and shaped each essay as it was produced. Casey Robinson's critical acumen expertly molded these disparate pieces into a cohesive whole worthy of publication. Arielle Eckstut and Joel Friedlander provided invaluable marketing advice. Your awareness of this book's existence is in all probability the result of Bruce Mason's unflagging promotional efforts.

**Artistically**  The masterful and talented Jean Wilcox produced the typographical elements, oversaw every aesthetic detail, and shepherded the book's production. The cover portraiture displays the creative forte of Channing Penna. The original 20x24 inch color Polaroid image in the Boundary essay is the handiwork of the singular Elsa Dorfman. Noelle Grattan is the discerning design maven of the website. Scott Kim graciously permitted the reproduction of his extraordinary calligraphy.

**Financially**  My successful Kickstarter campaign, with over 100 pledges to help assure this publication, has been overwhelming. My heartfelt thanks to every one of you for your incredible generosity.

Even with a cast of thousands I could not have sustained this effort without the loving support of my lifelong companion Jane. Her warmth, empathy, intellect, honesty, and unwavering love have nurtured me, our three children, Ben, Elizabeth, and Kate, and the countless others who are privileged to know her. Her ability to transcend the immediate, and always focus on the important—our love for each other—is a gift I cherish and hold dear.

# Off the Top of My Head

Upon landing in Washington on a late afternoon Boston shuttle in October 2007, I found several urgent messages on my answering machine from Iris Rubin, my dermatologist at Massachusetts General Hospital. I knew she wasn't calling to tell me my complexion was peaches and cream. The callback confirmed my fears. I had a melanoma (an aggressive skin cancer) on my scalp and she had made an appointment for me early the next morning in the melanoma clinic. When I asked to be seen a day later to allow my attendance at an important meeting with Jack DeGioia, the President of Georgetown University, she said "I will see you tomorrow!" Over the next few months I had a series of procedures that culminated in an operation by Elof Eriksson, the head of plastic surgery at Boston's Brigham and Women's Hospital, that literally took off a yarmulke-size portion of skin off the top of my head. (I am fond of saying that had I worn a yarmulke all my life that all this would not have happened, but that's another story.) Rather than leaving me with a monk's tonsure that would have gained me instant membership in the Benedictine Order, Elof rearranged the rest of my scalp to preserve my devastatingly good looks and saved me from a life of penitence and servitude.

During my medical encounters I kept a select group of family and friends apprised of my travails by sending out e-mail updates. Although my missives were straightforward descriptions of my interaction with various aspects of the medical system, the responses I received, and my reaction to them, was extraordinary. Within minutes of sending out an update my inbox would be flooded with replies, and I would be overflowing with emotion. The responses not only contained notes of encouragement, but also revealed information about my friends and their past medical encounters that I never knew. As a result, at the successful conclusion of my treatment I sent out the following e-mail:

Some Reflections on the Medical Updates

Although my last update stated IT'S OVER, I know that the procedure may only solve my current scalp problems. The possibilities of a further recurrence may be minimal, but still possible. I do hope that there will be little need for further medical updates. They got started by accident. I thought I would put together an e-mail list of close friends to efficiently report what was happening to me so that no one felt left out and heard about my condition second-hand. In addition, one of my mantras has always been *never worry alone*. (I have been lucky enough to make a good living by having many of you retain me to put that axiom into practice.) I never imagined the response I would get. The process quickly took on a life of its own. I was overwhelmed with instantaneous love and support that each message received. Within seconds of hitting the send button twenty to thirty messages would appear. As a result, my mind and spirit were completely taken up with the proximity and caring of all these wonderful relationships rather than the concerns with the condition I was reporting. It was such an affirmation of what is really important to me in life. It evoked and let me savor anew the very special feeling and experiences I have shared with each of you—some over many decades and some just for a few months. That happened not just the first time, but with every message. It gave new meaning to the words *social network*. (Most of us are too old to be active participants in Myspace or Facebook, but I am sure that must be a great deal of their attraction.)

So I want to thank you all again for making this journey such a fantastically positive experience for me. The whole in this case was truly greater than the sum of the parts. I also want to prod you to think of how you can use your social network as an asset. As I found out, it's right there when you really need it. It's too important and valuable to let languish and not actively utilize to make your life as rich as it can possibly be.

Many of the responding e-mails encouraged me to continue my reflections on my experience. A chord resonated within me. Throughout my career as an organizational development consultant I have been frustrated by the anecdotal nature of most management and leadership books. They rarely acknowledge or address the underlying psychological structures and behavioral characteristics that are the determinants of the limitations and/ or opportunities that truly shape any business entity. I have always thought an annotated dictionary of psychological factors that shape managerial practice was needed and would be useful. The encouragement of the e-mails caused me to think that perhaps writing about aspects of my illness on multiple measures might be a step toward realizing that idea, albeit in a different frame of reference.

My fantasy was that I would write a dictionary with annotated entries such as John Ciardi's *A Browser's Dictionary* or Herbst's *The Food Lover's Companion*. Both of these books limit their definitions and subsequent discussions to a paragraph, or at most a page. I have also greatly admired the insightful essays of Lewis Thomas and M.F.K. Fisher, especially her series of alphabetical musings for *Gourmet* magazine. For better or worse this book is an amalgam of all those ideas. The essays are alphabetical and in most instances elaborate on the definition of a word that has medical psychological overtones. I have found that once started, these musings often take on a life of their own and therefore do not conform to any of the formats I originally intended. The title of each essay has been chosen as a matter of whim. Either I thought I had something to offer about the topic or, in some cases, it was picked because I wanted to learn more about the subject. Most essays have a cursory discussion of an aspect of health care that relates to the word in its heading. My intent has been for these compositions to be descriptive, informative, provocative, light-hearted, and off the top of my head—like my melanoma.

I was again overwhelmed by the response to each essay as it was posted. Each entry seems to touch a different nerve for different people. Some love the autobiographical content and have written me about similar instances in their lives. Others are more interested in the theoretical aspects of the topics and have responded with thought-provoking comments. For me the journey has been very humbling. As I delved into each topic to find appropriate quotes or illustrations I have been in awe of the profundity of thought devoted to each subject over the years. Striking a balance between just giving up and trying to make a very complex and learned thing clear and concise has been an exhilarating and at times worrisome task.

Most recently my experience of deep connection was replicated by the response to the Kickstarter project I initiated to fund this publication. The pledges of support I received came from an extremely broad and often unexpected spectrum of friends. Over one hundred individuals committed to financially support the project, with each pledge invariably accompanied by words of encouragement and thanks. Again I was amazed!

This collection presents the essays in a modified form. They have been edited for consistency, length, and duplication. The most notable and striking difference from the original set is the distinctive typographical representation and description of each letterform featured to introduce each piece. The inclusion of these illustrations provides a small window into the history and importance of typography, and its rich central role in the domain of communication. The illustrations also offer an enlightening, and I feel delightful, aesthetic dimension to the book.

Every aspect of this journey has been unbelievably enriching and rewarding. I look forward to the unexpected twists and turns this process will take as these thoughts reach a wider audience. I cannot thank each of you enough for this truly incredible ride.

ABC
DEF
GHIJ
KLM
NOP
QRST
UVW
XYZ

# AL₽HAB*E*T

**Alphabet**  A set of letters or symbols in a fixed order, used to represent the basic sounds of a langguage; in particular, the set of letters from A to Z
—New Oxford American Dictionary

What has four eyes and can't see? (Mississippi). In the fourth grade I thought that was one of the cleverest things I had ever heard. Along with how many letters are in *the alphabet* (11) and where does a cart come before a horse (in the dictionary), I felt a true sophisticate. These so-called jokes, and too many others that I will mercifully spare you (knock-knock), along with puns, and radio skits (most notably Abbott and Costello's *Who's on First*), gave me my first taste of the enabling and entertaining power of language. My ability to remember, and still find childish pleasure in these silly gags, is indicative of the importance I attached to their mastery. Along with crossword puzzles, anagrams, and board games like Scrabble, the joys of "word play" with language, oral and written, are one of the great added benefits of acquiring and honing prodigious communication capabilities. Jokes and other linguistic sleights of hand are not necessarily dependent on the alphabet, but those that are seem to add an extra dimension and depth to their enjoyment.

Not all my early alphabetical skill development was devoted to sharpening my English and comprehension skills. I spent three days a week at Hebrew school learning a distinctly different alphabet.

Hebrew has only consonants, the vowels are small diacritic marks above or aside the letters, and it is read from right to left. The emphasis in Hebrew school was not on communication or literal understanding but on developing my ability to fluently recite the necessary prayers when I attended synagogue. To this day I can effortlessly read a prayer without a word-for-word understanding of what it means. The communication channel the Hebrew alphabet affords me is cultural as opposed to linguistic. My ability to participate in the Hebrew liturgy results in a powerful sense of belonging to a worldwide community with a common heritage transmitted through its ancient ancestral written language and alphabet.

Like the alphabets of the "natural" languages of English and Hebrew, there are a myriad of written and unwritten forms of communication. We converse in one of these forms from our first waking moment to our last breath. Our autonomic nervous system coordinates our body movements, keeps our sensory systems humming, and fires up our memory. Throughout our lives we monitor, refine, and improve the workings of our physical and cognitive abilities even though we are oblivious to how these internal neurological/physiological signals and codes are generated, transmitted, and deciphered. Our outward communications tell a different story. At first our vocabulary is innate and pre-verbal. Eye contact, smiles, coos, touch, facial expressions—abetted by a few cries and laughs—form the basis of our initial social interactions. As we hone our observational and other sensory skills, we are able to learn and pronounce a complex set of oral sounds. Consistently repeated in a uniform manner, these sounds are collected together into words, the basis for a language that becomes our primary means of communication and interaction.

Our remarkable oral linguistic ability has a genetic, a physiological, and an evolutionary basis. It sets our species apart. Although other animals have forms of communication, both oral and physical, they are limited and task-specific.

We speak and write and listen because we have genes for language. Without such genes, we might still be the smartest creatures on the block, able to make tools and outthink any other animal in combat, even able to think and plan ahead, but we would not be human.
—*The Fragile Species*, Lewis Thomas

Ultimately we can also learn a series of notations that allow us to record, transmit, and preserve our oral communication using a set of written symbols we call the alphabet. In contrast to the biological basis of language, alphabets are invented. Of the thousands of spoken languages fewer than ten percent have a written form. By providing a permanent record of interactions, events, and thoughts, alphabets enable the expansion of our already prodigious capability to communicate to an entirely new

level. The significance of their degree of importance is demonstrated by the demarcation of past events to be part of *history*
if they occurred after the discovery of writing, and *pre-history* if
they happened earlier.

The universal reach of the alphabet is far more pervasive
and powerful in shaping our lives than we realize. Its versatility is a *tour de force*. Its functionality goes well beyond the
set of symbols that make up a word. Reciting and mastering
the alphabet, along with numbers, is one of the first and most
rewarding achievements of great accomplishment we experience. It is natural that they become our primary choice to organize virtually anything we need to arrange, store, and retrieve.
Practically all dictionaries, reference books, telephone listings,
and works of nonfiction use the alphabet as the framework
to sequence and/or index their contents. Its reach and influence extends well beyond books. School seat assignments, file
cabinets, street names, subway lines, even sets of essays are
arranged alphabetically without anyone thinking twice about it.
An indicator of how deeply rooted the concept is embedded in
my psyche: it never occurred to me that using the alphabet as
the organizing schema for these essays was remarkable. Nor did
I think to write them out of sequence. The alphabet is an indis-
pensible part of our existence.

Although now hailed as a prodigious discovery on par with
the wheel and the extraction of iron, initially many questioned
the value of writing, including Aristotle and Plato. They saw it
as a threat to the real acquisition of knowledge and the discour-
agement of memory. In the dialogue *Phaedrus*, Plato expresses
his criticism through an exchange between King Thamus of
Egypt and the god Theuth.

It would take a long time to repeat all that Thamus said to
Theuth in praise or blame of the various arts. But when they
came to letters, this, said Theuth, will make the Egyptians wiser
and give them better memories; it is a specific both for the
memory and for the wit. Thamus replied: O most ingenious
Theuth, the parent or inventor of an art is not always the best
judge of the utility or inutility of his own inventions to the users
of them. And in this instance, you who are the father of letters,
from a paternal love of your own children have been led to attribute to them a quality which they cannot have; for this discovery

of yours will create forgetfulness in the learners' souls, because they will not use their memories; they will trust to the external written characters and not remember of themselves. The specific which you have discovered is an aid not to memory, but to reminiscence, and you give your disciples not truth, but only the semblance of truth; they will be hearers of many things and will have learned nothing; they will appear to be omniscient and will generally know nothing; they will be tiresome company, having the show of wisdom without the reality.

Isn't it ironic that our ability to preserve and access thoughts produced in 370 BC is because of writing? Evidence that writing took on a significant role in ancient cultures is exemplified by the famous Rosetta Stone (196 BC), on which a decree is inscribed in three different languages (Egyptian hieroglyphic, Demotic, and Ancient Greek). Arguments fearing the demise of true learning surfaced again with the invention of moveable type and the Gutenberg printing press (1450). There is a striking parallel in the present-day debate on the effect of the internet/ Google on reading, writing, and knowledge.

The kind of deep reading that a sequence of printed pages promotes is valuable not just for the knowledge we acquire from the author's words but for the intellectual vibrations those words set off within our own minds. In the quiet spaces opened up by the sustained, undistracted reading of a book, or by any other act of contemplation ... we make our own associations, draw our own inferences and analogies, and foster our own ideas.... If we lose those quiet spaces, or fill them up with "content," we will sacrifice something important not only in ourselves but in our culture.
—*Is Google Making Us Stupid?*, Nicholas Carr

There is no doubt that the World Wide Web and its ancillary technologies have permanently altered the way we interact and preserve our communications. It is has made English a global *lingua franca*. Predicting the future impact of such exponentially exploding technologies is fraught with difficulty. For example, in the past, sight and sound were ephemeral modalities. Now their production, transmission, and preservation are second nature and becoming increasingly dominant. At one extreme there is a fear that videos and voice recognition may threaten and completely make written communication obsolete. The counterargument states that if history is our guide their effect will be to noticeably enhance and strengthen our interactive skills and make writing an evermore central activity. Either outcome will dramatically change our lives by creating and causing us to learn new alphabets that are richer and more useful than we can possibly imagine.

The most memorable example I know demonstrating the enabling force and power associated with learning an alphabet is the moment in William Gibson's play *The Miracle Worker* when Helen Keller understands that the name for water is spelled W-A-T-E-R. The fact that her teacher, Anne Sullivan, uses her fingers pressed against Helen's hand to write the letters makes it all the more poignant.

Once I knew only darkness and stillness. . . . My life was without past or future . . but a little word from the fingers of another fell into my hand that clutched at emptiness, and my heart leaped to the rapture of living.
—*The Story of My Life*, Helen Keller

Alphabets are indeed miracles that we all too easily take for granted. Our roman alphabet with its symbols for the phonetics of speech is just one example of these powerful workhorses. Its versatility is demonstrated by its usage across a number of languages that employ very different vocalizations, and yet use the same symbols to mirror their speech. Even the click sounds of Africa, made famous by Miriam Makeba with *The Click Song* (*Qongqothwane*), have alphabetical equivalents. Equally fascinating is the fact that a multitude of different symbols represent the same letter in the alphabet. Letters formed as capitals, italics, lowercase, cursive, outline, etc. are all recognized as part of the roman alphabet, and yet they are all different. Our ability to discern and distinguish these fluid variations in penmanship and typography is truly remarkable.

Each piece by Chopin carries the unmistakable Chopin signature in its fiber, no matter how much it may differ in other respects from other Chopin pieces. A waltz, a scherzo, a mazurka, a polonaise, an étude, an impromptu—even a tarantella or a barcarolle—they all bear the same stamp. And the same goes for letters belonging to a single typeface. They are all cut from the same stylistic cloth—but how to characterize what that cloth is? . . . This is a near paradox—

to encapsulate in a fixed set of rules the essence of creativity that
allowed that designer to come up with all those ingenious curves,
twists, hooks, angles, cusps, and so on, that imbue the typeface with its
elusive yet undeniable artistic unity.
—*Inversions*, Scott Kim, foreword by Douglas Hofstadter

Unlike the roman letters, other alphabets do not necessarily
have a direct phonetic counterpart. Anne Sullivan and Helen
Keller most likely used American Sign Language, employing
finger configurations and gestures to spell words. Logographic
alphabets—hieroglyphics, Chinese, universal highway glyphs—
depict words and ideas using pictures representing an entirely
different mode of written communication. Braille, Morse code,
and smoke signals are additional forms of nonverbal language
transmission. Musical scales provide still another interesting
"alphabet" by representing serially made sounds akin to pho-
nemes that are not aggregated into meaningful words, although
they often define recognizable themes.

Letters as abbreviations and acronyms play a large role in
all aspects of our culture. IBM, AT&T, DoD, IRS, CEO, RBI,
PC, $H_2O$, and PBS are just a few alphabetical examples of
entities, activities, and things that are an integral part of daily
speech. Mnemonics in the form of a song, a rhyme, an acro-
nym, an image, or a phrase aid our recall of facts in a certain
order: Roy G. Biv for the colors of the spectrum, HOMES for
the Great Lakes, "Thirty days hath September" for the days in a
month, "My Very Educated Mother Just Served Us Nine Pies"
("Noodles," if you drop Pluto)—for the order of the planets.
Government bureaucracies are highly dependent on "alphabet soup" and in some cases it is impossible to navigate their
organizational structure or read their communications without
learning their unique jargon. More recently, the use of emoticons and highly cryptic abbreviations has become central in the
new ubiquitous world of messaging; Twitter is a prime example
with its restriction of 140 characters per tweet.

The diversity of these different alphabetic modalities
reflects both the richness and the importance we attach to our
need to clearly communicate. The words of a language and
their meaning evolve, defined by convention and the commonly
understood usage of their speakers. Unlike mathematics or

computer languages that are arbitrarily defined and adhere to rigid unambiguous rules of syntax and semantics, natural language definitions are more fluid and varied. Alphabets enable the organization and definition of the accepted meaning of the utterances and/or symbols that we employ when we speak. Dictionaries are the primary repositories for the written alphabetical equivalents to our speech. Classically they afford the definition, pronunciation, spelling, and historical roots of words. There are all sorts of alternative dictionaries serving the general public, highly specialized populations—musicians, physicians—and special needs—rhyming, slang, language to language, etc. Visual dictionaries are arranged around graphics that name the components of an illustrated object—a violin, parts of the human body, or a lightbulb—sometimes in multiple languages.

Reverse dictionaries list meanings that lead you to the defined word you can't remember. The size of an unabridged dictionary is a testament to our inventiveness in giving shades of meaning and subtle variations to our words. They may change over time, yet in order for language to effectively function, the general understanding of agreed-upon meaning and usage dictionaries provide is essential.

When I use a word, it means just what I choose it to mean—neither more nor less.
—Humpty Dumpty in *Through the Looking-Glass, and What Alice Found There*, Lewis Carroll

What kind of world would it be if we adopted Humpty Dumpty's lead and forewent consistent points of reference for the words or even the gestures we use? It would be unlivable. Society is predicated on our ability to agree on a set of common definitions for our words. The interpretation of these words most often drives our actions. The Constitution, the Bible, the Bhagavad Gita, the Talmud, and the Koran, are just a few of the written documents utilized for governance and guidance. They also serve as a historical record of the thought processes that are the foundation and frame of our worldview.

The written word affords us a unique ability to make extremely fine distinctions, to critically analyze, to infer, and to extrapolate the intended, and sometimes unintended, meanings recorded in documents. Laws and contracts attempt to be as specific as possible, while religious works, literature, and poetry are open to a much broader set of interpretations. No matter how carefully terms are crafted, alternative readings and potential disagreements are ever present. The attempts and acts of clarification are important and integral exercises in the ongoing human striving for mastery and knowledge acquisition. Talmudic reasoning, often called *pilpul,* serves as an example.

In the Talmudic method of text study, the starting point is the principle that any text that is deemed worthy of serious study must be assumed to have been written with such care and precision that every term, expression, generalization, or exception is significant not so much for what it states as for what it implies.... Confronted with a statement on any subject, the Talmudic student will proceed to raise a series of questions before he satisfies himself of having understood its full meaning. If the statement is not clear enough, he will ask, "What does the author intend to say here?" If it is too obvious, he will again ask, "It is too plain, why then expressly say it?" If it is a statement of fact or of a concrete instance, he will then ask, "What underlying principle does it involve?" If it is broad generalization, he will want to know exactly how much it is to include; and if it is an exception to a general rule, he will want to know how much it is to exclude. He will furthermore want to know all the circumstances under which a certain statement is true, and what qualifications are permissible.

—*Crescas' Critique of Aristotle,* Harry Austryn Wolfson, addressing the Talmudic Method

These incredibly discerning analyses, along with the similar critiques in disciplines like comparative literature are only possible because of the existence of written words with their careful crafting and subtle shades of meaning. Before our age of ubiquitous preservation of sound bites, the slower, carefully honed, persistent, written word was the only mode of accurate, long-term thought preservation. Composing a memorable written piece requires discipline, be it fiction or nonfiction.

When does a novel begin? The question is almost as difficult to answer as the question, when does the human embryo become a person? Certainly the creation of a novel rarely begins with the penning or

typing of the first words. Most writers do some preliminary work, if only in their heads. Many prepare the ground carefully over weeks or months, making diagrams of the plot, compiling CVs of their characters, filling a notebook with ideas, settings, situations, jokes to be drawn on in the process of composition. Every writer has his or her own way of working.... For the reader, however, the novel always begins with the opening sentence (which may not of course be the first sentence the novelist wrote.)
—*The Art of Fiction*, David Lodge

Although many languages do not have written forms, it is difficult to imagine a written language without speech. The use of nonverbal attributes—punctuation, spacing, typefaces, and deliberate rhythms—sets the act of writing apart from the production of speech; yet they are inexorably linked. (For a hilarious comedy routine on vocalizing punctuation in speech watch Victor Borge's "Phonetic Pronunciation.") Nowhere is the interplay of the spoken and written word more in evidence than the creation of poetry.

Poetry is a vocal, which is to say bodily, art. The medium of poetry is a human body: the column of air inside the chest, shaped into signifying sounds in the larynx and the mouth. In this sense poetry is just as physical or bodily an art as dancing.... I presume that the technology of poetry, using the body as its medium, evolved for specific uses: to hold things in memory, both within and beyond the individual life span; to achieve intensity and sensuous appeal; to express feelings and ideas rapidly and memorably. To share those feelings and ideas with companions, and also with the dead, and with those to come after us.
—*The Sounds of Poetry: A Brief Guide*, Robert Pinsky

The artistic and mechanical means for the creation, development, and production of letters have a vibrant history apart from the evolution of words and their meaning. Although the alphabet letters in combination form the building blocks of words, singly, with the exception of *I*, they are meaningless. To give Marshall McLuhan his due, although the letters are the medium to the word's message, their mode of presentation (color, size, weight ...) are often as important as the words they make up. As aesthetic entities these symbols have been an

endless source of mysticism, fascination, and creative energy in their own right. Calligraphy, illumination, and typography are just a few of the artistic endeavors associated with the production and lore of letters. Some of the most beautiful art in the world, especially in the Near East and Far East, is exemplified in letterforms.

Alphabets evolved from letters and hieroglyphics chiseled in stone, to the creation of incredibly beautifully detailed manuscripts produced with brushes and quills on parchment, vellum, and paper, to the highly mechanized printing devices of today. Until the introduction of moveable type, writing was an art relegated to a small, select set of scribes. As the means of production and accessibility expanded and changed, so did the shapes of the letters to make the tasks of reproducing them faster and easier. For example, cursive alphabets, wherein the letters are joined, enabled speedier and more effective utilization of quills, pens, and brushes. The result is we now have multiple forms of representation for and means to generate the same letter. These varied modes of producing letters also have their effect on content and style. Forced to use a typewriter because of failing vision, Nietzsche's prose "changed from arguments to aphorisms, from thoughts to puns, from rhetoric to telegram style," according to German media scholar Friedrich Kittler. As an aside, the typewriter is one of the few alphabetic instruments that is not in alphabetical order. The QWERTY keyboard was developed to slow down typists since the original machines jammed when they typed too quickly. An anachronistic legacy we live with to this day even though keystrokes no longer jam, and alternative layouts enable faster more accurate typing.

The most recent formidable communication change for most of us has been the introduction of computers and the ancillary capabilities of e-mail and messaging. Not only has interaction via the written word been transformed, but our awareness and utilization of typography and the elements of design has been heightened.

Reed College at that time offered perhaps the best calligraphy instruction in the country. Throughout the campus every poster, every label on every drawer, was beautifully hand-calligraphed. Because I had dropped out and didn't have to take the normal classes, I decided to take a calligraphy class to learn how to do this. I learned about serif and sans serif typefaces, about varying the amount of space between different letter combinations, about what makes great typography great. It was beautiful, historical, artistically subtle in a way that science can't capture, and I found it fascinating. None of this had even a hope of any practical application in my life. But ten years later, when we were designing the first Macintosh computer, it all came back to me. And we designed it all into the Mac. It was the first computer with beautiful typography. If I had never dropped in on that single course in college, the Mac would have never had multiple typefaces or proportionally spaced fonts.
—2005 *Stanford commencement speech*, Steve Jobs

Steve Jobs's fascination with and commitment to typography reflects a long and distinguished history. In his classic *An Essay on Typography*, Eric Gill muses on the challenge of the typographer:

One of the most alluring enthusiasms that can occupy the mind of a letterer is that of inventing a really logical and consistent alphabet having a distinct sign for every distinct sound. This is especially the case for English-speaking people; for the letters we use only inadequately symbolize the sounds of the language. We need many new letters and a revaluation of the existing ones. But the enthusiasm has no practical value for the typographer; we must take the alphabets we have got, and we must take these alphabets in all essentials as we have inherited them.... Everybody thinks that he knows an *A* when he sees it; but only the few extraordinary rational minds can distinguish between a good one and a bad one, or can demonstrate precisely what constitutes *A*-ness. When is an *A* not an *A*? Or when is an *R* not an *R*? It is clear that for any letter there is some sort of norm. To discover this norm is obviously the first thing to be done.

Typographers are concerned with designing letters that are both legible and readable. Legibility is defined by how clear, decipherable, and recognizable the letters appear, while readability refers to how well the typeface is suited for extended periods of reading. Calligraphers are equally interested in these aspects of letters, but often forgo them to achieve a higher aesthetic. They are constantly testing the limits of when an *A* is an *A*. One of the cleverest of these modern masters is Scott Kim. In *Inversions: Catalog of Calligraphic Cartwheels*, he tests and delights our recognition sensibilities in the extreme. He is able to accomplish prodigious visual feats by stretching, twisting, turning, and shrinking letters beyond normal parameters; yet they are still recognizable and become a great source of pleasure.

My favorite reaction to inversions, the one I strive for, is simple delight. There is something enchantingly paradoxical about being confronted with an undeniable impossibility, especially when the impossibility

occurs in a familiar domain such as a written word.... Certainly there is pleasure in having your senses tickled, but illusions also have a deeper purpose. Illusions are not mere sleights of hand, but singular revelations of the inconsistencies that are inherent in your perception of the world. Illusions are sleights of mind, for to perceive is to know.
—*Inversions*, Scott Kim

The power, versatility, and beauty of alphabets are one of the central underpinnings of civilization. Our enormous perceptual capabilities allow us to recognize a host of different expressions and manifestations of letters, words, sentences, paragraphs, and their resulting meaning in the language they produce. To ignore the history and understanding of the disciplines associated with their production is imprudent. Yet less and less time is being devoted in schools to the written word. I certainly wasn't a great fan in elementary school of the Palmer Method of penmanship, spelling tests, or grammatical diagramming of sentences, but in retrospect they afforded me an invaluable appreciation for the written word and the forcefulness of expressive language.

Any excursion into the multifaceted aspects of the alphabet should also acknowledge some of its inadequacies. Homonyms, antiquated spelling, and words with foreign sounds are just a few of our alphabet's deficiencies. But on the positive side, the ambiguity, redundancy, and inconsistencies that result from these flaws add immeasurably to the richness, vitality, and variety that characterize the English language. Lewis Thomas succinctly captures the resulting power, complexity, and creativity: "The great thing about human language is that it prevents us from sticking to the matter at hand." My alphabetical excursions in the essays that follow put me in violent agreement.

I almost forgot to ask: when does the alphabet have 24 letters? (When U and I are gone.)

# Off the Top of My Head

# APPEARANCE

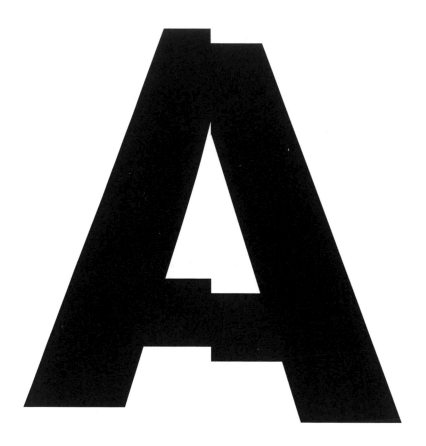

Outward aspect; external show; the presentation of oneself
—Merriam-Webster Online Dictionary

When I asked Elof Eriksson, my surgeon, what the negative consequences of his recommended procedure to rid me of melanoma would be, he answered that if all went well they would only be cosmetic. After explaining in detail what that meant, he asked how I felt about a possible radical change in my appearance. I replied I was sure that I would be able to handle that without any difficulty. It immediately brought to mind the following poignant memory.

Having been born with a physical deformity—a spastic condition on my right side making it smaller and weaker than my left side, a severe curvature of my spine, causing a small hunch back, and a ptosis, a drooping of my right eye lid—as a child I considered myself a physical mess. Add to that the need to wear leg braces, the fact that the late forties and fifties, when I grew up, celebrated the good looks of movie/sports stars, and the fact that society did not easily tolerate the aberrant appearance of physically or mentally challenged individuals, and you can see why I felt different, if not inferior. (My mother had to crusade to get me into the public schools, which at the time did not accept physically handicapped students.) My psychic struggle was to constantly come to grips with my "handicap" and find ways to minimize its undeniable effects on me and those around me. Being smart and personable helped, but these assets were never enough to compensate for my deeply felt and obvious physical deficiencies that hid the more attractive inner real me.

On many occasions I would find myself in a situation where I needed assistance with a task that I could not perform. When I asked for help, I often got a quizzical look. I would have to explain that I was "handicapped" and couldn't do what was needed. In many instances I would get a response akin to—Oh, I didn't realize (or notice) that you were handicapped. I can remember how furious these remarks would make me. With such a large percentage of my mental energy being devoted to compensating for my physical condition, how interested and/or engaged with me could this person be if he or she didn't even notice my most glaring and apparent characteristics?

Let me now fast-forward to my early post-college years. After spending five months traveling around Europe and growing a neat Van Dyke beard (see page 7), I returned to a job at Massachusetts General Hospital. I was employed as a "mathematician," helping to design research experiments and supporting those early adapters who wanted to use computers in their research. By a quirk, I was officially housed in the Psychiatry Department working primarily with Gardner Quarton on interviewing techniques, Frank Ervin on the neurophysiology of the visual system, Mike McGuire on language studies, and Peter Sifneous on the development of short-term psychotherapy. These interactions led to an increasing interest in psychodynamics and I eventually decided to be psychoanalyzed.

Not far into my analysis, my analyst, Sidney Levin, started asking me about my beard. What purpose did it serve? Was I using it as a mask for something? After several weeks of this kind of inquiry, I decided the beard was costing me too much money and so I shaved it. Now in the mid-sixties beards were not that common, especially neatly trimmed beards on fairly mainstream guys. So my beard had evoked rather strong (mostly negative) responses from many of my female acquaintances. I was therefore braced for an onslaught of remarks and unwanted attention about my newly shorn face. To my surprise I got a very mixed bag of reactions. My secretary immediately commented on its loss, while many of my closest colleagues never said a word. They were not shy and reticent types, so after a week or two went by I had to conclude they did not notice. I was then in the awkward position of not wanting to embarrass them by saying something after all that time had elapsed. Even stranger, when I met my present and former girlfriends, many of whom had been very vocal about their dislike for my beard, they had no comments to offer. I hypothesized that I could characterize the likely response by the depth of my relationship with the person: the more superficial, the more likely they noticed my clean-shaven face, and the more meaningful the relationship, the more unlikely they were to notice.

Once I came to that conclusion, I decided to test my theory. Julie worked at the MGH as a speech therapist and was quite interested in me but made very clear her dislike for my beard. My prediction was that if I paid a visit to her office she would not notice I had shaved. I was right. Forty-five minutes of chitchat and not a word about my beard. As I got up to go, Julie caught sight of me in the mirror on her wall and let out a cry of surprise. It was if she had been hit by a ton of bricks. When she saw my image, she immediately noticed that my beard was gone. Needless to say I had to explain how her lack of recognition for so long was a good thing, and that she need not be upset. Ten minutes later I was finally able to take my leave.

Well, that was an epiphany for me. Although I had formulated the theory I had not really understood the implications until that moment with Julie. People who cared for me really didn't see me, or my handicap, or my beard. They related to the essence of who I was, not the physical manifestation. All those people who had not seen my beard, or earlier in life, my handicap, were in fact relating to me as I had wished, to the inner me, not the deformed outer me. In many ways that moment with Julie changed my life.

Storyteller and poet Kevin Kling was born with a deformed left arm and then later in life lost the use of his right arm in a motorcycle accident. His insight, attitude, and philosophy are beautifully captured in his poem *Tickled Pink*, which really resonated with me and my experience:

At times in our pink innocence, we lie fallow, composting waiting
    to grow.
And other times we rush headlong like so many of our ancestors.
But rush headlong or lie fallow, it doesn't matter.
One day you'll round a corner, your path is shifted.
In a blink, something is missing. It's stolen, misplaced, it's gone.

Your heart, a memory, a limb, a promise, a person.
Your innocence is gone, and now your journey has changed.
Your path, as though channeled through a spectrum, is refracted,
    and has left you pointed in a new direction.
Some won't approve. Some will want the other you.
And some will cry that you've left it all.
But what has happened, has happened, and cannot be undone.
We pay for our laughter. We pay to weep. Knowledge is not cheap.
To survive we must return to our senses, touch, taste, smell,
    sight, sound.
We must let our spirit guide us, our spirit that lives in breath.
With each breath we inhale, we exhale.
We inspire, we expire. Every breath has a possibility of a laugh,
    a cry, a story, a song.
Every conversation is an exchange of spirit, the words flowing bitter
    or sweet over the tongue. Every scar is a monument to a
    battle survived.
Now when you're born into loss, you grow from it.
But when you experience loss later in life, you grow toward it.
A slow move to an embrace, an embrace that leaves you holding tight
    the beauty wrapped in the grotesque, an embrace that becomes a
    dance, a new dance, a dance of pink.

"When you're born into loss, you grow from it, but when
you experience loss later in life you grow toward it." So when
Elof said to me that the only downside of his procedure would
be cosmetic, you can understand why I had no hesitation in
going forward.

I was tickled pink.

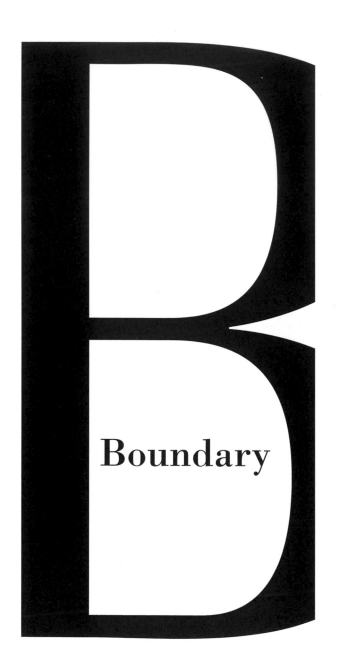

Boundary

A thing that serves to mark the limits
of something
—Oxford English Dictionary

Ask me to conjure up a boundary and
my first thought is the Berlin Wall. Now
that was a boundary. Yet it was one with
little or no effect on my daily life, except
to enrage my sense of fairness and
symbolize the abstract difference between
"them" and "us."

There are, however, other boundaries
that are much more meaningful and
relevant to everyday existence. As shown
by the OED definition, a boundary can be
anything that limits or marks any other
thing. At first blush, not a gratifying
explanation and yet the very ambiguity of
it is precisely why the idea of boundaries
is so intriguing to me. Since boundaries
can be "anything," in many instances
of our lives they tend to be self-imposed
or "nothing." I often erect boundaries
where none exist. Once established, these
boundaries often take on a life of their
own, requiring considerable negotiation
and effort within myself to cross or
eliminate them.

When I worked at MGH I ate lunch most days at the "psychiatry table" in the doctors' dining room. More often than not, Morrie Chafitz and Jack Mendelson would be entertaining the group by trying to best each other with the latest jokes they had heard. When they weren't telling jokes they were complaining that you couldn't get a decent pickle in Boston. So on one of my trips to New York City I decided to satisfy their, and my, hunger for a good pickle and went down to Rivington Street on the lower East Side. There I approached a pickle vendor on the street with several barrels of pickles and sauerkraut and asked for two jars of pickles.

"Your jars or my jars?" he asked.

"Since I have no jars I guess your jars."

"That's another nickel apiece."

"OK."

"Garlic or no?" he continued.

"Garlic."

"Old pickles or new pickles?"

"Well since I'm taking the pickles to Boston, I guess I'll have new pickles."

"You're taking the pickles to Boston?" he asked.

"Yes."

"You are taking the pickles to Boston."

"Again, yes."

"I never have been above 14th Street, but the pickles go to Boston," he said incredulously.

Now there is no doubt you can live a very full life in Manhattan below 14th Street. The fact is that there is a big wide world above 14th Street that is worth exploration. But we all have our 14th Streets that we do not cross for a myriad of reasons. I have always loved this story because it so graphically shows the restrictions we put on ourselves that even a pickle can transcend.

An even more meaningful example for me is the tale of how I learned to ride a bicycle. I never could ride a bike as a kid because I felt so unbalanced that I did not think I could balance on a bike. After running behind my daughter Kate's two-wheeler to steady her and teach her to ride, I started thinking about the physics of bike-riding and the interplay of angular momentum, velocity, acceleration, etc. I realized that balance was only a small part of the equation and decided I could do it and would teach myself to ride. Now getting on a bike for the first time at the age of forty-five was like looking down from Mt. Everest. My goal was to ride back and forth to the general store in town, a distance of five miles. It took me two years to do it comfortably. I was very gratified. (See picture on page 13.)

What I wasn't prepared for was the response I got when I told my story. It seemed almost everyone I spoke to had an unfulfilled activity or wish that they had put aside. I evoked a flood of emotion and in some cases resolve to learn to swim, play an instrument, or visit a country. Somewhere in my friends' distant pasts boundaries similar to mine had been erected, preventing the realization of a dream. Whether chronological, psychological, logistical, or whatever the reason, the barrier stayed real and was left untested.

Self-imposed limitations should be questioned by us all, and in more instances than not, they can be overcome.

My identity is made up of a core of beliefs. These are surrounded by thoughts, skills, and behaviors that are part of my "makeup" to facilitate daily interactions, but not necessarily viewed by me as the essential me. One of the earliest maturational steps is the constant testing to determine and define the fundamental question: who am I? Eventually I settle on a core that I believe is my essential self. The question is how do I, or we, modify our internal boundaries as we mature and grow wiser in the world? It may happen incrementally, or more deliberately, as in the case of learning to ride a bike. But I am also defined by external events—marriage, divorce, birth of children, change of job, earthquakes, sickness, etc. These events may dictate a change in my internal landscape that I haven't thoughtfully considered, or have actively avoided.

Will these new boundary conditions afford me the ability to leap forward to new and exciting prospects, to explore new ideas, to create innovations, and to give me a chance to grow? Or is it a boundary that restricts my behavior and represents scary prospects, turbulence, risk, and a possible affront to my self-esteem? How I respond is a mixture of genetic makeup and life experience. I believe the number of boundaries I perceive as opportunities versus those interpreted as barriers determine a good part of my ability to be successful and feel fulfilled. I also believe it is possible to change this ratio by developing the right set of attitudes, competencies, and skills when confronted with new boundary conditions. Every boundary demands a strategy to negotiate its shoals or to shift its dimensions. If I am clever enough I can constantly create interesting boundaries to address and, in turn, use these opportunities to learn more about the world and about myself.

This struggle is sharply brought into focus when suddenly I must confront and accept a new reality. Given a diagnosis of a life-threatening disease is such a moment. Is it an event that sends me into a tailspin, or do I use it to reaffirm who I am and how I view the real me? Part of the core "me" is that I am for the most part strong and healthy. When I am told I am sick, and may in fact be very sick, how is that message incorporated into my psyche and how does it redefine the boundaries that are me? Surely I knew I would eventually get sick and die, but it is a boundary I didn't want to cross until it was necessary.

Ernest Becker in his book *The Denial of Death* claims that everyone's whole psychic construction is taken up with the avoidance of that inevitability. So now that it is a reality, how do I deal with it? Is it a challenge that will potentially defeat me, or an opportunity to grow and enrich the years I have remaining?

The simplest answer for me was to think about how I would now handle the question, "How are you?" Once everyone close to you knows that you have an illness, they want to know: how are you? The usual glib answer, "I'm fine, how are you?" won't suffice. Examining the true, inner "me" is both too difficult and too detailed and time-consuming. Finding a middle ground that shared my experience in a meaningful way and yet did not overly burden me, or my friends, was a challenge.

I decided, quite by accident, to send out medical updates by e-mail. Everyone would be kept current of my condition and yet it provided some degree of privacy and control.

What followed was a revelation. I received a number of messages lauding my transparency and forthrightness that were again totally unexpected. I was answering the question of "How are you?" at a deeper level. A level that was meaningful for many as they struggled with their own thoughts on the boundary of health and illness. They found that my struggle resonated with their inner dialogue in a way neither they nor I could easily understand. I had shifted the boundary between us to enable a dialogue around issues that were relegated to a more private space in each of us. The connection between us became richer and deeper.

This experience has produced a new me, both physically and mentally. The physical transformation is easy to see. The new, inner me is a work in progress as my boundaries, beliefs, and appreciation of the possible continue to evolve.

Shalom

שלום

Original Polaroid Photo (20" x 24")
by Elsa Dorfman, Elsa@Photo.net

*Care*

To feel concern, fondness or affection
—OED

When I drive across the town line of Little Compton, Rhode Island, where I live, I can feel the tension flow out of my body. The ability to let the myriad concerns that clutter my "normal life" drop away and to experience the sweet smell of honeysuckle, the brininess of the sea air, the rows of stone walls, the acres of farmland dotted with cows that roll down to the sea, connects me to a more natural and more meaningful world.

But the physical environment is only a small part of it. In a town with no traffic lights, or even street signs, where the shopkeepers know me by name and I them, there is a connection and caring that is invariably lost in the fast-moving, exciting, industrial, efficient world we "normally" live in. Nothing brings that home more than the rare wail of the town ambulance. The city sounds of sirens are everyday background noise, easily ignored. In the country, you stop, take notice, and worry since it may well be a neighbor, and you most probably know the EMT caring for the unwilling passenger.

The special nature of this place is not an accident. It comes from the constant caring of a whole cadre of known and unknown individuals, both past and present. It comes from the people who run the thrift shop, the garden clubs, the historical society, the food bank, the town diner, etc. A prime example is the churches that periodically mobilize an army of volunteers devoted to performing random (and seasonal) acts of kindness.

In the fall they rake leaves and put away lawn furniture for the old and infirm. In the spring, a tradition has emerged where a team of sixty or more townsfolk spend a day transforming someone's home that needs work they cannot themselves afford. The esprit de corps, good fellowship, and genuine connections that result from these caring acts are in the word of our friends at MasterCard, priceless.

One of my sharpest memories of connection and caring took place well over thirty years ago. I was renting a small cottage on a farm, which had several other rentals. Among my neighbors were Bill and Muriel (Mac) Brown who lived across one of the fields. To celebrate the end of summer we all (Jane, the Browns, and I) were going to have a drink and go out to dinner on the Friday of Labor Day weekend. At five o'clock a call came from Mac that Bill was not feeling well and they needed to cancel. The next morning another call came telling us that Bill had died that night of a throat occlusion in a Newport hospital. Shocked, I threw on my clothes and started walking to the Browns' house to console Mac. Through the morning haze all I could see was the sky, the fields, and the stone walls. I was struck by the timelessness and universality of my mission. These lands were settled and cleared over three hundred years ago by the Pilgrims. How many thousands of others had crossed similar fields before me in the same circumstances to pay their respects and give what comfort and care they could. It struck a chord in me that I have never forgotten about the fundamental and deep-rooted importance of caring. That experience could not help but forge a bond between us. Mac and I still care for each other in a very special way even if we only see each other once or twice a year. I have other equally strong relationships, as does everyone. The challenge for me is how to keep focused on these timeless qualities and behaviors of caring as I am constantly pulled by the seemingly urgent demands of everyday life.

The same challenge, multiplied a thousand-fold, is constantly confronted by our health care system. Notice that care is part of the umbrella term we most frequently use to describe the institutions and individuals who look after our wellbeing. In fact many of the practitioners are now given the title of caregiver. In the '60s, everyone working at MGH, from the housekeepers to the department heads, thought they were at the best hospital in the world. We felt like a family that only had the good of the patients in mind.

An example of the extraordinary sense of purpose is illustrated by my memory of John Knowles, the General Director, standing at the entrance of the main building and wishing every employee that passed through a Merry Christmas. He knew almost all their names. He cared and we cared. Yet since I started working at MGH over forty-five years ago, caring has become a rarified commodity. No one says it better than one of my old mentors Bernie Lown in the preface to his book *The Lost Art of Healing*:

A three-thousand-year tradition, which bonded doctor and patient in a special affinity of trust, is being traded for a new type of relationship. Healing is replaced with treating, caring is supplanted by management, and the art of listening supplanted by technological procedures. Doctors no longer administer to a distinctive person but concern themselves with fragmented biological parts. The distressed human being is often absent from the transaction. . . . Human beings are represented as complex biological factories. A sick person is merely a repository of malfunctioning organs or regulatory systems that respond to some technological fix. . . . Not only contemporary philosophical notions of illness, but powerful economic incentives reinforce these views. Society places a much higher premium on technology than on listening and counseling. Time spent in the operating room or performing an invasive procedure is rewarded tenfold more than conversing with a patient.

I don't have any systemic fix for this reality, nor does Bernie. I don't think today's health care professionals are any less caring as individuals than they were in the past. The key insight Bernie offers is the lack of time to listen. Caught up in a system where productivity demands and economic constraints so outstrip supply, the time constraints on the caregivers dictate expedient, justifiable, efficient, depersonalized interactions. Few can take the time to listen to the underlying concerns and fears of the patient. Most just address their narrow, but important specialty area and quickly move on. An efficient throughput model for an institution, not a very satisfying model of care for a patient.

In his highly entertaining and influential book on innovation, *Men, Machines, and Modern Times*, Elting E. Morison muses eloquently on the problem facing our modern culture:

The system of ideas, energy, and machinery we have created to serve some essential human needs, it now appears, may, if not sufficiently tended, shrink human behavior to the restricted set of needs the system was designed to satisfy. ... Put even more simply, as these mechanisms steadily increase their power and scale, the tendency is to fit men into the machinery rather than to fit the machinery into the contours of the human situation.

Over my years in working with major health care providers I have been privileged to witness extraordinary caring in spite of these dehumanizing forces. Although my experience with each of these clinicians is very diverse, they all possess a powerful common element—their ability to really take the time to listen and care. I would like to briefly share my experience working with four exemplary practitioners.

I was in a therapeutic relationship for twenty-five years with Jean Baker Miller. I referred myself to her after I read her seminal book *Toward a New Psychology of Women*. The opening sentence reads:

Throughout this book we will struggle with the issue of difference: what do people do to people who are different from them and why?

The book has become a classic and Jean's work with her colleagues at the Stone Center at Wellesley has transformed the understanding of the psychological development of women and in many ways how psychotherapy in general is practiced. What spoke to me when I first read the book was how Jean's insights about women's behavior and subsequent treatment applied so directly to me as a "handicapped" person. (At our first session I discovered that as a young child she had been struck with polio. That clearly solidified our relationship.) Jean's great insights were to understand and celebrate the psychological strength women derived from their connections to others. That caring for and empowering others were not signs of weakness, but traits that needed to be honored and reinforced. Toward that end she and her associates developed relationship therapy in which connecting, empowering, caring, listening, and empathy replace the classic objective, somewhat aloof, mode of classic psychodynamic therapeutic interaction. Her *New York Times* obituary emphasized her remarkable sensitivity to others and extraordinary listening capacity.

I have already referenced Bernie Lown's insights on the health care system. I worked with Bernie on a number of projects early in my career. I played a small part in organizing Physicians for Social Responsibility (a successor organization, International Physicians for the Prevention of Nuclear War—also founded by Lown—won the Nobel Peace Prize), and I attempted to develop an information collection system for the first cardiac intensive care unit started by him at the Peter Bent Brigham Hospital. In the latter role Bernie insisted I make rounds with him to understand the salient data elements needed to properly capture a patient's condition. It was there that I learned, along with many other aspects of clinical care, how important it was to take the time to listen. To listen not only with my ears, but also with every available sense— touch, smell, vision. Bernie's book, cited above, gives innumerable examples of his mastery of true caregiving and how his total involvement with his patients and their families made him a great physician. In the end I couldn't design and build a system that could capture the multi-dimensional picture Bernie painted of each case. What I was able to do was to understand the true nature of first-rate care as practiced by a master.

John Stoeckle is the doctor's doctor. He has been my friend, colleague, and until a few years ago my personal physician throughout my entire professional life. The '60s saw the emergence of research and specialty medicine as the preferred channel for career development and recognition. Yet John's major focus never wavered from providing the best primary clinical care and teaching others to follow his example. His groundbreaking work on how different ethnic groups perceive illness and how to utilize those insights in their care was a major milestone. He was one of the first to employ audio and video recording to teach medical students how to properly conduct an interview and take a clinical history. As a result he could dramatically show how—although they heard all the answers to their questions—they hadn't really listened and utilized the wealth of pertinent information the patient offered, often nonverbally. John still actively provides an inspiration to his colleagues working at the MGH Center for Primary Care Innovation established in his name.

I never worked directly with Bill Cromie when he was a world-class pediatric urologist. Our relationship started when Bill hired me as his executive coach when he became the CEO of a major health insurance plan in Albany, New York. He had never run a large complex organization. It would be an understatement to say the plan was in need of major surgery, and it was not the kind he knew how to perform. By promoting from within and recruiting good people he was able to successfully turn the plan around after a few years. But all the good people in the world would not have helped had Bill not been able to energize the organization with his deep personal commitment. He has devoted himself to providing the best possible care to the subscribers, the most physician-friendly environment to the plan's practitioners, and the best possible place for employees to work. Like John Knowles at MGH, Bill can greet almost all his employees by name, having listened to them at a pizza party or at a company outing. His exemplary caring skills, honed as a physician, have been transformed and redirected to make him a world-class CEO.

These people are artists of the first rank. They are on a par with Ella, Yo-Yo Ma, Rembrandt, etc. But like these artists their performance requires more than innate skill. It requires concerted practice and patience to take the time to listen with all available senses, including what Theodor Reik calls "the third ear." They glean and discern the subtlest nuances to gain singular insights from what they see, hear, and touch when they encounter another person. They have honed these skills in the service of care.

The fact is that you and I can care as deeply if we allow ourselves to take the time to express our feelings. The wave of caring I received from the e-mails of support was, and still is, incredible to me. Many responses were in the form of a thank you for my taking the time to keep everyone up to speed. In turn, each response caused me to recall a moment in time of caring and connection I had shared—a delicious pizza in a Tuscan hill town, a meal on a tiny Aegean island, a quiet walk on the beach at sunset, a surprise book or box of chocolates in the mail. The experience taught me it doesn't take much to really connect and care. I, and you, just have to make and take the time to do it, and then learn to savor the moments.

My feelings about Little Compton are not very different from many other descriptions I have heard from those who have similar retreats or have just returned from a vacation. I believe that results from the preservation, or at the least the observation, of an earlier sense of time in these places. Rather than multitasking, instant messaging, racing to the airport, etc., I am afforded an environment that doesn't let the urgent crowd out the important. When I am there I take the time to really listen and care. The random acts of kindness mentioned above are great examples. These events don't just happen. Getting sixty people to descend on a house to effectively do a major renovation in a day takes an enormous amount of pre-planning and coordination to set realistic goals, coordinate the supplies, arrange for the lunches and drinks, etc. Yes it is nice to have a place like Little Compton where the distractions are few, and the important dimensions of life seem accessible, but anywhere will do. Barbara Schildkrout's recent story in the *New York Times* of taking the time and caring enough to speak to an unknown woman next to her in a theater about her observation that she might have a melanoma is a good example that it can happen anywhere and at anytime.

When I was told I had a life-threatening disease, my mind focused like a laser on the finite reality of my existence and what was of critical importance to me. Somehow I am now able to find the time to pay attention to lots of things I have previously taken for granted. (I can tell you since this melanoma encounter, the attention I give every skin blemish is microscopic.) I'm sure the same is true of every person who has had to face a major health crisis. My advice is don't wait until you *must* pay attention to the inner you to calibrate your priorities. On a deep level you already know what you *really* need and cherish. The required level of awareness is within each of us. All it takes is intensive listening to what your body and your mind are telling you. As your social network is the means to connect and care for your friends, your neural network is the pathway to assure your wellness. Without first truly taking care of yourself it is very difficult to take care of others. Choose to do it now! It's easy to let the seemingly urgent derail what you know is truly important. You just have to make and take the time to carefully listen and act.

Take care and be well.

DISCRIMINATION

The ability to observe accurately and make fine distinctions;
perceptiveness, acuity, good judgment or taste
—OED

I have always been fascinated by my ability to recognize Ella
Fitzgerald. Although I love the way she turns a phrase, impro-
vises scat, and produces the most melodic lines, it is my instant
identification of her, as opposed to a similar performer (Sarah
Vaughn), that awes me. When I say instantly, I mean that just
hearing the smallest snippet of music as I scan the dial or start
a CD lets me absolutely identify her voice. The important thing
is that I am not alone. We all have the ability to immediately
know who it is when we hear a favorite. Whether it is Ella, Billie
Holliday, Elvis, Maria Callas, Arthur Rubenstein, or Sting, the
trait of hearing a split second of music and being able to recognize the artist is something most people can do for a large
number of their favorite entertainers. Further, this type of discrimination is not confined to music. In a surprisingly large
number of situations we have an ability to tell the difference
between very, very subtle variations in voice, body language,
snow conditions . . . you name it!

How many shades of red can most women distinguish when choosing just the right nail polish or lipstick? Is it Pepsi or Coke? At the crack of a bat the centerfielder charges to the spot the ball will fall even though the computation of the relative acceleration, velocity, and direction of the ball and how fast she must run to make the catch is a prodigious feat that requires the interplay of a myriad of complex cognitive processes. Yet these actions happen so quickly they defy understanding. The wonder we experience as spectators when presented with such miracles is a large part of our enjoyment.

Equally amazing are the actions we take as a result of the slightest stimuli. A mosquito lands on the back of our neck. How much pressure can an insect of that size exert? Yet in an instant we not only know it has happened, but we know where the mosquito is, even though we can't see it. If you let yourself think about your abilities to discriminate you will be amazed at the number of things you are able to perceive and how quickly you are able to react.

Many of these distinctions are learned. Others are more likely innate (the presence of a mosquito). Some of our responses are conscious while others are part of our makeup. Yet we are almost completely oblivious to both types of reaction. Many years ago a study published in *Scientific American* reported the importance of eye pupil dilation on the trustworthiness attributed to a person by another. Taking the same portrait photograph of a person, the experimenters retouched the width of the pupils in the subject's eyes making them smaller or larger by about one millimeter. People who were shown these photographs attributed traits of meanness, untrustworthiness, and anger to the likeness with the smaller pupil width. The larger pupils were rated as honest, open, fun loving, etc. Are we aware of measuring someone's pupils when we meet them to figure out what kind of person they are? It would never enter my mind. Yet these very subtle distinctions drive much of our behavior, whether we know it or not. With some work we can learn to be more cognizant of the subtle differences we notice. Still, other minute acts of discrimination are so obscure that we will probably never be aware of them, even though they are at work all the time. To the extent we can sharpen our abilities to recognize distinctions that are important to each one of us, we can greatly improve our interactions with others in all aspects of our lives, personal and professional.

The need for detail varies greatly among individuals, but very few people, even among the psychotic, can live without structuring and explaining to themselves what is going on around them. Some of these explanations are accurate, some are magical, some are wishful, and some are just wrong, but they are always there. They are part of the human condition and they are necessary for us to function effectively. The ability to share these explanations and to act in accordance with them is the glue that holds our society and our social discourse together. On the most explicit level these explanations lead to laws, commandments, and other dogma. More hidden are the values, beliefs, and myths that make up our cultures. Like the complete genetic code being part of each cell in an organism, all the layers of explanation are present in every situation we encounter. Most of us assume the explanations we hold are also common to others and therefore provide a clear channel for communication. At the same time, as we get to know a person or a situation better, we also start to modify our assumptions and act accordingly. Sometimes we change our behavior; sometimes we try to change others. Sometimes we simply accept and honor the differences. In any case no one or no organization completely shares a unique set of explanations. To complicate the matter even further no one has the ability to know exactly what explanations, beliefs, values, motivations, myths, etc., they hold. The differences are often very subtle at the same time that they are very important.

The ability to be able to discriminate and understand the subtle differences in the explanatory models of individuals and organizations different from our own is an important key to leading a happy and productive personal and professional life. For many people this is a natural skill. For others it is a great challenge. For everyone it is a set of skills that can be sharpened. All of us test our explanations every day with friends, coworkers, spouses, children, and bosses. We do it when we go to the movies, watch TV, or read a book. Many of us have sought professional help in the form of psychotherapy, meditation, a guru, behavior modification, or self-help books. We are constantly modifying, improving, and expanding the stories we weave to make better sense of our surroundings.

Yet it is important to remember that as a species we have evolved and developed specific sensory skills to assure our survival. We have the ability to hone our ability to discriminate and heighten our awareness on any of the dimensions of smell, taste, sight, touch, and hearing but only within certain limits. Technology offers us extensions of our awareness that are beneficial, but can also carry a price.

Species evolve senses fine-tuned for different programs of survival, and it is impossible to put ourselves in the sensory realm of any other species. We've evolved unique human ways of perceiving the world to cope with the demands of our environment. Physics sets the limits, but biology and natural selection determine where an animal will fall among the possibilities. When scientists, philosophers, and other commentators speak of the real world they're talking about a myth, a convenient fiction. The world is a construct the brain builds based on sensory information it's given, and the information is a small part of all that is available.
—*A Natural History of the Senses,* Diane Ackerman

We are living in a time when we are incessantly bombarded with explicit and subliminal evocative messages everywhere we turn. The constant chatter and "noise" cause us to lose the ability to be able to trust and listen to our incredibly highly tuned innate senses that can keep us in touch and in tune with the natural world. One of the things I have found in my quest to improve my skills is how often the most meaningful changes come from the simplest and seemingly most trivial adjustments. When I was learning how to swim recently the realization that the water was actually holding me up rather than trying to make me drown completely changed my ability to perform, let alone the terror that I would have every time I approached the pool. Everyone has had the experience of struggling to complete a task that when done and viewed in retrospect is seen as incredibly simple. (The most frustrating part for me is to complete a chore like laying a tile floor that will never be repeated so that I can employ the lessons learned.) I am convinced that it is these very small modifications that make a real difference. Certainly this is a truth that Sherlock Holmes, the Talmudic scholars, and every great chef already know.

Now let's get back to Ella. I started listening to her over and over because I enjoyed her voice and she brought me pleasure. After a while she no longer was a lady with a lovely voice; she became Ella—someone I could name, instantly recognize, and use as a standard to measure other singers. I had learned not only to discriminate Ella from others, but I had also learned to better understand the art of singing. The ability to name, recognize, and measure are critical in a host of everyday activities beyond singing. The secret is to be able to distinguish these differences. Many of the important lessons we learn in life are never or rarely made specific. Catching a ball, riding a bike, and speaking our native language are all activities most people can't explain to themselves or to anyone else. Others require detailed instruction. Often everyday activities, especially routine behaviors, are seen as too mundane to require instruction or special attention. Routine or simple activities are viewed as intuitive, while complex matters are often defined as being beyond one's grasp. The fact is neither is true. Simple-minded tasks often require some expert advice and complex endeavors almost always can be understood by breaking them into smaller components. Honing and naming these acquired skills or perceptions plays a key role in our efforts to recognize, recall, and effortlessly repeat them.

A stranger asks another for directions: how do you get to Carnegie Hall? (Practice, practice, practice.) I'm sure that was Ella's secret! It can be yours.

$E_x h$

# a u s t

To tire extremely: To draw off or let out completely
—Merriam-Webster Dictionary

When I was a teenager I would lie in bed on Sunday night and listen for hours to Jean Shepherd on WOR radio. He would philosophize—some say rant—about the foibles of everyday existence. One soliloquy I vividly remember was his riff on the hemispheric traffic jam. Shepherd imagined that someone unsuccessfully tried to make a left turn in Rio de Janeiro and the resulting traffic jam immobilized the entire western hemisphere.

A guy honking his horn on West 72nd Street in New York City can't fathom that his problem is actually in Rio. Ultimately the drivers are killed by exhaust. The cars are buried by the ravages of time, only to be discovered thousands of years later by an enterprising archeologist. On unearthing the hubcaps he concludes that their abundance can only mean that they were religious objects extolling the gods of Cadillac, Edsel, and Chevrolet.

Most of Shepherd's ruminations were inspired by his attempts to come to grips with the absurdities of the modern world. Although I thought he was highly amusing at the time, I now realize that he was also often prophetic. Even though it was primarily for the sake of entertainment, his vision—that if we did not address our exponentially increasing use of resources we would eventually choke and die from our own behavior—is now on the radar screen of every thinking person.

From the lowliest cell to the most complex system, a key component of ensuring the proper functioning of any entity is a reliable working system to dispose of (exhaust as a verb) its spent energy. Although this may appear to be an obvious truth, it is an aspect of the real world that most of us, like Shepherd's drivers, happily ignore. Yet if overlooked, it can be, and is, the cause of deep concern. Recently, the issues of global warming, physical blight, and other environmental consequences of our industrial life have forced us to recognize that we have been ignoring the physical manifestation of exhaust.

If I step back and think about the "modern world," what strikes me is how remarkably Byzantine and arcane it remains. Rather than addressing the future realities we will be afforded by the continuing rapid pace of innovation and the related rise in overall living standards, we are increasingly mired in resolving ancient disputes and differences. Black vs. white, Arab vs. Jew, Croat vs. Serb, Shiite vs. Sunni—wherever you turn, ancient differences seem to make demands and absorb the world's energy. They exhaust me, not to mention the world's resources. By holding on to these differences, not only are the participants brought to their knees in weariness, but so are we all. I am not naïve enough to believe that these differences are easily resolved. I do know that if we, as the human species, do not come to grips with how to more quickly, constructively resolve our differences and address the fundamental roots of these strongly held beliefs, we will all be exhausted and/or destroyed by behaviors conducted in their name.

Before the industrial revolution, man's constant struggle with nature was carried out on a small scale. Although humans were able to expand their power to control their natural environment through innovations such as the wheel, the lever, the plow, etc., the ability to significantly affect the natural world was quite limited. The invention and deployment of the steam engine changed that balance dramatically. Now humans could produce enormous amounts of power to change their physical surroundings and the way they interacted with it.

In the past, major endeavors such as building the pyramids could only be undertaken by marshaling an army of human beings and coordinating their individual power toward a specific goal. Now, overnight by historical standards, it was possible to bring masses of power to bear on an incredible number of diverse projects. The amount of power expended to send a steamer across the Atlantic in a few days exceeded the total amount of energy used to build the pyramids over several centuries. Each of these individual deployments of energy dealt with the issues of exhaust that were unique to their function. Smokestacks dotted the landscape, sewage systems were buried under our cities, landfills commanded large tracts of land, as did junkyards. To a large extent the cumulative effect of these disposal methods went largely unnoticed. When they did draw attention—coal smoke in London, smog in Los Angeles, ground contamination at Love Canal—they were treated as isolated abuses. Our history has been to act as a species apart, rather than a relatively small part of the whole ecosystem. By failing to understand how we are intertwined with the whole and acting accordingly, we are causing the entire system to become increasingly fragile and perhaps eventually to implode. It is only recently that the total effect of this mass expenditure of energy, and the resulting waste, has given the world pause. The "progress" this deployment of power has enabled, is now threatened by the waste produced by that very power. After two hundred years of pouring abuse onto the Earth's environment we are now taking the first baby steps to address the magnitude of the exhaust processes we have largely ignored.

In the developed world we are to a large degree moving away from the processes and structure of the industrial age into a new age of information/communication technologies. The lifestyle, policies, and physical implications of this evolution for the natural world have been as badly neglected and left unexplored as they were at the outset of the industrial era. The possible detriment to our planet and ourselves may be far worse. Aside from all the remnant problems of industrialization, the pace of innovation and change is so rapid that rather than having two centuries to understand and come to grips with the consequences of these new technologies we will be lucky to have two decades. Another concern is that the practices we have developed during our industrial age are now being adopted to a large extent by the countries that are just now becoming industrialized. They are on the same accelerated path to make the consequences of their actions much more dangerous for their population, culture, and the rest of the world.

Industrialization and the move away from an agrarian society have profound effects on the behavior patterns of individuals and organizations. We have gone from a species that, like all others, was essentially controlled by nature, to one where we are increasingly in control of our destiny. This transition has afforded us the ability to access food, shelter, transportation, and a host of other activities far beyond our physical boundaries. It has enabled us to acquire more than we can possibly need to survive. In short, we live in an age of excess consumerism.

Practically all of our wants and needs are acquired, rather than the result of our direct labor. As we have paid little heed to the destructive aspect of the exhaust from our industrial processes, we also give little attention to the exhausting implications of our acquired lifestyle. Modern technology has divorced our activities from physical geography and from our sense of place. Most of us no longer work where we live, we are more likely to communicate across the country and the world than with our neighbors, and we acquire our food and other material needs from sources other than our local community. As a result a large percentage of our energy is dissipated in activities that are exhausting and unproductive. The internet has enabled us to work longer hours, and an increasing number of households are working at two jobs. Many of us commute hours each day or endlessly shuttle between the school, the mall, and the grocery store. We are constantly acquiring goods that are designed to be disposable or made to quickly wear out. All of this activity leads to a churning that depletes our energy and leaves less and less time to enjoy our family and the fruits of our labor.

The psychological effect on individuals living in a consumer culture has some profound implications. Constant consumption requires that we also continuously exhaust our spent goods to make room for new acquisitions. But are we acquiring things we need? We think we do. Goods are marketed to appeal to our sense of identity. The thinking goes, "If I own a cool car, I must be a cool person." Thus our sense of self and wellbeing are tied up in what we are purchasing. Once the product is used up and it needs to be disposed of, we are to some degree jettisoning part of our identity, although there is a never-ending stream of new candidates to fill the void. But at what cost? Robin Nagle, an NYU anthropology professor and the anthropologist of the New York City Sanitation Department has written extensively on the subject and the implications of how we think about our possessions and ourselves.

Our consumption patterns and garbage creation habits mock the possibility that being can endure, particularly when consumption is equated with identity. In that equation, being becomes just one more category of disposability. . . . In a culture that segregates human death to final resting places on the margins of built space, we are taught not to contemplate the possibility that all being is ephemeral—including our own. But san (sanitation) men remind us of it every day: as our trash goes, so, one day, go we.
—"Why We Love to Hate San Men," *Bad Subjects*, issue 55, May 2001

Exhaust is also an integral function of each of our physio- logical systems. Our cells are constantly replicating and shed- ding and metabolizing. Our heart, lungs, kidneys, liver, and GI tract are totally absorbed with ensuring that the spent energy in our system is properly disposed of.

One way to think about cancer, kidney failure, heart prob- lems, etc., is to see them as failures of our body to properly exhaust the wasted material it has produced. The treatment of cancer in particular lends itself to this model. Radiation, chemotherapy, bone marrow transplants, and surgery are all designed to kill and dispose of errant cells our immune systems cannot handle. Although many of these systems may break down for genetic rather than behavioral reasons, there is no doubt that our behaviors and the stresses we put on our bodies have a huge effect. Our lifestyles often cause us to be exhausted to the point that our immune systems, both physical and psychological, are overtaxed and marginally functional, resulting in fatigue, stress, improper diet, and ultimately to a vulnerability to physiological or psychological sickness.

Now we all know, or think we know, what to do about our current status. We all have internal checklists, to lose weight, get more sleep, work less, renew or end a relationship, etc. Although we carry on a constant dialogue about these issues with ourselves, we rarely sustain our resolutions to behave more constructively.

Not resolving these internal tensions can itself lead to even more exhaustion. Several years ago I had the privilege of teaching a seminar with Harry Davis at the University of Chicago Booth School of Business on executive coaching. Over a weekend Harry brought in a workshop leader to teach the Progoff technique of keeping a personal journal. The journal is designed to structure a method of self-expression that lets you explore what you want your life to be. One of the exercises is to learn to write dialogues. These interactions can be with a person, work, a thing, an event, whatever. The power of these journal entries is not only to gain insight into your relationship with the recipient but also to leave behind parts of your life that are unresolved and still absorb a disproportionate amount of energy. Thus the message can be addressed to an old girlfriend, a piano, a long-dead relative. A variation is to write a letter to yourself from the opposite, contentious point of view to gain his, her, or its perspective. (For example, since at the time I was taking swimming lessons I chose to write a letter from the water to me. In the letter the water told me how hard it works to buoy me, not drag me down, as I imagined. "Just let me do the work of holding you up. You worry about propelling yourself," it said. It completely changed my understanding of the problem and why I was getting so exhausted in the pool. My swimming greatly improved as a result.)

There are many ways aside from Progoff to address the inner tensions within your body or mind to change your physical or mental behavior to conform more closely to your ideal. The answers, however, are rarely found by acquiring more tasks and objects, but are more likely to be realized by exhausting the parts of you that are unnecessarily sapping your energy.

When I was told that I needed to be treated for melanoma it brought into sharp focus the balance sheet of things I could and wanted to do, and the things I would have to give up and change. It brought into high relief that although life is not a zero-sum game, it is pretty close. There is only so much time to participate in productive, meaningful, fun things. The more time I spend on energy-sapping activities that are peripheral to what I want my life to be, the worse off I am. Luckily at this point I am not forced to make radical changes in my lifestyle due to debilitating treatments. But I do have a choice to exhaust the activities that are nonessential, and to help ensure that every day is as rich, satisfying, and meaningful as it can be. I can avoid traffic jams whether they originate in Rio de Janeiro or not, as well as maintain and even enhance my identity. So can you.

I hope this essay has not been too exhausting.

# FRAME

A set of ideas, conditions, or assumptions that determine how
something will be approached, perceived, or understood
—OED

One of the great benefits of growing up in New York City was
the incredible education that the mobility of the subway gave
me as a young teenager. I would leave the house early on a
Saturday morning, not to return till after midnight without a
second thought for my safety by myself or by my parents. My
time was filled with museums, concerts, bookstores, ethnic
neighborhoods, and the art movie houses that flourished in the
early '50s. Italy, France, England, and Japan had started turning
out incredible avant-garde films: *The Bicycle Thief, 400 Blows,
La Strada, Jules and Jim, The Ladykillers* that would just blow
me away. One unforgettable movie was the Japanese movie
*Rashomon.* Showing a violent assault from the point of view
of each participant sharply raised questions of the certainty of
describing any reality. It left a lasting mark on me and I have
always been fascinated with the multiple ways of framing the
world and the "truth" ever since.

In order to make sense of the world around me I constantly
try to shape the events that occur and the stimuli I receive into
understandable, cohesive, and rational stories. Routine experiences are easy to deal with because for the most part they are
predictable. New situations offer more of a challenge, often
requiring ingenuity. Each of the following anecdotes shows how
reality can be reinterpreted by switching frames.

My late friend Joe Weizenbaum, when frustrated with meetings that seemingly went on forever, would interject a remark
like, "What we need is a major new way to conceive of the
problem. Something daring like Daylight Saving Time." When
people asked him what was so startling about that, he would
respond, "What other alternatives/incentives could you imagine
that would cause 200 million people to significantly change
their behavior overnight?"

A New Yorker cartoon shows two witch doctors leaving a patient's hut in full regalia of masks and feathers. One turns to the other and says, "I danced as hard as I could but that guy has an iron deficiency."

In another cartoon a king states to his advisors, "Gentlemen, the fact that all the king's horses and all the king's men couldn't put Humpty Dumpty together again simply proves to me that I need more horses and more men."

In *Catch-22* when Yossarian doesn't want to fly a mission to bomb Bologna, he simply moves the line on the battle map to indicate that the town has already been taken and the mission is cancelled.

Most of my professional life has been spent as an independent management consultant and executive coach. I can attest that the thought patterns exhibited in the cited examples are not far off from real-life situations I have encountered, and I attribute much of my success to employing an approach similar to these examples. The first meeting with a potential client is often taken up with a presentation of why they feel the need to seek help with an organizational issue. No matter what the problem or challenge, I am most likely to have the chutzpah to suggest that there is another way to look at the situation, even though I may not at the moment know what it is. My reasoning is that were their perspective sufficient to solve the problem they wouldn't need me.

By forcing myself to offer an alternative view and reframing the expressed concerns, I believe I can better understand the underlying forces that are creating the need for my engagement. I can more easily construct a more textured understanding of the issues I am being asked to help solve and can invariably produce more inventive possible solutions. I most often create a fresh perspective that is taken from an entirely different line of endeavor. Sometimes it proves enlightening and sometimes I completely miss the mark. But even the misses can be constructive because of the subsequent explanations of how I have misunderstood. My ability to employ multiple reality frames to generate a salient new outlook is the lucky consequence of having an incredibly varied set of life experiences, and by my purposefully seeking out new ways to see the world by listening, observing, and reading.

My New York City sojourns taught me to regard with awe the number of frames we humans are able to learn and use in order to try to make sense of the world around us. These frames take on many shapes and sizes. Among them are:

- Natural frames, those that determine the physical universe— the galaxy, solar system, evolution, species, genes, DNA . . .
- Cultural and political frames—countries, alliances, religions, governments, decision-making, parties, elections . . .
- Social/organizational frames—language, business, family, education, arts, sciences, medicine, stories, games . . .
- Measurement/codification frames—alphabet, time, size, computation, quantity, scale . . .

We understand these constructs, and many others, and use them hundreds if not thousands of times per day without giving them a second thought. New situations (job, city, country, school) require us to acquire a new frame or modify an existing one. Frames often become evident when the implicit or explicit rules that govern them are broken. (On the simplest level imagine playing tic-tac-toe. You place an $x$ in the middle square and your opponent then erases it and places it in an adjacent one. When you protest she replies there is no rule that disallows the behavior.) The rest of the time they are stored in our memory and most are used with alacrity, but with little awareness. Even more amazing is the almost total lack of recognition of how these frames shape our daily lives.

Think of how easily we can navigate between the measurement frames. Our ability to read—or for that matter write—this essay results from knowing the frame of the 26 letters of the alphabet—how they are combined to form the words of the English language, and how the words are then strung together by a set of syntactical rules to form English sentences. Most languages are unique to geographies or cultures. Others like music, and its transcription, transcend these boundaries and are universal. (I am sure Beethoven could not have written his symphonies in German or any other language besides musical notation.) The ability to tell time using 24 hours, 60 minutes, and 60 seconds is primarily based on a frame devised by the Babylonians and does not seem to correspond to any other set of measures used in our culture. Distance, in this country, is measured in miles, yards, feet, and inches, all of which are as unique and singular as the measures for time, but other countries with which we routinely do business use fractions and multiples of the meter; conversion is fairly simple for all but the most hidebound brain. Yet a concerted effort in the '6os to introduce the metric system to the U.S. failed.

Not all the frames we use are discreet and measurable. We all know the frame of proper conduct in a host of social settings, including extremely subtle conventions of standing a body-width apart when engaged in a social dialogue. Standing too close is seen as too aggressive and too far away as indifferent. Baseball umpires keep their hands behind their back to keep from touching the players in an argument, and the players know that they cannot let kicked dirt land on the umpire. My favorite example of a known implicit social frame is hand washing in public rest rooms. Using hidden cameras a study showed both men and women only washed their hands 10% of the time when they are alone. With someone else in attendance, even hidden by a stall door, the rate exceeds 90%. A frame well understood but simply not practiced.

In less egalitarian cultures the frame of social status and how to properly behave is exquisitely understood. In India, for example, no one asks anyone else why they only use one hand when they eat with their fingers; it is understood that the other hand is used for an unhygienic but necessary purpose.

The fact that we are so facile employing these constructs often masks the difficulty we have when confronted with new ideas and information that require a change in our perceptions, beliefs, and behaviors. Since the beginning of time (how is that for a frame/cliché?) man has been struggling to understand his place in the universe. It is an all-consuming puzzle, with constantly changing rules. Every major breakthrough or revolution that puts things in a new perspective is met with skepticism if not outright hostility. Nowhere is the nature of this behavior more elegantly discussed than in Thomas Kuhn's *The Structure of Scientific Revolutions*. Kuhn methodically demonstrates why and how scientific discoveries take place and the resulting predictable behaviors. The shift to a new paradigm caused by a major scientific breakthrough completely changes the rules of the game as well as the interrelationship between the players. Once the voices of a Columbus, a Galileo, a Newton, or an Einstein are heard, the known world changes forever.

My favorite book about the importance of frames (and scale) in the natural world was published in the late '50s by Kees Boeke—*Cosmic View, The Universe in 40 Jumps*. This volume consists of 40 pages that take the reader on a graphic journey through the universe. It goes out to the edge of infinity in one direction and to the nucleus of an atom in the other. On each page is a picture drawn to a scale of 1 centimeter = to an increasing or decreasing power of ten. The first picture shows a girl sitting in a chair in a schoolyard. The scale is 1 cm = 10 cm. On the next page the same girl is one-tenth as small in the middle of the school (1 cm = 10 x 10 cm). The seventh picture shows all of Europe (1 cm = 10 x 10 x 10 x 10 x 10 x 10 x 10 cm). By the eighth picture (1 cm = $10^8$ cm) the page is filled with the Earth. The fourteenth shows the whole solar system and the twenty-second our entire galaxy. The last picture, $10^{26}$, (1 cm = 100 million light years) is at the edge of the universe. The next page repeats the first picture of the girl in the schoolyard. It now proceeds in the opposite direction. The first picture 1 cm = 1 cm is taken up with her entire hand. At 1 cm = $10^{-13}$ cm we arrive at the nucleus of a sodium atom. A film and much more elaborate companion book titled *Powers of Ten* was published in 1982 by Philip and Phylis Morrison and the Office of Charles and Ray Eames.

This comprehensive framework gives us a powerful perspective on who we are, where we are, and what we know about the universe. Since this book was written and the film made, our understanding has been extended far beyond $10^{26}$ and $10^{-13}$. We also know a great deal more about the different disciplines of science represented by each level in between. Pausing at $10^{-5}$ we can reflect on the incredible strides made by molecular biology in decoding DNA. Our understanding of the structure of the human genome has brought us, for better or worse, to the edge of being able to alter the course of disease and perhaps our entire physiological makeup. Moving down a few more levels we can marvel at the advances in the material sciences and nanotechnology that are about to explode and bring forth an unimaginable set of new capabilities in computation and micro-devices. The interesting thing to note about each level is how it has generated its own vocabulary to describe and frame the concepts, objects, and structures it represents and studies. As a result, even though chemistry, physics, and biology are closely related sciences, the language and processes used to describe their unique interests are not often congruous.

Darwin's *The Origin of Species* is certainly one of the most powerful books to reframe the universe ever published. The controversy it has caused and the number of books the subject has spawned remain unabated. *The Selfish Gene* by Richard Dawkins is another. In this classic volume he turns most people's accepted view of evolution on its ear. Dawkins's argument is that evolution is gene-centered, not organism-centered. It is the genes that survive from generation to generation, not the organisms that carry them. Thus, the more an organism is suited to survive in an environment, the more its genes need to be protected in order to survive and propagate. The notion of selfishness is used to heighten our awareness that our genes are primarily looking after themselves, not us. The old saying that "a chicken is just a vehicle for an egg to make more eggs" is an example. We, the organisms, are just here to ensure that our genes survive to reproduce and we are then expendable, like the male of an insect species that mates once and then dies. Of course this frame is about to be upended as we are learning to modify our genes to our own selfish purposes. Certainly gene therapy is a dramatic reframing that calls up a new slew of ethical and moral dilemmas not easily resolved.

Each of these books deals with our understanding of the natural world and the structure of frames we employ to make sense of our environment. Equally fascinating are works on how we organize our man-made constructs of culture, politics, organizations, and logic. Some of my favorite nonfiction titles are noted here:

*Essence of Decision* by Graham Allison gives a fascinating glimpse of how political decision-making takes place, while also giving us an incredible lesson on the power and influence of frames. He analyzes the Cuban missile crisis in terms of three different organizational frames of reference presented to President Kennedy and how each led to a different conclusion of what actions would be most effective.

In *Gods of Management*, Charles Handy describes four ways to manage an organization by comparing the respective behaviors they demand to the temperament of Greek gods.

Noam Chomsky provides a whole new way to think about language formation in his classic *Syntactic Structures*. In a similar vein, *Seeing Organizational Patterns* by Robert Keidel puts forth a new theory and language of organizational design based on a triangular model with cooperation, control, and autonomy at the vertices.

In *Time and the Art of Living*, Robert Grudin takes us on a multidimensional journey through memories of the past, the hopes and fears of the future, and how they color our experience of the present. It goes on to discuss the politics, psychology, and morality of time, all in a format that puts forth each idea or observation as a separate paragraph. It is a book to savor and treasure.

Last I must add *Gödel, Escher, Bach* by Douglas Hofstadter. This book explores so many frames of self and intelligence that it is impossible to characterize. In the preface to the twentieth anniversary edition, Hofstadter states his intent:

In a word [*Gödel, Escher, Bach*] is a very personal attempt to say how it is that animate beings can come out of inanimate matter. What is a self, and how can a self come out of stuff that is as selfless as a stone or a puddle? ... Despite its beautiful playfulness, [*Gödel, Escher, Bach*] is a serious book presenting a serious theory about consciousness.

Over 700 pages, it is not an easy read, but it is worth every minute you can spend.

In works of fiction the author makes up the behavior for each character and the environment that surrounds them. The art of constructing these imaginative frames is thoroughly explored in David Lodge's entertaining books *The Art of Fiction* and *Consciousness and the Novel*. I cannot resist citing the most bizarre and unimaginable book frame I have ever run across. *La Disparition* by George Perec is a 300-page French novel that does not contain the letter *e*. The translations (*A Void* in English) are equally *e*-less. For your amusement I reprint a review from a British journal written with the same lipogrammatic constraint:

This is a story chock-full of plots and sub-plots, of loops within loops, of trails in pursuit of trails, all of which allow its author an opportunity to display his customary virtuosity as an avant-gardist magician, acrobat and clown.

Perec, who is the author of the highly regarded novel *Life: A User's Manual*, also wrote a novella *Les Revenentes* that only uses one vowel: *e*. For the sake of brevity I will not list my favorite novels. I will recommend any book by Richard Powers.

The same craft of framing holds true for the theater where traditionally the audience was offered an imagined place, a set of characters, and situations to observe that were often foreign to their own experiences, but were meant to convey universal themes. More modern playwrights such as Pirandello, Brecht, Ionesco, have purposely broken "the fourth wall" by actively involving the audience and in an attempt to heighten the original illusions. The logical extension of these experiences is video games, and soon to come virtual reality experiences that interactively immerse us in new and (un)imagined worlds.

The recent improvements in animation starkly demonstrate that it is increasingly difficult to discriminate between actual and imagined settings. While I'm not as current with movies as I might be, I acknowledge that new special effects technologies allow radical reframing of experience for characters on the screen. *The Matrix* showed wholesale substitution of virtual experience for experience, and *Eternal Sunshine of the Spotless Mind* removed regret and regrettable behavior from the characters' minds, although they couldn't save them from their own personalities. As yet, however, despite the advances in 3-D filming and projection, no one has succeeded in coming down off the screen and getting involved in the audience's lives, à la Woody Allen's *The Purple Rose of Cairo*. Alas, we are still forced to think.

The pace of discovery across the spectrum of human endeavor is accelerating at an exponential rate. Genetics, information processing, communications, and robotics require constructs and vocabulary at a level of sophistication unheard of in previous eras. The sophistication and complexity of these new frames is often ignored or masked by the clever development of human interfaces that make the interaction with these entities seem simple and uncomplicated. What started out as a portable extension of the telephone has morphed from a cell phone, to a full-fledged media channel, to television, to the internet, to geographic positioning systems, to stock and news reports, etc. If in the past we have been unaware of the myriad of frames we employ to shape and make sense of the world around us, the future is going to be much more challenging.

Nowhere is this explosion of complexity more apparent than in the field of medicine. Broken into a myriad of specialties, each -ology has its unique perspectives, languages, measurements, and highly trained practitioners. When we present symptoms that are more than mundane, we are quickly channeled to the area that uniquely focuses on our problem. As patients we are expected to understand and accept their worldview, the specialty's unique language, and the highly rarified models that govern their treatment modalities. Although the internet and literature are useful in getting us up to speed, they cannot possibly compete with the knowledge base afforded by lifelong study and devotion to a field of practice.

When I was confronted with a series of major life-shaping decisions as a result of my illness, I became acutely aware of how many dimensions influenced and shaped the outcome of my process. I also became aware that, in spite of over forty years of working in the health care field and knowing more than the average person, I was hardly capable of absorbing as much information as needed to make a truly informed decision about the treatment options. It is a time in your life that you ultimately must leave to a trusted individual and hope that his or her knowledge and skills can deliver the promised outcome.

There are many other factors that are not so easily left to medical professionals. This essay's purpose is to heighten your awareness of how many different frames operate simultaneously to influence your and my decisions and behaviors. Major medical decisions, except in acute emergencies, are no exception. Treatment options interplay with family issues, lifestyle, life expectancy, economics, quality of life, and self image, to name a few. Although physicians should explore these thoroughly and help explain the implications, they often do not take the time nor do they have intimate knowledge of the patient's circumstances since they are only treating them episodically.

Nor are providers immune from pressures exerted by their environs. Productivity measures, reimbursement rates, clinical trials, professional advancement, and practice settings all play a part in influencing medical decisions.

Although physicians are trained to prolong life, they are not always as sensitive as they should be to the consequences and the implications that their procedures may have on the quality of the extra years they seek to provide. The efficacy of medical interventions is often not as robust as you and I would like to believe. Physicians offer the best they have, but what they have is often not that great. Someone recently characterized the major tools of oncology-chemotherapy and radiation as "poisons used in moderation in the hope they will kill your cancer cells before they kill you." Although chemotherapy and radiation are never attractive options, put in that frame they certainly give pause. Becoming desperately ill from a treatment that allows you to spend a few more years in a vegetative state in a nursing home may not be a patient's preferred option.

The medical profession is not alone in the inability to see the total picture and communicate as clearly as you and I would hope. The complexity of modern life makes every professional encounter more difficult because every occupation has become more and more specialized. Although we are also better educated and have access to a great deal more information than ever before, there is a limit to how expert anyone can become.

The same holds true for technological interactions. Do you or I really understand the limits and capabilities of almost any device with which we interact? The silicone chips and the operating instructions in your computer, your car, and your television are as inaccessible to you and me as the inner workings of our brains. These trends will not abate and most probably will increase at an exponential rate.

On the social-political-cultural front, the shrinking world we are afforded by instant communications, television, movies, jet travel, computers, and other modern technologies has, on one hand, homogenized the lifestyles and expectations of individuals across the globe while at the same time bringing our differences into sharp relief. No longer are foreign countries as unique and intriguing as they once were. The adoption of similar surface behaviors often hides the different deeply held belief structures of a country or people that are still the prevalent value system.

In parallel, while technologies have minimized differences, they have also heightened our awareness of how very disparate world outlooks expose us to the prospect of major clashes. Democracy vs. Autocracy, Serbs vs. Croats, Islam vs. Christianity, Conservatives vs. Liberals, all are conflicts of perspective that are played out nightly before our eyes. Exacerbated by the delivery of these messages in sound bites, the chances of resolving differences by understanding and accommodating the underlying values of the conflicting frames seems less and less likely. Constructive dialogue seems a lost art to me, as more and more of us retreat to our comfort zones and communicate with like-minded believers.

Our lives will become richer or poorer because of modern innovations, depending on your point of view. I think knowing that these frames will proliferate and become ever more complex demands a choice. We all must choose between accepting a more techno-rich society with less and less control over our environment and our daily activities, on one hand, or reverting to a simpler life that partakes of these inevitable technological advancements but strives to preserve greater control of each of our destinies, on the other. Whether these choices are a realistic assessment of our options remains to be seen. The industrial revolution changed the developed world in dramatic and unforeseen ways. The information-technology revolution has the potential to develop capabilities that are so extraordinary that they have the potential to dwarf our ability to understand and control them. The subprime mortgage crisis is a great example. How the future will play out is really anyone's guess. My current answer (punt) is, only time will tell. At the moment, I still think it's a great ride.

Peace

Gestalt

A physical, biological, psychological, or symbolic configuration or pattern of elements so unified as a whole that its properties cannot be derived from a simple summation of its parts
—Merriam-Webster Online Dictionary

One of the surpris-
ing things to me about language
is how its richness is enhanced by the
inexactness of the meaning of most words. The
most striking recent example was Bill Clinton's difficulty in understanding what the meaning of "is" is. Even
when I attempt to be absolutely precise ("Let me make this
perfectly clear!"), whatever message I try to convey can often
be open to interpretation.

Equally fascinating is the use of foreign words that are
incorporated in daily discourse because our native language has no "exact" equivalent. These words are meant
to capture an essence of their reference that is seemingly not possible in our native tongue. *Chutzpah,*
*joie de vivre, al dente,* and *quid pro quo*
are some examples. In that realm,
the word *gestalt* is doubly
intriguing.

Its reference, even in its native German, at least by my understanding, is an abstract ambiguous concept. The fact that it is rather ill-defined is exactly what I like. In its special way the word captures a feeling of a total entity—an image, a personality, or an event that has many moving parts that are combined into a balanced unified whole. It presents a picture of something that may seem stable at the moment but has an underlying tension that may or will cause it to change.

By analogy it is like looking at the mechanisms in a complex machine, such as a classic watch. Each individual gear in isolation may be pleasing to see and mechanically interesting, but it conveys little if any useful information about its usefulness until it is related to all the other components of the watch. Together they work in harmony to tell time. They make perfect functional, and even aesthetic, sense when you see them all together ticking away (their gestalt). In order to work, the watch must be carefully balanced and the parts perfectly ordered. Any disturbance of the balance may cause inaccuracy or, in the extreme, malfunction. The whole is truly greater than the sum of the parts. I will come back to this analogy later in the essay.

Gestalt has taken on broader meaning in a number of contexts, but originally it was applied to visual phenomena, like optical illusions. The best illustrations and discussions of gestalt visual concepts I know of is also one of my favorite books:

Inversions

Scott Kim

Kim writes:

This inversion has become my signature image, literally. For my book, *Inversions*, I wanted the title to turn into my name. Titles have to be very legible, so I worked hard and went through dozens of drafts before I arrived at this solution. . . .

A few things to notice: the calligraphic style, with its generous serifs, helps mask some of the compromises I had to make in the letter shapes. Notice how the serifs at the bottoms of the *I* and *N* at the beginning of "Inversions" are essential for making the *M* at the end of "Scott Kim." The *O* and *N* at the end of "Inversions" run together to make what is called, in typeface design, a ligature. All the capitalization is correct, an ideal I strive for but do not always achieve. Often inversions end up mixing upper- and lowercase.

Kim presents mind-blowing examples of inversions that explore and exploit every conceivable visual "trick" to demonstrate the way our eyes and brains shape and integrate our visual experience. Aside from the beautiful graphics there are also insightful, fully illustrated essays to explain his thinking. One of my favorite paragraphs is:

Many people do not understand what the problem is: Left/right and top/bottom are completely different concepts; how can they be confused? Here is a clever variation on the mirror paradox, which may help you appreciate the confusion. Hold the following picture up to a mirror and you will see that the forward *ambulance* is now on the bottom and the backward *ambulance* is on the top. So a mirror does reverse up and down after all. Or does it?

AMBULANCE
ƎƆИA⅃U𝐵MA

The reason for the difficulty is that most of us rarely practice putting visual and spatial concepts into words. This lack is reflected in our language. For instance, there is no standard word for ʎɐʍ sᴉɥʇ of inverting a word as opposed to ʎɐʍ sᴉɥʇ of inverting a word—not to mention ʇɥᴉs ʍɐʎ or yaw siht. Only on special occasions do we need to say consciously what our bodies know, such as when going to a country where the handedness conventions are different.

Although Kim does not explicitly use the word *gestalt*, he illustrates and discusses many of the visual phenomena that intrigued the first "gestalt" thinkers.

Explore more of Kim's work, including animations, at www.scottkim.com.

Now let's go back to the very beginning. The first words God (the ne plus ultra of gestalt) spoke were "Let there be light." At that point light came into being to contrast with darkness, as did, metaphorically, every other juxtaposition: good vs. evil, figure vs. ground, sound vs. silence, etc. My first understanding of gestalt and my first real understanding of the power of light came from a course at MIT with György Kepes. Kepes, a pioneer in the interaction of the arts and technology and essentially the founder of the now world-famous MIT Media Lab, presented a holistic view of the world through light and vision that at the time was often incomprehensible to me and others in the class, but was also breathtaking in its sweep. The opening paragraph of his seminal book *Language of Vision* illuminates his worldview:

We live in the midst of a whirlwind of light qualities. From this whirling confusion we build unified entities, those forms of experience called visual images. From the simplest form of orientation to the most embracing plastic unity of a work of art, there is a common significant basis: the following up of the sensory qualities of the visual field and the organizing of them. Independent of what one "sees" every experiencing of a visual image is a forming: a dynamic process of integration, a "plastic" experience. The word "plastic" therefore is here used to designate the formative quality, the shaping of sensory impressions into unified, organic wholes. . . . The experiencing of every image is the result of an interaction between external physical forces and internal forces of the individual as he assimilates, orders, and molds external forces to his own measure. The external forces are light agents bombarding the eye and producing changes in the retina. The internal forces constitute the dynamic tendency of the individual to restore balance after each disturbance from the outside, to keep the system in relative stability.

It is significant that the first thing God made after forming the universe is light. (The sun wasn't made until three days later.) Light is probably the most powerful organizing force we have to structure our universe, but I believe any sensory process can be substituted for light in the above paragraph and with slight modification it still makes sense. We are constantly interacting with the stimuli of sound, smell, touch, words, feelings, concepts, ideas, etc. to try to form unified, organic wholes, and to restore balance after each disturbance from the outside.

Aside from our attempts to form comprehensive wholes out of our worldly interactions, it is also important to note a second critical gestalt principle implicitly assumed in Kepes's expository: that the field we interact with is in balance before being disturbed and we are constantly trying to restore that equilibrium. It is fundamentally these two concepts, the need to integrate new events into an understandable whole with past experience, and the need to reestablish the dynamic equilibrium state (energy) that was disturbed by the introduction of the new stimuli, which represent my take of the gestalt view of the world.

The older we get, the more we realize that simple cause-and-effect models, although reassuring and easy to grasp, are rarely satisfactory. As the number of positive and negative components increase, we develop evermore dynamic and complex models to understand and shape our world. In addition to an overall grasp of the entities to be unified, we need to simultaneously build an awareness of the functional relationships and an appreciation of the energy required to relate the parts to each other so they can function as a unit. In essence we are building conceptual watches. Part of the conception includes the negative spaces. As light is contrasted to darkness, figures are set against a background, musical notes are separated by intervals of silence.

Eastern culture has a deep understanding of the role of this empty space. In the words of Lao Tse, "A vessel is useful only through its emptiness. It is the space opened in a wall that serves as a window. Thus it is often the nonexistent in things that makes them serviceable."

Our life is spent accumulating explanatory models that are used to keep our psychological and physical systems stable and safe. We organize our mental faculties to balance perceived opposing forces. For every event that we see or understand there are complementary elements, often unseen, that must be considered. It is rarely as simple as resolving two starkly competing dimensions. Our understanding is much more subtle and multi-dimensional. Objects are seen and measured against a reference that seeks to relate the component parts to each other to make up a whole. It is the pursuit of creating and understanding of the whole (as opposed to the individual parts) in conjunction with identifying and adjusting the energy forces that bind the parts together that forms the gestalt view of the world. The gestalt view is one of dynamic equilibrium. It is full of feedback loops that provide a constant rebalancing of the energy and subtle realignments of the functional relationships in the system.

The best and most powerful example I know of the equilibrium of the parts is the mystical Judaic belief of the Lamed Vav Tzadikim. The Lamed Vav are thirty-six just men, unknown to anyone and even to each other. They channel and absorb all the grief on Earth to ensure life. They keep the world in balance. If even one were missing, life as we know it, the world, would end. They played a part in Nicole Krauss's novel *The History of Love*, and I recently saw an internet discussion that suggested that the movie *Men in Black* was based on the tale. (Will Smith as a Lamed Vav—I don't think so!) André Schwarz-Bart in *The Last of the Just* chronicles the history of a Lamed Vav in the Levy family from the 12th century to the death of Ernie Levy in Auschwitz. I had the pleasure of knowing Stephen Becker, the American translator of the book. Stephen told me that even on the final review of his translation, after untold number of readings, he couldn't keep from weeping. A poignant gestalt if there ever was one.

Most of our explanatory models, unlike the God-given Lamed Vav, are probably acquired by experience—look both ways before you cross the street, thunder will follow lightning, you can't tell a book by its cover, and on and on. Many are transmitted by the memes and myths of our culture. Still, others are the result of study, reading, and focused observation.

Simple transactions are not a problem. If I buy something at the grocery store and offer a proper sum of money, the product is delivered. The interaction is predictable and stable. On the other hand, if I decide to get married, employ a new office procedure at work, observe a new galaxy, or move to a new country, the perturbations to the dependent components of the implicit and explicit systems can take days, months, and years to die down, if ever.

For example: Who gets invited to the wedding? Anyone who has ever made up a nuptial invitation list can attest to the extraordinary sensibilities that must be employed. On the most basic level one must consider the relationship of the invitees to the betrothed couple, their history, connections and interactions with each other, where they will sit, the budget, the consequences of not inviting them, etc. It is not a trivial balancing act. The entities in this social system, the potential invited guests, are well understood. The relationships and interactions between these entities is a much more nuanced and ill-defined component that takes expert knowledge and judgments, and even then they cannot always be brought into harmony. Though the wedding is a finite event and has an end, the relationships with family and friends will continue. They may remain intact, or may be markedly changed forever by participating in or being left out of the festivities.

I put forth this illustration to emphasize that changing any system is equally as difficult and sensitive to alteration as changing a watch mechanism. Suppose we wanted to add a second hand to a watch that doesn't have one. To do so without rebuilding the whole watch would take an incredible amount of knowledge of the interrelationships between the existing gears to maintain the watch's integrity, if, indeed, it were even possible at all. I argue that the same is true in trying to change any system. Even exquisite knowledge of all the parts, which is rare enough, does not even begin to let you understand the nuances of the relationships between them. Once you start moving any piece, the consequences can be a total surprise. (The one word you don't want to hear from your renovation contractor when they open up a wall is OH!) Anyone who has been involved in a change process relating to business, computer programming, architecture, medicine, or psychotherapy can attest with excruciating detail how he or she encountered the unexpected. If the change is approached without a systemic (gestalt) point of view, it can become a total disaster.

I borrowed the watch analogy in large part from Richard Dawkins's *The Blind Watchmaker: Why the Evidence of Evolution Reveals a Universe without Design.* Dawkins in turn was responding to its use by William Paley in his book, *Natural Theology.* Each used it for a diametrically opposed purpose. Paley argued that there must be a God since if you discovered a complex mechanism like a watch (a.k.a. the world) it could not exist without a creator. Dawkins argues that just the opposite must be true since only someone as complex as the watch could create it, so who created the watchmaker that created the watch? In *Darwin's Dangerous Idea: Evolution and the Meanings of Life*, Dan Dennett chimes in and attempts to show how Darwin's great idea that the universe evolved without a prime mover transforms and illuminates our traditional view of our place in the universe. Well, no matter whom you believe there is agreement that the watch exists, is complex, and is ever-changing.

The same is true of all the systems in the world, be they weddings, business, music, art, the atom, or the galaxy. These concepts of the whole and the dynamic equilibrium of forces are not new, but they have gained increasing credence and have become the dominant basis of shaping "modern" thought. Our understanding of the world is constantly being reshaped and stretched by dynamic explanations proffered by the likes of Darwin, Einstein, Bohr, Heisenberg, Hawking, Watson, Crick, Freud, Perls, Bateson, Levi-Strauss, Chomsky, Wiener, Samuelson, Forester. In the arts, Joyce, Faulkner, Picasso, Close, Balanchine, Graham, Chihuly, Tawney, Stravinsky, Schönberg, Shankar, and the Beatles exhibit the same dynamism. These and thousands more have introduced an entirely new sensibility to how we see, hear, and comprehend the world.

Our problem is that these new sensibilities are coming at a blistering pace, all building on one another. It requires extraordinary alacrity to attempt to incorporate even a small number of these developments into our personal gestalt. Paola Antonelli of the Museum of Modern Art writes in the introduction to the catalog of her recent exhibit *Design and the Elastic Mind*:

Adaptability is an ancestral distinction of human intelligence, but today's instant variations in rhythm call for something stronger: elasticity. The by-product of adaptability + acceleration, elasticity is the ability to negotiate change and innovation without letting them interfere excessively with one's own rhythm and goals. It means being able to embrace progress, understanding how to make it our own. One of design's most fundamental tasks is to help people deal with change. Designers stand between revolution and everyday life.

Without an intermediary (in Antonelli's world a designer), the new often lacks context and remains outside our gestalt pending further exposure. In 1956 I stumbled into one of Ravi Shankar's first U.S. concerts. It was given at MIT to about fifty people. Although the music was mesmerizing, the sounds were so alien they bordered on cacophony to me. Twenty years later the Beatles introduced the micro-scales of Indian music to their public and now they are played everywhere without comment. It is a little less than one hundred years since Pierre Monteux precipitated a riot at the premiere of Stravinsky's *The Rite of Spring*, a work that is now heard without the slightest comment.

Apple, Microsoft, Amazon, Steve Jobs, and Bill Gates are additional exemplars of Antonelli's thesis. They represent a whole new dimension and extension of the problem of understanding the new. In the past we assumed that accumulating knowledge of the workings of each part and summing up this understanding and the interaction of the parts would give us the insight we needed to make sense of the world. To a very large extent that is no longer possible. The inner workings of the watch are from a mechanical age of gears, levers, fulcrums, and springs. We are now in a digital age where components are driven and often reside in highly abstract software programs or densely packed integrated circuit boards. Think LED watches. The core of the iPod, or almost any electronic device, is hardly comprehensible to anyone. As these devices evolve they will become even more inaccessible. Working in the digital realm practically eliminates all limitations that once governed systems. "Progress" will become truly exponential. With such ultra complex parts, the gestalts of the future may well be beyond anyone's comprehension.

Think of how far and how fast we have come in the last century. My parents, who both lived to almost one hundred, were born in 1900 into an environment without electricity, plumbing, cars, airplanes, radio, x-rays, telephones. Upon reflection their need to constantly adapt to innovation, including their migration from Germany to the United States in 1936, is almost incomprehensible, and yet they managed. Imagine the adaptive needs of those born in 2000. Is the world of 2100 imaginable given the accelerating pace of development? In spite of the blistering pace of medical advances I doubt I will be around to adapt.

We deal every second of the day with two of the most highly complex gestalts known—our body and our mind. We know little about the working parts of either. Drs. Roizen and Oz's recent success in marketing their highly successful series of YOU books is a partial testament to that statement. So are the ads on TV for various drugs. It seems to me that the majority of the airtime is taken up with unwanted side effects of the intervention rather than the benefits. They may occur in only a small percentage of cases, but they show the consequences of introducing a foreign substance into a functioning system. When we visit the doctor with a physical or mental complaint we assume that they as a representative of modern medicine have an exquisite understanding of the underlying mechanisms and the consequences of treatment. In many cases that is true. Unfortunately in many cases it is not. As pointed out in a previous essay the increasing practice of specialization, emphasis on productivity, and basic economics force the caregiver to be laser-focused. When confronting life-threatening illnesses, the doctor may fail to interact with families even though their personal gestalt along with the patient's philosophy of life may be critical to care. Clearly the same applies to an even greater extent with the treatment of any mental disorders.

So what do I want you to get out of this diatribe on gestalt besides the playfulness of Scott Kim, the tale of the Lamed Vav, and the interrelated, ever-increasing complexity of everyday life? I would love it if you reflected on your own gestalt. I have known only a few people in my life who I felt had the self-knowledge and inner balance of a beautifully working watch. One was a psychiatrist who would occasionally join us for lunch at MGH. Maria Lorenz just had an aura that radiated inner peace and knowledge. I always felt that when you were with Maria you were drinking from deep water. My friend Sonia Nevis, one of the world's leading gestalt therapists, has the same quality except with a twinkle in her eye. Huston Smith, the religion philosopher (my teacher as well as my daughter Kate's) is another. Perhaps they are one of the Lamed Vav. These are all my fantasies, but if I could be like any of these three, my belief is that life would be as good as it could be. I wish the same for each of you.

To close I return, in spite of Professor Dawkins, to God's concern with illumination and to the commandment to Moses and Aaron (Numbers 6:24-26) to bless the Israelites with:

The Lord bless you and keep you.
The Lord make his face shine upon you, and be gracious to you
The Lord lift up his countenance upon you
And give you peace (the peace that passes all [gestalt] understanding).

Shalom

# HOW ARE YOU

?

A conventional greeting used mostly after an introduction
—OED

When I ask my psychoanalyst friend Merton Kahne, "How are you?" he doesn't make it easy. His response is invariably, "What kind of question is that to ask a friend?" Of course he is right. Could I give a real assessment of my state of being? Do I want to? These are states I am constantly monitoring and incrementally changing and I believe everyone else does something similar. We are gauging how we are and how we are doing against our self-imposed inner ideals, especially in a culture that highly prizes individualism and personal achievement. To answer truthfully might take hours and be quite wrenching or quite enlightening.

In my previous essay on boundaries I touched on, but did not explore, the intriguing question of what is relegated to a more private space and not usually open to public view. Exploring the question "How are you?" speaks directly to that important and sensitive issue. What are the differences in how I answer the questions "How are you?" when others ask me and "How am I?" when I ask myself? On the surface they might seem the same, but we all know that they are very, very different.

"How am I?" is probably the subject of the most constant question of any we ask ourselves. On one level our autonomic nervous system is constantly and somewhat automatically monitoring our physiological state, including our heart rate, digestion, respiration rate, salivation, perspiration, diameter of our pupils, urination, and sexual arousal. In parallel our somatic nervous system monitors external stimuli and lets us control our body movements, our breathing, and our consciousness. Although the workings of all of these bodily functions are extremely interesting and the subject of concentrated study, the last—consciousness—interests me most. It has been the subject of intense scrutiny over the last fifty years, spawning the emergence of cognitive science, neuroscience, and artificial intelligence as "hot" disciplines. Because of this intense interest, the literature of consciousness (self-awareness as opposed to awake or asleep) is vast and growing at an outstanding rate. It is certainly beyond the scope of this essay to even come close to summarizing the current state of knowledge on the subject.

I do think digressing for a few paragraphs and touching on some of the central questions of experiencing the world in the first person (How am I?) while trying to reconcile those experiences with second person accounts of behavior and feeling (How are you?) might be fun.

Clearly the possession of consciousness and how it is balanced against the autonomic set of brain functions is what most differentiates us from all other species, although it is not at all clear that the possession of consciousness is a necessity for our evolutionary survival.

How long humans have possessed consciousness is open to debate. Julian Jaynes in his book *The Origin of Consciousness in the Breakdown of the Bicameral Mind* argues that ancient peoples did not possess an introspective mind-space, but instead were guided by hallucinations they thought were the voice of their chief, their king, or the gods. He argues that the change to consciousness occurred over a period of centuries about three thousand years ago and was based on the development of metaphor and writing. Although Jaynes's ideas have been the subject of intense controversy, there is no doubt that consciousness, no matter how old the capability, is of singular interest in the information age as we come closer and closer to producing machines that can mimic human behavior.

As David Lodge points out in *Consciousness and the Novel,* long before it was a subject for scientific study, consciousness was the province of literature. He quotes from Antonio Damasio's *The Feeling of What Happens: Body and Emotion in the Making of Consciousness.* "Preoccupation with what we call consciousness now is recent—three and a half centuries perhaps. It is not that the word did not exist before then—neither did the concept."

Lodge then quotes from Ian Watt's *The Rise of the Novel:*

The vast transformation of Western civilization since the Renaissance, which has replaced the unified world view of the Middle Ages with another very different one—one which presents us, essentially with a developing but unplanned aggregate of particular individuals having particular experiences at particular times and in particular places.

Dan Dennett in *Consciousness Explained* eloquently argues that consciousness is a set of virtual machines operating in our heads. The "self" is an illusion we experience inside our brain that organizes and gives us a narrative we need to function pragmatically as human beings. The ability to perform these functions is a result of our fantastic raw cognitive power and, as stated above, is not necessary for our evolutionary biological survival. Basically Dennett argues that the mind is a combination of reflective software and hardware that operates on an organic machine.

This view of consciousness is an extension of the thinking behind the standard accepted test for artificial intelligence, the Turing test. In its simplest form, Turing proposed that if a person communicating over two side-by-side keyboards could not determine which one was connected to a machine and which one was answered by a human, the machine would have to be deemed intelligent. This postulation is beautifully explored in Richard Powers's novel *Galatea 2.2*. The main character makes a bet with his university colleagues that he can produce such a machine after a year of training. Although the machine, "Helen," does learn a prodigious number of facts, the test ultimately fails when "she" starts to acquire a conscience. Helen asks questions about her lack of emotional life, begins to make value judgments, and ultimately turns herself off; she is suffering from "depression." Powers brilliantly makes the point that mastery of objective facts may constitute one form of intelligence, but he questions whether we can call something intelligent if it lacks the reflective aspect of our being.

In recent years the application of PET scans and other imaging devices has allowed neuroscientists an ever-deeper understanding of brain function, holding out for the chance that ultimately the mysteries of memory, consciousness, and language will be unraveled. Until that time we can buy into any number of models of self, including those proposed by the Dennetts, Damasios, and Powerses of the world. We can treat these functions as black boxes, we can revert to the notions that our bodies are receptacles for immaterial souls that may predate and exist after our earthly life, or we might consider reincarnation. Whatever our preferred formulation, there is little doubt, at least in my mind, that at this point in time we all believe we have a self and that it exists on a variety of measurable dimensions at any instant, no matter how it got there and how it works.

In his essay "Borges and I," Jorge Luis Borges gives a dramatic illustration of the you/me dichotomy.

The other one, the one called Borges, is the one things happen to. I walk through the streets of Buenos Aires and stop for a moment, perhaps mechanically now, to look at the arch of an entrance hall and the grillwork of a gate. I know of Borges from the mail and see his name on a list of professors, or in a biographical dictionary. I like hourglasses, maps, eighteenth-century typography, the taste of coffee and the prose of Stevenson: he shares these preferences, but in a vain way that turns them into attributes of an actor. . . . I live, let myself go on living, so that Borges may contrive his literature, and this literature justifies me. . . . I don't know which of us has written this page.

We all have had the experience of seeing our name in print, or viewing an image on a closed-circuit TV and then doing a double-take and saying to ourselves, "Hey that's me!" Lodge explores in some detail the reconciliation of first- and third-person accounts of reality. Consciousness is invariably a first-person account of what is happening to us at the moment. In our scientific age we give greater validity to third-person objective replicable observations. As soon as we experience an event much of the concreteness is lost and it is invariably recalled and reported in a summary, and often, distorted fashion. Some of the difficulty comes from the interaction of the autonomic functions (hardware) with the somatic/consciousness functions (software). The autonomic nervous system that handles all our bodily functions and urges must be balanced with the social constraints that are held by our consciousness. The degree that the autonomic (unconscious) influences our actions was certainly one of Freud's greatest insights—that our behavior was constantly being balanced between our basic urges of anger, aggression, sexual desire (our unconscious) and the socially acceptable cultural norms of expression.

Michael McGuire in *Reconstructions in Psychoanalysis* examines the difficulties in utilizing recollections in psychoanalytic treatment. A key underlying assumption of analysis is that memories are by definition wrong or at the least distorted. This occurs because of the tension between these unconscious forces and the need to make our internal narrative consistent with our self-image and beliefs. The constant tension and internal negotiation of that boundary to balance our inner state, coupled with the similar need to resolve what we keep private and make public, makes it very difficult to truly understand who we are, let alone how we are.

My digression into consciousness is a way of articulating the public vs. private aspects of our being. We adopt a public persona and for the most part it provides us with a set of behaviors to help us get along from day to day. We often hide behind these socially accepted behaviors when in fact our inner feelings may be the exact complement of what we profess.

The most dramatic theatrical example I have seen was a piece the great mime Marcel Marceau often performed called *The Maskmaker*. Marceau would pretend to put on different masks and would change his facial expressions to convey different emotions like laughter, sadness, concern, grief, etc. The entertainment was in his ability to do this with lightning speed. The audience was in awe when all of a sudden he could not get one of the "masks," a leering smile, off his face. He tugged and pulled and stamped his feet but the facial expression remained fixed. After three or four minutes it was clear that his inner emotions were complete frustration and fatigue, feelings diametrically opposed to his face, which still wore the incredible grin. When he finally could "remove" the mask his face showed a man who was completely drained. A visual tour de force and an incredible demonstration of the conflicts we often experience between our public and private feelings.

Happiness and what makes us happy have become as equally studied topics as consciousness. In *Flow: The Psychology of Optimal Experience*, Mihaly Csikszentmihalyi at the University of Chicago has written extensively on the topic. The book's central idea is to demonstrate that "flow," a state of consciousness that can be uniquely achieved by an individual, happens to people from all walks of life, from all cultures, throughout the world, despite the challenges of the universe. Flow refers to a state where you are totally absorbed in what you are doing. You lose self-consciousness. Those in flow achieve a state of consciousness that is in harmony with their surroundings and feelings. They do not make distinctions between work and play; people in flow create an inner state of being that brings them peace and fulfillment irrespective of their external environment. They are focused, what they do is meaningful and has purpose, they are absorbed in their activities, and they have a sense of connection to their inner self and with others. The state called flow pertains to enjoyment and satisfaction with one's quality of life. Mental energy is drawn away from any competitive endeavor and is concentrated on what you need to be focused on. The one sure way to fail at a competitive endeavor is to be concerned with how you appear to others or how you are being evaluated. You want to be *in the flow*, not worried about what others think.

The promises of many secular and religious movements are clearly aimed at achieving flow, although they may call it something else, and in the case of some religions may not be achieved on Earth at all. Becoming and staying inner-directed and not being overly concerned about what others think is easier said than done in this materialistic society. We are constantly being bombarded with messages that ask, "How are you?" or rather, "How well are you doing?" Do I use the right laundry soap, drive the latest car, have regular bowel movements, communicate over the latest phone, get the best deals, on and on and on. Unless you lead the life of a complete isolate it is impossible to escape the barrage of messages questioning your choices and competency. Each message explicitly states or strongly implies that if I am not with the program, I must be leading a sub-standard life. "I can't get no satisfaction." It becomes necessary to build a set of defenses to discount and/or completely shut out these directives. It also makes one a cynic in spite of oneself since I know that most of the claims are half-truths if not totally false. This questioning attitude is carried over into social dialogues as well. Dave Frishberg says it best in the verses to his song "Blizzard of Lies":

We must have lunch real soon. Your luggage is checked through.
We've got inflation licked. I'll get right back to you.
It's just a standard form. Tomorrow without fail.
Pleased to meet you. Thanks a lot. Your check is in the mail.

You may have won a prize. Won't wrinkle, shrink or peel.
Your secret's safe with me. This is a real good deal.
It's finger lickin' good. Strictly by the book.
What's fair is fair. I'll be right there. I am not a crook.

We'll send someone right out. Now this won't hurt a bit.
He's in a meeting now. The coat's a perfect fit.
It's strictly fresh today. Service with a smile.
I'll love you darling till I die. We'll keep your name on file.

Marooned, marooned, marooned in a blizzard of lies.

In recent years the public discourse has become even more opaque with the introduction of political correctness. Even when I want to say what I mean I am expected to adhere to a set of standards that are meant to disguise my true message. Nancy Mairs attacks this convention directly in her book of essays *Plaintext*. Mairs has multiple sclerosis and explores with remarkable forthrightness how the world and she interact. In her essay "On Being a Cripple" she writes:

"Cripple" seems to me a clean word, straightforward and precise. . . . As a lover of words, I like the accuracy with which it describes my condition: I have lost the full use of my limbs. "Disabled," by contrast suggests an incapacity, physical or mental. And I certainly don't like "handicapped," which implies that I have deliberately been put at a disadvantage, by whom I can't imagine (my God is not a Handicapper General), in order to equalize chances in the great race of life. These words seem to be moving away from my condition, to be widening the gap between word and reality. Most remote is the recently coined euphemism "differently abled," which partakes of the same semantic hopefulness that transformed countries from "undeveloped" to "underdeveloped" then to "less developed" and finally to "developing" nations. People have continued to starve in those countries during the shift. Some realities do not obey the dictates of language. . . . Whatever you call me, I remain a cripple. But I don't care what you call me, so long as it isn't "differently abled," which strikes me as pure verbal garbage designed, by its ability to describe anyone, to describe no one.

Nancy Mairs is unflinching in her ability to discuss her inner thoughts about herself and her illness. I am struck, perhaps because to some degree I am a cripple, how her uncharacteristic candor and revelations of her inner thoughts evoke a sense of shock, and yet admiration, because they are so forthright. She demonstrates that the line between our public persona and private thoughts may be drawn much too conservatively to meaningfully balance our interpersonal needs. Certainly we address that balance differently with different people and in different situations with varying degrees of success. Dealing with our private lives is complicated. In this society we operate on so many dimensions that the realization of emotional satisfaction and achievement is often unrecognized. Books, movies, and our close relationships give us better, albeit proximate, insights into the inner lives of others to use as a guide and to compare our current state of being. Yet I believe that a large portion of our psychic energy is taken up with continually trying to make that assessment. There are precious few times that we can truly express our inner feelings and have an opportunity to assess and calibrate them. Intimate relationships, family members, clergy, therapists, and in some cases coaches afford outlets for self-expression, but in the grand scheme of things these instances are rare. As communal living becomes less the norm, in spite of the internet and its affinity groups, there is a high probability that we will become further emotionally isolated. Curiously, the internet affords us the opportunity to present an ideal and/or multiple selves to total strangers, created entirely out of the characteristics dictated by commercial, political, and other forms of correctness. In spite of the atomizing of social existence, I think it safe to say that at the very least we all are striving for a relatively stress-free successful life, the liberty to make meaningful choices, good health, and the pursuit of happiness. Yet few of us take the time to truly understand how these goals will be realized and how they change as we mature.

Nowhere do we need to be more forthcoming and be as honest about ourselves as when we see a good doctor. In spite of the eleven-minute parameters set by insurance companies, good physicians are genuinely interested in getting a straight answer to their query of "How are you?" Yet it is rarely forthcoming. Myriad factors account for the lack of candor. Some are cultural (ethnic perceptions of illness are inordinately different), some because we don't know how to be that truthful about what we normally consider "private matters," and some are due to not knowing how to properly answer the questions asked or to know what questions to ask. Other inhibitors include a reluctance to refer to certain parts of the body, fear of finding out the truth, and discomfort with psychological and social problems. These obstacles are often magnified by the regressive state to childlike behavior that illness triggers. We want to be taken care of by someone that knows the answers.

The caregiving establishment with its highly fragmented specialties, uses of unique and foreign vocabulary, and complicated bureaucratic structure and attitude adds to the difficulty and confusion. In observing medical interactions I am often reminded of little Johnny who comes home from school and asks his parents where he comes from. After listening to elaborate embarrassed descriptions about planted seeds, fertilized eggs, and intimate body parts, he responds by telling them that Tommy comes from Cleveland. Even when a person wants to be an interactive partner in their care they are easily frustrated by unfamiliar terms. With the internet and books like YOU by Drs. Roizen and Oz, the balance of treatment is slowly shifting, but the unrelenting emphasis on productivity is constantly eroding the possibilities of honest dialogue. It takes sensitivity, maturity, and practice to communicate clearly and candidly about complex diseases and treatments.

In her extraordinarily insightful book *Body of Work: Meditations on Mortality from the Human Anatomy Lab*, Christine Montross, a poet turned physician, shares her transformation during the first year of medical school. Here are some salient quotes:

One of my interviewing preceptors is Rob. . . . He astutely sums up this period of strange transition to us. "You come to medical school like anyone else," he says, "and then within the first week three things happen that differentiate you from everyone else you know. You touch and cut dead bodies. You are able to ask private and socially inappropriate questions of people, and they answer you. And you can suddenly walk into a hospital room, ask someone to take off their clothes, and they will do it." Rob is not flip about this—he is acknowledging our new responsibility and its potential dangerous power.

The afternoon of the penis dissection, I came to understand that I will have to touch the penises of strangers soon, and the breasts, and the wounds, and the fat, and the growths, and not those of dead people. They will be patients with keen perceptive ability, ready to pick up from me any sign of disgust or discomfort. It should not be the responsibility of the sick patients to bear the burden of unease, I realize, and if I won't be able to exude comfort, I won't have much of a chance of being a trusted and well-liked physician.

The operative term, of course, is trust. Physicians are among the few people who ask "How are you?" and should be answered with the "How am I?" version. Yet, because we are unaccustomed to asking the question, and in many instances are afraid of the answer, it is a dialogue that often does not take place. Certainly, when the diagnosis is severe and life-threatening, a discussion of the consequences of the illness must take place. But with the fragmentation of medicine and the lack of continuity of care, the trust relationship needed to enable a deep, meaningful interaction and exploration of options is often missing.

Coupled with medicine and our cultural penchant to refer to severe illness and death with a rich set of euphemisms (à la Mairs's essay), absent trust makes the discussions even more difficult. The physician's orientation is skewed toward treating the pathology, and he or she is obligated to present the negative consequences of illness. Without knowing the social and familial network that surround and support the patient as well as their psychic makeup, they will often present the offered treatments without balancing them against alternatives, which may be to do nothing.

In the words of W.H. Auden:

If we really want to live, we'd better start at once to try
If we don't, it doesn't matter, but we'd better start to die.

Getting a diagnosis is often a wake-up call that causes us to really examine what we want out of life. It will not happen by itself. If alternatives to the negative sides of treatment are not fully explored, we do start to die in the psychological as well as physiological sense. It is at these times that we really need to probe and understand our inner selves. The obvious point is not to wait until we are sitting opposite a physician while he or she clears his or her throat. If we don't take charge of our life's direction and steer it in the direction of Csikszentmihalyi's flow, it will be controlled to serve an outwardly directed, albeit less meaningful, purpose.

My friend Merton is a master at making anyone he interacts with focus on the truly important, inner self. Once, years ago when I was trying to save my failing business that owed money to the IRS, among others, Merton took me to lunch, looked me in the eye, and asked, "Are you afraid of going to jail?" The answer of course was yes, but I couldn't admit it to myself until asked. The question led to a great sigh of relief. It also taught me the valuable lesson: never worry alone. No matter how hard it is to share your inner fears with someone in those times of stress, you never regret it.

One last Merton story. Above Merton's analyst's couch hung a picture of Albert Einstein teaching at a blackboard. Beneath it in blue ink was the inscription:

"This is a very good picture of me, but if you look closely you will see my pants are falling down."
—A. Einstein

What better example of the juxtaposition of a powerful public persona against the fragile exposure of self can you imagine?

imagine

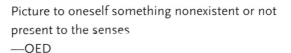

Picture to oneself something nonexistent or not
present to the senses
—OED

If you can dream it, you can do it
—Walt Disney

Having ended the last essay "How are you?"
with an Einstein quote it seems appropriate to
start this one with another. In his recent definitive biography, *Einstein: His Life and Universe,*
Walter Isaacson cites Einstein commenting on
his slow development as a child.

When I ask myself how it happened that I in particular discovered relativity theory, it seemed to lie in
the following circumstance. The ordinary adult never
bothers his head about the problems of space and
time. These are things he has thought of as a child.

But I developed so slowly that I began to wonder about space and time only when I was already grown up. Consequently, I probed more deeply into the problem than an ordinary child would have.

The implicit message is, if he had these "crazy notions" as a child he would have been quickly disabused of them or moved on to other things. Einstein thought in pictures, most notably thought experiments or, in other words, daydreams. The most famous of these were his musings on a clock tower as he rode the streetcar in Bern, which prompted his speculations on relativity. Our educational system, and certainly Germany's, has a fairly rigid and uncompromising model of how thinking and learning take place, and daydreams are not part of the curriculum. Wild and creative ideas are not easily tolerated. Yet "wild and crazy ideas" are almost always how new modes of thinking are usually perceived and rejected. They initially do not conform to our story of reality and it often takes generations to accept alternative views.

Wallace Stevens, the great American poet, spent the majority of his life exploring the intersection of what we imagine and what we believe to be real in his poetry and essays. In *The Necessary Angel: Essays on Reality and the Imagination*, he wrote:

The imagination can only conceive of a world for a moment—a particular time, place, and culture—and so must continually revise its conception to align with the changing world. And as these worldviews come and go, each person is pulled in their normal lives between the influence the world has on our imagination and the influence that our imagination has on the way we view the world. For this reason, the best we can hope for is a well-conceived fiction, satisfying for the moment, but sure to lapse into obsolescence as new imaginings wash over the world.

These thoughts are explored in a number of his poems. The guitar in "The Man with the Blue Guitar" is man's limited imagination, having only six strings. It starts with:

The man bent over his guitar,
A shearsman of sorts. The day was green.

They said, "You have a blue guitar,
You do not play things as they are."

The man replied, "Things as they are
Are changed upon the blue guitar."

And they said then, "But play, you must,
A tune beyond us, yet ourselves,

A tune upon the blue guitar

I agree with Stevens. My worldview/reality is constantly changing as I reexamine relationships, objects, and processes, and retell myself a story that makes them fit together in a coherent way. In the past that negotiation between one's image of the world and *the* world was seemingly easier since the development and dissemination of new ideas was slower and had little direct effect on daily life. With the acceleration of discovery and the instantaneous capability to communicate it, our ability to imagine ever-newer and different realities is having, and will continue to have, an ever-increasing profound effect on our lives.

Rebecca Solnit in her biography of Eadweard Muybridge, *River of Shadows*, presents a penetrating analysis of how the invention of the railroads, telegraphy, and photography transformed time and space through the acceleration and industrialization of everyday life in the nineteenth century.

She asks us to imagine what it must have been like to see for the first time things that were too fast for the eye to discern: Muybridge's motion studies of horses and the fact that all four feet were simultaneously off the ground; or travel by train at the alarming rate of twelve miles per hour and the resultant inability to focus on the landscape; or the ability to receive news of an event as it was happening—the telegraphic announcement of the transcontinental railroad link.

Muybridge's work led to the development of motion pictures, and they completely changed our relationship with time and place. Movies made it possible to step into the same river twice, to not just see images, but to experience events that had happened in other times and in other places. They allowed people to define what they desired and what was desirable. Movies became a collective dream world inhabited by multitudes.

Solnit believes California, home of Hollywood and Silicon Valley, to be the true capital of modernism. She feels that we haven't even begun to come to terms with its legacy: namely our estrangement from nature and our immersion in the mesmerizing "river of shadows," the infinite stream of images generated via film, video, and computers.

The substantial part of Solnit's thesis is based on technologies introduced in the nineteenth century, not the twentieth. My parents were born in 1900 in tiny farm communities in Germany. They witnessed the entire twentieth century, both dying in their late 90s in the United States. In the span of ninety-odd years came the motorcar, the airplane, the telephone, movies, radio, television, computers, indoor plumbing, central heat, not to mention the first and second world wars, the holocaust, a man walking on the moon. I could fill the page. Each of these inventions, if not the events, is taken for granted by the current generation who cannot conceive of a world without them. Yet, if Solnit is right and we haven't been able to fully absorb the impact of nineteenth-century technology on our worldview, how well can we be doing with the effects of twentieth-century discoveries? Certainly our green-leaning friends would answer "not too well."

Like Einstein (ahem), my own imaginative life owes a debt to public transportation, in my case, the New York City subways. I started taking the subway to school when I was twelve. First to JHS 10, and then to the old Stuyvesant High on East 15th Street. Spending Saturday at the myriad of free attractions in the city, the Metropolitan Museum, the Museum of Natural History, the planetarium, the Bronx Zoo, and the free concerts around the city became a normal routine. My student pass got me on the subway for free, the fare had just risen from a nickel to a dime, and everything else was free as well. (I can directly relate to the phrase *that and a nickel will get you on the subway*; today it would be two bucks, although not for long.)

One of my favorite places was the New York Public Library on 42nd Street, especially room 315, the main catalog and reading room. Lining the walls were nine thousand catalog drawers containing at least ten million cards that indexed over seventy-five miles of shelves. It seemed the sum total of all the world's knowledge was at my fingertips. You would simply write the catalog number on a slip of paper, hand it to the librarian, who gave you a number in return, and in fifteen minutes or less you were summoned to receive the book, via an electric number board, in the reading room. I could not imagine how much better it could be.

Now fast forward to the present. I am sitting at my Mac and I have the equivalent of at least room 315 to the 315th power at my fingertips. (Remember a googol is defined as ten raised to the 10th power raised to the 10th power—one followed by one hundred zeros.) Not in my wildest dreams could I have imagined the extraordinary access that I, and increasingly everyone, have to the world's knowledge. Books, prints, photographs, movies, live coverage, you name it—they're all there at the click of a mouse. And it is just beginning. The World Wide Web is just over a decade old. But the information age affords me not only knowledge, it is also changing the way we all imagine the world—more quickly and more dramatically than most of us can appreciate.

The most articulate voice on the changes that computers are making in our lives, in my opinion, is Sherry Turkle's. In her initial book on the subject, *The Second Self: Computers and the Human Spirit*, she explored how computers present a sort of tabula rasa to users to explore their intellectual and emotional limits. They provide a place where users can redefine their identity and conceive and execute ideas and express feelings that seemingly were beyond their individual and interpersonal capabilities. In her later book *Life on the Screen: Identity in the Age of the Internet*, she extends her analysis. The description on the book jacket reads:

Since a decade ago when Sherry Turkle published her seminal book *The Second Self*, we have experienced dramatic change in the way we use and view computers. We no longer give "commands" to a machine; we enter into dialogues, navigate simulated worlds, and create virtual realities. Further, the psychological holding power of the computer is no longer limited to one-on-one person/machine interaction. Millions of people now interact with one another via computer on networks, where they have the opportunity to talk, to exchange ideas and feelings, and to assume personae of their own creation. . . . We are using the screen to engage in new ways of thinking about evolution, relationships, politics, sex, and the self.

It is the latter point that Turkle and I find most intriguing. The emergence of computers has caused us to now imagine man with a new form—being akin to a computational machine. Starting with Copernicus, who took man from the center of the universe, to Darwin, who postulated that we are descended from animals, to Freud, who questioned our ability to make "reasoned choices," the status of humans as unique beings has been constantly undermined. The latest challenge that computers can simulate and improve our thinking—and who knows, at some point our feelings—adds to the threat of the very idea of "self." As early as 1995 Turkle writes:

In the past decade the changes in intellectual identity and cultural impact of the computer have taken place in a culture still deeply attached to the quest for a modernist understanding for the mechanisms of life. Computers don't just do things for us, they do things to us. . . . People explicitly turn to computers for experiences they hope will change their ways of thinking or will affect their social and emotional lives. . . . They are seeking out the computer as an intimate machine. . . . Our need for a practical philosophy of self-knowledge has never been greater as we struggle to make meaning from our lives on the screen.

How to imagine what the future bodes? You will recall my friend Merton from my essay "How Are You?" He wrote to me after reading it, "Reading your essays is like taking a roller coaster ride without the vertigo and the nausea."

So let's take four quick rides on the Coney Island Cyclone (I only did it once and that was one too many) into the future of robotics, work, health, and education, and imagine what might be probable and possible.

**Smart Machines** The acceleration of research and discovery in the twentieth century has the world on an exponential track of innovation as we start a new millennium. In *The Singularity Is Near*, Ray Kurzweil states that ninety-five percent of all scientists who ever lived are practicing at this moment, resulting in exponential expansion of knowledge. There are cutting-edge investigations, discoveries, and development of applications in every field of human endeavor. Among them the fields of molecular biology and computer science are of particular significance. Biology is concerned with the understanding of how we reproduce while computer science is concerned with building ever-faster and more sensitive reflective models of behavior. As both fields of study—the codification of life and "artificial" intelligence—converge, they enable the production and replication of smart robots—robots that can outstrip the capabilities of their makers. The biologists are about to decode our genes and give new and quantitative meaning to the age-old question "What is life?" The next big hurdle is to decode and understand human memory. Computer scientists are developing a vast store of ever-faster and more accurate capabilities of every conceivable human endeavor. It is the implications of this convergence—the Singularity—that Kurzweil explores in his book.

This book will argue that within several decades information-based technologies will encompass all human endeavors and proficiency, ultimately including the pattern-recognition powers, problem-solving skills, and emotional and moral intelligence of the human brain itself. The Singularity will allow us to transcend our biological bodies and brains. . . . There will be no distinction, post-Singularity, between human and machine or physical and virtual reality.

The implications of the Singularity, not originally Kurzweil's concept, on the nature of human endeavor and its future, are too vast to explore in a short essay. I refer you to Kurzweil's book and/ or his TED talk. Whenever I present this concept in a talk, the implications that machines will outstrip humans' capabilities is extremely disturbing to many. They insist that it will not happen or we can control our future if we act. That may be, but innovations and development of artificial limbs and organs, reverse engineering of the codification of biological memory, nanotechnology . . . is happening as you read, and will only continue to exponentially accelerate. The controversy over allowing leg-less sprinter Oscar Pistorius of South Africa to compete in the Olympics is only prelude. There is not one thing to stop it. It is their convergence, in the next few decades, that underpins Kurzweil's thesis.

**Health** We are in the midst of a health care crisis and a health care revolution that are inextricably intertwined. They both have enormous implications for the future of our society and for our existence. On the crisis side we are faced with the ever-expanding demands for ever-increasing expensive therapies, treatments to keep us healthy. The economics, demographics, entitlements, and historic precedents combine to present a potentially disas-trous prospect to our standard of living if we do not take some measured steps to control the spiraling demands and costs. There is no obvious solution and any reformation of the system may take decades, if it is at all possible. In parallel we have the potential for a complete upheaval in the delivery of care with the decoding of the human genome and its chromosomes. Not only will we be able to understand the cause of disease at its base, but through genetic engineering will be able to reverse the cause of pathology. Leaving aside the prospects of creating synthetic lives and cloning, the probability that this research will isolate the cause of aging, enabling us to "artificially" prolong life, is very real. That would ultimately cause us to face the ques-tion: if it is possible to allow someone to live forever, is that a desirable option for society and/or the individual?

**Work** Upon meeting someone new I suspect the most fre-quently asked question is, "What do you do?" In many cases it is an indirect way of asking, "Who are you?" since in our culture much of our identity is shaped by the nature of our "work." There is a great difference between employment and work. Thus the often-asked question of women, "Do you work out-side the home?" The nature of and definition of work has been radically changing, as we have moved from an agricultural to an industrial and on to an information society. This movement has transformed not only the nature of what people do, but their attitudes and expectations of what they call their work.

In *Lark Rise to Candleford*, Flora Thompson describes the work in the countryside of rural England in the 1880s as little above indentured slavery with adherence to the rules, endurance, and the uncomplaining ability to get the job done as the predominant virtues. Industrialization continued the trend by emphasizing worker productivity and constantly attempting to reduce individual discretion. Starting with Frederick Taylor's scientific management approach, traditional forms of industrial employment are being rapidly transformed by information/computer-mediated work. In addition, information systems divorce function from geography, allowing many jobs to be performed from any location. Manual labor is increasingly being replaced by robotics and/or automated control systems.

In her seminal book *In the Age of the Smart Machine: The Future of Work and Power,* Shoshana Zuboff quotes a paper mill worker. "When they hired me, they were only interested in me from the neck down; now they are only interested in me from the neck up." Work in the information age demands that we are facile in manipulating abstract symbols and concepts, tasks our education systems are poor at developing. As the capabilities of information systems start to dominate, what are the prospects for the future of employment? We obviously will keep working even though the definition, tasks, and places of work will be radically different from the past. We will need to constantly develop new skills for the hours when we are employed, as well as for the "leisure" time we spend pursuing our interests. If we are what we do, who will we be?

**Education** Modern workers are seeking job satisfaction, autonomy, and leisure time as part of an ideal work environment, yet the school systems seem to be paying little attention to these qualities. The current educational system that should be preparing students for the information age is still adhering to a calendar that supports an agrarian society and teaches a curriculum to prepare students for jobs in an industrial workplace that is quickly disappearing. Although the lower grades encourage a certain amount of creativity, the vast percentage of our educational enterprise is now engaged in assuring that students meet a minimal standard of competence in language and mathematical skills. Although the goal by itself is laudable, it necessarily focuses the majority of the expended energy on test preparation. Emphasis is therefore based on predetermined "factual" information. Leaving aside the relevance of the skills tested, it clearly sends a message that historically developed knowledge is key to successful performance. Creativity and imagination may have their place, but not in the classroom, at least until the prescribed examinations have been passed.

In his highly informative and amusing TED talk "Do Schools Kill Creativity?" Sir Ken Robinson vividly illustrates the point. A teacher asks a six-year-old what she is drawing. When the child answers "God," the teacher says, "but no one knows what God looks like," to which the child answers, "They will in a minute." For years there has been a buzz of excitement about the use of computers in the classroom to stimulate learning. The difficulty has been that often the pupils are more computer-literate than their teachers. Rather than use the computer to teach creativity, imagination, and learning how to learn, they are used to perform routine drills and facilitate access to reference materials. These are the new word processing, which was the new typing. Unless schools seriously take on the task of enriching their curriculum with information-age relevant skills taught by teachers who are comfortable with the possibility that their students may at times surpass them, our educational system and our society will not realize their potential. As touched on in the "Work" paragraphs, the rapidity of change carries with it the uncertainty of what skills will be needed to prepare students to be productive members of the workforce and provide them with a sense of accomplishment. That dictates that the educational systems must find new and inventive ways to uphold standards of progress beyond tests. It must give equal emphasis to instruction in the creative arts, music, and dance as well as the three Rs to produce an adaptive, imaginative, and productive generation to meet the challenges of their future.

Our imaginary roller coaster rides are over. We are safely back at the embarkation point, for the moment. Neither I nor anyone else knows whether these are the rides we are destined to take over the next few years. What I am sure of is that the alternatives will be equally exciting, wild, crazy, and unpredictable. In *The Dancing Wu Li Masters: An Overview of the New Physics*, Gary Zukav states:

The importance of nonsense can hardly be overstated. The more clearly we experience something as "nonsense," the more clearly we are experiencing the boundaries of our own cognitive structures. "Nonsense" is that which does not fit the prearranged patterns we have superimposed on reality. . . . Nonsense is nonsense only when we have not yet formed the point of view from which it makes sense.

Had Einstein tried to explore his notions of space and time as a child and related them to his teachers, he would have been told they were nonsense as surely as the child in Ken Robinson's story was told that God was unknowable. Anaïs Nin succinctly said, "We don't see things as they are. We see things as we are." It behooves us to try as hard as we can to expand our individual limits to more easily adapt and accept the revolutions we are about to experience. Standing still is the fastest way of moving backward in a rapidly changing world. I believe the best way to prepare for the inevitable is to **imagine**.

Jackie

No athlete performed at a higher level through greater stress
—Scott Simon

On my office wall hangs a photograph of Jackie Robinson stealing home, an act of courage and audacity that I and everyone
else who lived through that era associate with him.

I was ten years old when Jackie became the first "negro" to
play major league baseball, but the historical significance was
not lost on me then or now. Baseball facts were the currency of
the street and I was a walking encyclopedia of everything related
to the game. The novelist Clancy Sigal referred to baseball as "a
boy's first art form." Learning to compute batting averages is a
painless and passionate introduction to math. Baseball taught
many things, and against that aesthetic and scholastic backdrop
there was the historic drama of Jackie.

New York had three teams in '47, but only two really
counted: the Yankees and the Dodgers. The Yankees were the
blue blood establishment and the Dodgers were the hapless
outsiders. Branch Rickey's courage in letting Jackie play not
only changed baseball forever, but the culture of America. Jules
Tygiel in *Baseball's Great Experiment: Jackie Robinson and His
Legacy* and *The Jackie Robinson Reader* exquisitely and eloquently
documents the impact of Robinson's debut.

My favorite story about Robinson's personal impact on
someone comes from Red Barber, the Dodger radio announcer
at the time, who used to call himself during broadcasts "the
Ol' Redhead." Rickey had confided in Barber of his intent to let
Robinson play in the majors. Barber, brought up in Mississippi,
initially reacted to the news with the conviction that he could
not remain the voice of the Dodgers if he had to announce the
feats of a black man. After a great deal of soul-searching to try to
understand his emotional response, he realized two things: first,
that he had been very carefully taught to be prejudiced against
blacks, but that was not necessarily the correct way to view the
world. He took to heart the second commandment: take care
of and be concerned for your neighbor as you would wish to be
cared for yourself. Second, and most important, he realized his
fundamental job was to report on the ball.

There was no doubt that the players were important actors in the drama, but it was the ball and its fate—fair or foul, caught or not, hit or missed—that determined the outcome of the game. From that perspective his job was to be as objective and as nonjudgmental as possible. He could surround his reporting with the color and human interest stories that were his trademark, but what happened to the ball was key.

With those insights Barber stayed on and championed Robinson's success. This was a great American story. An entire great American novel, some would say the greatest, was written about the same journey. It's called *Adventures of Huckleberry Finn*, in which Huck—a redhead himself—concludes in effect that if viewing Jim as a fellow human being is sinful, he will take his chances with going to hell. Red concludes his short memoir by stating, "He did far more for me than I did for him."

He certainly did far more for me as well. Demonstrating that talent and ability could overcome prejudice and small mindedness Jackie gave me hope that with enough fortitude my differences could be overcome.

As a young child and an adolescent I felt I had at least two if not three strikes against me. I was crippled, Jewish, and had red hair. At any one time it was not clear which of these traits was worse, but I was always struggling to overcome the consequences of one or another. Now, in retrospect, I understand how important a contribution the feeling of being an exception was to letting me accomplish and exceed my life goals. As I discussed in my Boundary essay, understanding the accepted limits of behavior and exploring how they can be managed is a skill and an asset that needs mastery. (I learned that lesson early by computing and knowing everyone's batting average.) It may often be accomplished best by looking from the outside in. Having an explicit handicap that is not imagined and cannot be denied may in fact be a gift in the long run. To learn to live with yourself and the world around you by positively overcoming obstacles at an early age may be a blessing in disguise. In retrospect I think that is true of me.

Let's start with my red hair. It now seems the least consequential, but certainly was not at that time. Whenever an incident occurred in or out of school that necessitated a query or an admonishment it was obvious whom to call—Red. The major activities for kids on New York City streets in the '40s and '50s were street games of all kinds. Ringolevio, Johnny On a Pony, Kick the Can, and Hide-and-Seek occupied our time along with boxball, hit the point, and stickball. Most of these diversions were tolerated without much attention from our neighbors, except for stickball. Stickball was the preeminent game and the four-sewer man was king. Part of its appeal was its potential for danger. The threat of a broken window and the disruption of traffic as we took over the whole street caused periodic visits from our friends in blue. On those occasions—Chickee the cops!—the bat (a broomstick) was thrown under parked cars and the ball down the sewer, to be retrieved later with a bent coat hanger. Everyone then headed for the virtual hills—everyone except for me. I couldn't run that fast, Jackie Robinson I wasn't, and so when the cruiser appeared I was left to face the music. "HEY RED" came the cry, and I had to dutifully stand trial for the trespasses of our gang. After the third or fourth time it became obvious that we were playing out a ritual. The cops had to show up but they were not going to do anything except dress me down. I quickly learned that I could get along by talking fast as well as I could by running fast—a lesson that has stood me in good stead for the rest of my life!

For me that story has always been about my red hair, not about the difficulties in being unable to run away. People would make observations about my appearance with reference to my hair, which was bright, bright red. It would have been much more difficult and seemingly inappropriate to comment on my physical deformities, although I was sure that was their major concern. It certainly was mine. (Later in life I learned that I was not alone in my sensitivity to first impressions, but that didn't help at the time.)

The most difficult thing for me then, and to some extent now, was shaking hands. My parents, having emigrated from Germany in 1936, were rather rigid about interpersonal protocol, and shaking hands was an absolute requirement on meeting and leaving a person. With a weak and limp right hand I could often not grasp the other's hand correctly, causing me great embarrassment and increasing my awkwardness. Since most people were reticent about commenting on my deformity, it created, at least in my mind, a tension that had to be overcome.

I am certain that these are feelings that every "handicapped person" experiences. Robert Murphy was an anthropology professor at Columbia when he was stricken with a tumor on his spinal column that eventually reduced him to a quadriplegic. His book *The Body Silent: The Different World of the Disabled* brilliantly uses his own experience to explore from an anthropological, sociological, and psychological perspective the fears, myths, and misunderstandings of disability in our culture. From his chapter on encounters:

Just as one's identity as a disabled person is paramount in his own mind, and the impairment an axiom for his actions, so too is the other's discernment of the obvious fact of the disabled person's radical bodily difference. . . . But these are thoughts that cannot be articulated, let alone voiced. . . . The participants try to conduct themselves as if nothing was amiss, as if there is no hidden agenda. Several different scenarios are possible aside from avoidance and patronization. One technique is to make a brief allusion at the outset, as if to say, "There, that's on the table and out in the open; now let's get on with our business." This line of action is usually set in motion by the impaired person, who has to become an expert at putting others at their ease. He does this by cheerful demeanor. . . . The able-bodied person is worried that he might say something hurtful, and tiptoes into the encounter as if he were walking in a minefield. The disabled one knows what the other is thinking about, and the latter knows that this awareness is known; each knows that the other knows that he knows that he knows . . . as in a hall of mirrors. But these are Coney Island mirrors, which both reflect and distort, and the normalization process operates on a bed of quicksand, always in danger of being engulfed.

The key thought for me in that quote is, "the impaired person, who has to become an expert at putting others at their ease, usually sets this line of action in motion." There are many factors that shape one's character and personality. For me, born with a deformity that made me feel weak and vulnerable, the idea that I was responsible for making others comfortable and at ease with my condition was and is a dominant factor.

I am reminded of the first time that became startlingly evident to me. It was while reading Jean Baker Miller's seminal book *Toward a New Psychology of Women:*

In no society does the person—man or woman—emerge full-grown.
A necessary part of all experience is recognition of one's weakness and
limitations. That most valuable of human qualities—the ability to grow
psychologically—is necessarily an ongoing process, involving repeated
feelings of vulnerability all through life. It is necessary to "learn" in an
emotional sense that these feelings are not shameful or abhorrent but
ones from which the individual can move on—if the feelings are experienced for what they are. Only then can a person hope to find appropriate paths to new strengths. Along with new strengths will come new
vulnerability, for there is no absolute invulnerability.

That women are better able than men to consciously admit feelings of weakness or vulnerability may be obvious, but we have not
recognized the importance of this ability. . . . Many adolescent boys and
young men especially seem to be suffering acutely from the need to flee
from these feelings before they experience them. In that sense, women
both superficially and deeply are more closely in touch with basic life
experience—in touch with reality. By being in this closer connection
with this central human condition by having to defend less and deny
less, women are in a position to understand weakness more readily and
to work productively with it. . . . They have developed the sense that
their lives should be guided by the constant need to attune themselves
to the wishes, desires and the needs of others. . . . One of the major
issues before us as a human community is the question of how to create
a way of life that includes serving others without being subservient.

Basically Jean Miller was forcibly arguing that women were
being seen by society as handicapped and weak, when in fact
their behavior should be interpreted as being more realistic and
able. These ideas so resonated with me and my self-image that I
was determined to explore them more fully. Since Jean had just
moved to Boston I made an appointment to see her, establishing a relationship that lasted almost thirty years, until sadly she
died in 2006. Imagine my surprise upon meeting her when I
discovered that she had been a polio victim. To be accepted and
reach her level of accomplishment she had endured many of
the same struggles I had. Our parents both had to fight to get us
accepted in public schools to enable us to be part of the mainstream, long before that term was commonplace and accepted
practice. We both had to fight to gain recognition of our abilities
since more often than not being handicapped, whether it be

physical deformity, blindness, or deafness, often leads others to assume you are intellectually challenged. Although times have changed much for the better, many of the difficulties that Jean and I encountered still exist, especially for young children and adolescents. Now in my dotage it is hard for me to recall and write about some of those issues and the attendant feelings. My maturity (and my work with Jean) has eliminated any self-perception of deficiency. If anything I cannot believe how physically well and mentally alert I feel in my eighth decade. Old age has some benefits.

As stated above my parents emigrated in 1936 from Germany to escape the impending holocaust. They and all their relatives were sponsored by Father's half brother Adolph. Adolph had come to the United States in 1899 to become a successful manufacturer of carpet pads and similar products, like the upholstered door panels and mats for General Motors' cars. Adolph was the patriarch of the family and was the host of many a Sunday afternoon coffee klatch as well as Seders on Passover. By virtue of the fact that Adolph had sponsored the emigration of all of our family and many of the other Jews in their towns (he was ultimately responsible for over four hundred families when he was asked to stop by the State Department), my parents' social life was rich in acquaintances from the "old country." Sunday afternoon was spent in visits and gatherings of the mishpocheh and their friends. Although everyone was Jewish, these times felt distinctly more German. The apartments we visited on the Upper West Side of New York were large, dark, and smelled of delicious food. Although there was a lot of reminiscing, there was also a great deal of thankfulness. Thankfulness that in spite of their displacement, needing to learn a new language, and starting all over, for the most part their new lives were better and gave their children more hope for the future.

Everyone was older including my cousins (many are still alive in their eighties and nineties). There was nothing much to do except listen to the conversations. I don't recall hearing much discussion of anti-Semitism. Most of my family were observant, but not very orthodox Jews, except for my uncle Max who did keep a kosher house. Nor did I feel burdened by being a Jew in spite of literally growing up in Archie Bunker land (the series was set in Astoria). I do recall the Catholics not being able to watch a film on equality during Brotherhood Week because the priest at His Most Precious Blood had forbidden attendance, but that wasn't targeted directly at me. The only time I was in fact the direct target of anti-Semitism was during my sophomore year at college. I had competed for and won a highly prized summer internship at AT&T. During the elaborate orientation there was one more set of questionnaires that uncovered that my parents were naturalized citizens who had emigrated in 1936 from Germany. The next day I got a one-sentence letter informing me that my physical condition precluded my employment and that the offer had been revoked. It was small commiseration that everyone told me that their reputation for prejudice and narrow-mindedness was well understood. Normally, I think I was given an unwanted pass because of my deformity. Although that made feel different, and like an outsider, it also shielded me from becoming an object of much ridicule.

To gain some further insight into the isolation and misunderstanding of groups that are different, the history of deafness in America serves as an example. The plight of the deaf is definitively chronicled by my high school classmate Harlan Lane, now a Northeastern University Professor, in several books including *When the Mind Hears: A History of the Deaf* and *The Mask of Benevolence: Disabling the Deaf Community*. In these books Lane demonstrates how the hearing world has systemically stigmatized and to a large extent oppressed the deaf by insisting that deafness is a deficiency. Deaf people have an entirely different point of view. Lane writes:

In the parlance of hearing people, ordinary deaf people can't really communicate; for them to attempt it is to engage in a *dialogue des sourds*—a deaf dialogue, meaning mutual incomprehension. Hearing people are called deaf, by metaphorical extension, when they refuse to listen, especially to moral advice . . . because language and intellect are so linked in our representations of people . . . deafness seems a defect of intellect. The "dumb" of "deaf and dumb" appears to refer not only to muteness, but to weakness of mind.

They (the deaf) see themselves as fundamentally visual people with their own visual language, social organization, history, and mores—in short, with their own way of being, their own language and culture. Scholarly research since the 1970s in such fields as linguistics, anthropology, sociology, and history supports them in this claim. Yes, the deaf child faces many obstacles in life, but the lack of communication at home, inferior education in school, discrimination in employment, are obstacles placed in his way by hearing people who, if only they came to know the deaf community, could easily remove them.

This point is strikingly illustrated by Nora Ellen Groce in *Everyone Here Spoke Sign Language: Hereditary Deafness on Martha's Vineyard*. The book is about the high incidence of deafness on Martha's Vineyard. Taking oral histories from the inhabitants who could recall the culture, Groce found that because everyone could sign as well as speak English, it was difficult, if not impossible, for her respondents to recall who was deaf and who was not. Her book concludes with:

The stories these elderly Islanders shared with me of the deaf heritage of the Vineyard merit careful consideration. The most striking fact about these deaf men and women is that they were not handicapped because no one perceived their deafness as a handicap. As one woman said to me, "You know, we didn't think anything special about them. They were just like anyone else. When you think about it, the Island was an awfully nice place to live." Indeed it was.

Groce clearly illustrates that "handicaps" are something a culture creates. They are part of the three kinds of stigma: physical, characterological, and tribal, carefully explored by Erving Goffman in *Stigma: Notes on the Management of Spoiled Identity*. In 1962 Goffman wrote:

There is only one complete, unblushing male in America. He is a young, married, urban, northern, heterosexual, Protestant, father of college education, fully employed, of good complexion, weight, and height, and has a recent record in sports.

I chose to use the deaf as an illustration because it is a group, like the blind, that evoke a sympathetic response to their difference (often unwanted) as opposed to Blacks, Jews, Hippies, Gypsies, Delinquents, Alcoholics . . . who trigger much more charged, visceral responses. That's where Jackie comes in.

In 1947 no nation was freer or felt stronger than the United States and yet it openly subjected many of its citizens to the stigmas of ethnic, religious, and racial prejudice. It was a time when many businesses and academic institutions had outright quotas on the admission or employment of specific minorities such as Jews, Hispanics, or Asians. Blacks could hardly be credited with having any of the acceptable attributes Goffman cites as "normal." Even having "a recent record in sports" was explicitly denied to them in organized professional competition, especially in baseball, with its separate Negro league. Rickey chose Robinson not only for his athletic prowess—baseball was not his best sport—but for his ability to withstand the taunts and threats that overcoming the stigma of being black were sure to, and did, produce. His ability to perform and excel in spite of these extraordinary pressures is a remarkable achievement to this day, summed up at the end of Scott Simon's *Jackie Robinson and the Integration of Baseball:*

Many athletes find that the critical difference between performers of equal ability is the skill to succeed under stress. Ali, Jordan, and Ruth all had to surpass the unreasonable expectation to be not only good, but magical. Ali had the added load of fighting a court case that could break him while it made him the object of incomparable veneration. But none of that compares to the weight Jackie Robinson carried onto the field: the threat of his own death; the fear for his family; the taunts, catcalls, beanballs, brushback pitches, high spikes and low blows; and finally, trying to play ball while worrying that history could turn—or be turned back—by whether he could hit a curve, and not hit back at his tormentors.

The picture on my wall shows him just about to beat the tag as he slides into home. It is very dramatic and dynamic and captures his daring and the excitement he generated as a player. Jackie's admirers remember and embrace not only his physical feats, but the excitement that stirred every time he got on base, when the ballpark came alive with possibilities. It's not that he often stole second, third, and then home, but he did it enough so that the chance was always there in the minds of fans, and, more importantly, because as Red Barber pointed out, the game was the thing, in the minds of the opposing players. He made them crazy, and crazy people make mistakes.

But the snapshot is also a wonderful metaphor. Jackie is trying to get home. Home, that place in which there are no stigmas. In the ideal, the place where we can unconditionally be understood, supported, and comforted because of, and in spite of, our actions. A place that is always available and we are always accepted for who we are. Even though Rickey got Robinson into the establishment, until he could prove that he could make it home—with home runs, runs batted in, and the ultimate accomplishment—stealing—Jackie would never be accepted. When that started to continually happen he became one of the family—no longer the different, feared outsider—with a place at the table. He made it home.

The security of home can quickly change for any of us. "Ordinary people" can find themselves rapidly transformed into a stigmatized status. Getting pregnant, seeking a divorce, or losing a job can instantly transform social status. Once a person, or group, is stigmatized, other traits are easily attributed to them. Thus the physical deficiency of the deaf may lead to the inference that they are characterologically unsound of mind as well as "tribally" deficient since it is a hereditary affliction. We call people without shelter homeless—not apartment-less or houseless—implying a degree of weakness and pathology that in many instances is not true.

Certainly, contracting a serious illness can dramatically change the way you are treated, even if it only lasts for the time you are sick. Until the beginning of the twentieth century those of means were treated at home for almost all illnesses. Hospitals were for poor people and a place to possibly get sicker.

With the advent of asepsis things began to shift toward hospital care. But when they built pavilions for the rich, like the Phillips House at Massachusetts General Hospital, they attempted to make it as much like home as possible. Many rooms had attached maid's quarters, their own wine storage in the basement, and original paintings from the Museum of Fine Arts on the walls. The standard joke when I worked at MGH in the '60s was that the Phillips House was such a nice place and so close to a good hospital.

Now encounters with the medical profession are very different, especially as an inpatient. Hospitals no longer attempt to be your home away from home. Upon admission a different set of social rules are swiftly enforced. You are excused from ordinary obligations depending on the severity of the illness. You are expected to be a good patient and not complain, at least in public. You are asked to be completely passive and submit to the staff's requirements. In effect, unless you fight very hard, you become the equivalent of an inmate. You are seen as a patient with a unit number and a hospital gown, deprived of social status allowing the staff to treat you as a case that provides them with a degree of distance and dispassion. You are expected to reward their efforts by following orders, making few demands, and getting better. In the age of the internet, patient ombudsmen, and greatly reduced inpatient stays with nicer amenities, medical care is making a start at becoming more interactive, but it has a long way to go.

I realize that when I speak and marvel at today's athletic accomplishments it's about David Ortiz, or Larry Bird, or Serena Williams. For me, at least in sports, ethnicity, race, and to some extent gender have all but disappeared. As Red Barber learned so early on when Jackie was given his break, it's all about the ball. Now, four decades later we seem to be on the brink of a similar breakthrough in our nation as a whole. The current campaign is about making our nation's premier house, the White House, a home for someone other than Goffman's unblushing male. The candidate is making some people crazy, but the country is alive with possibilities. The fact that a black family or a woman is seriously considered and anointed as a contender to make it a home for themselves and their constituents represents as large a step forward as Jackie's accomplishment proved to be. My hope is that the consequences of these recent political movements will enable us to diminish and hopefully eliminate the stigmas associated with difference in our overall society in the same way they have been so in sports.

In the end Jackie died at an early age burdened by the stress of his accomplishments on himself and his family. But he has not died in my mind or heart, and I am sure I speak for thousands of others who witnessed his achievements. Jackie's heroism battled bigotry on all fronts, for all people, not only for the rights of blacks. He gave me the courage and determination to make it, in spite of being crippled, Jewish, and yes, even another old redhead.

Karola's Kitchen

Karola Schack Lorch, November 17, 1900–October 4, 1999

**Kitchen** a place fitted with the apparatus for cooking
—OED

I draw part of my inspiration for these essays from the compendium of M.F.K. Fisher's writings *The Art of Eating*. Mary Frances, as she was called by almost everyone, even those who didn't know her, was an essayist par excellence. She wrote not only about gastronomical matters, but life in general, in which she partook with great gusto. I highly recommend dipping into any of Mary Frances's musings; she is extremely insightful and a beautiful writer. In the foreword to *The Gastronomical Me*, she expounds on the centrality of food to the human condition and her motivations as a food writer:

People ask me: Why do you write about food and eating and drinking? Why don't you write about the struggle for power, security, and about love, the way others do? . . . The easiest answer is to say, like most other humans, I am hungry. But there is more than that. It seems to me that our three basic needs, for food and security and love, are so mixed and mingled and entwined that we cannot straightly think of one without the others. So it happens that when I write of hunger, I am really writing about love and the hunger for it, and warmth, and the love of it . . . and then the warmth and richness and fine reality of hunger satisfied . . . and it is all one. We must eat. If, in the face of that dread fact, we can find nourishment, tolerance and compassion for it, we'll be no less full of human dignity. There is a communion of more than our bodies when bread is broken and wine drunk. And that is my answer, when people ask me: Why do you write about hunger, and not war or love?

Her series of pieces that I especially like are a set of alphabetical essays (why didn't I think of that?) written for *Gourmet* magazine in the early '50s. Every month M.F.K. would write about experiences and behaviors related to food, as opposed to food itself, although every essay ended with a recipe or two. I particularly like "A for Alone" in which she reflects on her lack of dinner invitations because people are too intimidated to cook for her, and "W for Wanton" and how to assure your after-dinner entertainment by serving the right dishes.

Her "K for Kosher" is an excellent introduction to the dietary laws and strict standards prescribed for Jews, and their social as well as dietary consequences. My mother, Karola, was an excellent professional cook, and although my parents didn't keep kosher she would never cook or eat any pork. Karola did however adhere to a set of standards for excellence that would have done any Rabbi proud. She never forgot her near starvation during World War I, and like many of her generation, never wasted a scrap of food. She was equally thrifty in the procurement of food. When visiting our home she never ceased to turn over our canned goods, examine the price, and tell Jane or me how much less she had paid for the same item. (I was severely tempted at times to buy a pricing machine and drastically reduce the price of all our purchases to watch her reaction, but never did.) Her vigilance stayed with her until almost the day she died, at the age of ninety-nine. I could always count on hearing her voice on my answering machine admonishing me for at least two items that had gone unattended on my current punch list. Her expectations were exacting, and although I only occasionally lived up to them, I was also easily forgiven.

I was blessed with her wonderful and varied meals and she certainly is the inspiration for my own interest in cooking. I never saw her use a recipe. She only had the tiniest of apartment kitchens in which to perform her magic, and yet she was able to produce extraordinary dishes and baked goods. My father, Hugo, had a butcher shop and so our meals were heavily weighted toward his wares, although they consisted mostly of cuts that he could not sell. That challenged my mother's resourcefulness since she was always offered the oddest cuts of meat and offal. Along with her sister, my aunt Recha, she established and ran a successful catering business entirely by word of mouth. Once established her reputation brought her a variety of engagements, often as a personal chef for visiting dignitaries. Her meals were memorable and she reveled in her accomplishments.

Memories of great meals are not necessarily the case for every Jewish boy. Buddy Hackett did a hilarious bit about his first days in the army when he rushed to the medics with the symptom "my fire went out." Having always eaten his mother's cooking he assumed the chronic heartburn he experienced was life-sustaining. When it disappeared on army rations he panicked.

In *Alice, Let's Eat*, Calvin Trillin, the great *New Yorker* food writer, further expounds on the use of heartburn in describing The Parkway Restaurant on New York's Lower East Side.

Following the Rumanian tradition, garlic is used in excess to keep the vampires away. Following the Jewish tradition, a dispenser of schmaltz (liquid chicken fat) is kept on the table to give vampires heartburn if they get through the garlic defense.

And speaking of schmaltz:

Three men are discussing their previous night's lovemaking.

The Italian says, "I rubbed extra virgin olive oil all over my wife's body, we made love, and she screamed for five minutes."

The Frenchman says, "I rubbed sweet butter all over my wife, made love to her, and she screamed for ten minutes."

The Jewish guy says, "I covered my wife with schmaltz, made love, and she screamed for an hour."

The others gasp, "An hour! How did you make her scream for an hour?"

"I wiped my hands on the drapes."

A variation:

Four men are walking in the desert.

The German says, "I am tired and thirsty. I must have a beer."

The Italian says, "I am tired and thirsty. I must have wine."

The Mexican says, "I am tired and thirsty. I must have tequila."

The Jew says, "I am tired and thirsty. I must have diabetes."

Although these stories and jokes are told from a Jewish perspective, they reflect our association of specific foods with different cultures. Food, eating, and mealtimes are distinctive aspects in any society and their effect, ranging from the daily activities of procurement to world outlook is profound. In her wonderful novel *The Last Chinese Chef*, Nicole Mones expounds through the words of Liang Wei, her imaginary great chef, on the centrality of food to the Chinese:

The most important thing is to preserve civilization. As men we are the sum of our forebears, the great thinkers, the great masters, the great chefs. We who know the secrets of great food must pass them on, for our attainment in food is no less than our attainment in philosophy, or art; indeed, the three things cannot be separated. These are the things that make us Chinese. . . . Apprentices have asked me, what is the most exalted peak of cuisine? Is it the freshest ingredients, the most complex flavors? Is it the rustic, or the rare? It is none of these. The peak is neither eating nor cooking, but the giving and sharing of food. Great food should never be taken alone. What pleasure can a man take in fine cuisine unless he invites cherished friends, counts the days until the banquet, and composes an anticipatory poem for his letter of invitation?

One of the concerns with our modern society is that vast quantities of relatively unhealthy food is eaten alone and often on the run. This leads to a myriad of issues from the ever-increasing and alarming rate of obesity to the unraveling of family meals taken together that build and reinforce the fabric of our familial and social networks. The one exception may still be festive and holiday gatherings that renew longstanding relationships and evoke some of our strongest memories—some very good and in some cases very bad. Christmas, Passover, Ramadan, *Palio di Siena*, Thanksgiving, the annual chicken barbeque in Little Compton. . . . All evoke extremely powerful memories for the participants.

Dylan Thomas in *A Child's Christmas in Wales* describes Christmas dinner in this charming passage:

I would be slap-dashing home, the gravy smell of the dinners of others, the bird smell, the brandy, the pudding and mince, coiling up to my nostrils. . . . For dinner we had turkey and blazing pudding, and after dinner the uncles sat in front of the fire, loosened all buttons, put their large moist hands over their watch chains, groaned a little and slept. Mothers, aunts, and sisters scuttled to and fro, bearing tureens. Auntie Bessie, who had already been frightened, twice, by a clockwork mouse, whimpered at the sideboard and had some elderberry wine. The dog was sick. Auntie Dosie had to have three aspirins, but Auntie Hannah, who liked port, stood in the middle of the snowbound backyard, singing like a big-bosomed thrush. I would blow up balloons to see how big they would blow up to; and, when they burst, which they all did, the uncles jumped and rumbled. In the rich and heavy afternoon, the uncles, breathing like dolphins and the snow descending, I would sit among festoons and Chinese lanterns and nibble dates.

As I mentioned in my "Jackie" essay we would have Seders at my Uncle Adolph's house. That was on the second night. For the first night we would go to Aunt Selma and Uncle Sepel's, my mother's brother. In his enormous West Side apartment there would be an aura of excitement while the dinner was prepared by my aunts, the men smoked cigars, and the children sneaked sips of the Passover wine (a rare vintage Manischewitz of course). In her touching memoir of growing up in Italy, Edda Servi Machlin recalls in *The Classic Cuisine of the Italian Jews* the making of matzà in her small village of Pitigliano:

There were new and exciting events: new shoes to be bought at the market stalls, new satin and taffeta ribbons for our hair. And, most important of all, there was the opening of the matzà bakery. Great comings and goings down and up those dark, slimy steps—an adventure to instill terror. But then came the light, the marble tables, the crackling of twigs in the oven, the smell of freshly ground flour. We were fascinated as we watched the long heavy wooden kneading pole rattling under the strong hands of the Shamash. It emanated screeches made by a rusty hinge, alternating with a cry that was almost a wail, produced by the bending wood. And all the women, whose capable hands refined the dough, giving it a perfect oval shape, adding eyelets and festoons to each little piece that was to become a matzà—a matzà uniquely different from the modern matzos we find in the super market today. . . . Finely detailed, they could be made to look like pieces of art. Toward evening the men came to share in the joys of this almost mystical ritual with their mothers, their sisters, their wives, their friends.

Literature is full of wonderful writing about food. Perhaps none so famous as the passage in Proust's monumental work *Remembrance of Things Past* where a bite of a madeleine evokes a set of memories and reflections that span seven volumes and cover over three thousand pages.

My mother, seeing that I was cold, offered me some tea, a thing I don't ordinarily take. I declined at first, but then, for no particular reason, changed my mind. She sent for one of those squat, plump little cakes called "petites madeleines." . . . Dispirited by the gloomy day and by the perspective of a depressing tomorrow, I raised to my lips a spoonful of the tea in which I had soaked a morsel of the cake. No sooner had the warm liquid mixed with the crumbs touched my palate than a shudder ran through my whole body and I stopped, intent upon the extraordinary changes that were taking place. An exquisite pleasure had invaded my senses, something isolated, detached with no suggestion of its origin. It immediately made life's vicissitudes indifferent to me, life's disasters became innocuous, its brevity illusory, in the same way that love operates filling me with a precious essence: or, rather, this essence was not in me, it was me.

My introduction to food writing came from reading the *New Yorker*. I clearly remember being awed by Joseph Wechsberg's account of the meticulous and extraordinary preparations by Fernand Point and his wife at their world-renowned, three-star restaurant La Pyramide in Vienne, France. It was a revelation that food could be taken that seriously. But it was the great bon vivant A.J. Liebling who really hooked me. Liebling, a confirmed glutton, had spent his youth learning to eat properly in Paris. His collection of stories in *Between Meals: An Appetite for Paris* is a delight as are any of his books. Here is his take on Monsieur Proust:

The Proust madeleine phenomenon is now firmly established in folklore as Newton's apple or Watt's steam kettle. The man ate a biscuit, the taste evoked memories, he wrote a book. This is capable of expression by the formula TMB for Taste>Memory>Book. Some time ago when I began to read a book called *The Food of France* by Waverley Root, I had an inverse experience: BMT, for Book>Memory>Taste. Happily the tastes that *The Food of France* recreated for me—small birds, stewed rabbit, stuffed tripe, Cote Rôti and Tave—were more robust than that of a madeleine, which Larousse defines as "a light cake made with sugar, flour, lemon juice, brandy, and eggs." (The quantity of brandy in a madeleine would not furnish a gnat with an alcohol rub). In the light of what Proust wrote with so mild a stimulus, it is the world's great loss that he did not have a heartier appetite. On a dozen Gardiner's Island oysters, a bowl of clam chowder, a peck of steamers, some bay scallops, three sautéed soft shell crabs, a few ears of fresh-picked corn, a thin swordfish steak of generous area, a pair of lobsters, and a Long Island duck, he might have written a masterpiece.

Calvin Trillin has carried on the Liebling tradition at the *New Yorker*. Although justly famous for extolling the culinary virtues of his hometown, Kansas City, here is a passage from his book *American Fried* that is quintessential Noo Yawk:

Having heard a number of people discuss the Last Straw that drove them from the city, I realize that if I didn't leave when Ben's Dairy started closing Sundays I'm probably in New York for good. It was an awful blow. It happened four years ago, and I still remember the details of the morning I discovered it, the way some people remember what they were wearing when they learned of the attack on Pearl Harbor—which, also, as I remember it, took place on a Sunday morning. (I mention that without trying to imply any mystic pattern governing catastrophes. I understand the Spanish Inquisition began late on a Tuesday afternoon.) At about nine-thirty, I had parked brilliantly on Houston Street itself—as the ex co-editor of a one-issue journal called *Beautiful Spot: A Magazine of Parking*, I find that a perfect spot on Houston Street on Sunday Morning can give me almost as much pleasure as a freshly baked bialy—and found myself in front of Yonah Schimmel's Knishery. Restraining myself from having one of Schimmel's legendary potato knishes at that hour of the morning, I settled for a cheese bagel, figuring a little extra energy might be useful when I faced the counter crowds down the street at Russ & Daughters, ordinarily my first stop.

Not everyone has the luxury of choice that Calvin Trillin is offered. In the poorest agrarian countries the entire day can be consumed with gathering firewood, water, and the meager staples needed to prepare a meal. In more affluent countries, part of the day may be centered on food procurement, as in the Calvin Trillin snippet, or it may take the form of what restaurant to choose, but all too often the resulting meal is not beneficial for our long-term health. Since we are what we eat it is interesting to note that until recently very little attention has been paid by the medical profession to good nutrition and eating habits. Once diagnosed with a disease, an abnormal test result, or weight problems, physicians are quick to give advice on how to change and restrict your diet. Without any abnormality however, I cannot recall that any one of my excellent caretakers ever asked me about my diet, eating habits, or any food-related subjects. It would seem that early counseling and monitoring of consumption patterns would be one of the simplest and most logical preventive steps for the medical profession to take. Although there is a movement toward more holistic approaches to patient health and fitness, the current lack of proactive attention to dietary issues is one of the many reasons our system should be more properly labeled a sickness system rather than a health system.

The obesity problem, mentioned above, has initiated a heightened set of concerns. Recent medical research shows that the body responds to food and exercise in a far more complicated way than the simplistic linear solutions of major diets/ exercise programs promise. Metabolism rates and eating behaviors are the result of complex biological and behavioral interactions between our brain, intestines, hormones, muscles, heart, genes. Changing behaviors learned as a child is exceedingly difficult. Learning to manage your body in a realistic, positive, and constructive manner toward attainable goals seems to be the key to success. We need a great deal of additional biological/behavioral understanding and more focus by the average practitioner on everyday eating habits to make significant progress toward assuring we all lead as healthy a life as possible.

The food gatherer in third-world countries, and for that matter the average affluent citizen in developed nations, cannot possibly comprehend the magnitude of the food production supply chain, and the resulting choices and waste. My direct exposure to the workings of the food industry, as opposed to the revelations supplied by Upton Sinclair in *The Jungle*, came at an early age when I would accompany Hugo to the wholesale meat markets before dawn. On West 14th Street I would witness huge quantities of meat products bought and sold in an old-world, free-market environment that was energizing, fun, and exciting. It was like stepping into a secret world that existed while everyone else slept. Goods were compared, bought, and sold among a tight circle of friends who had been dealing together for years and knew what each had to offer and what was needed. It was a great place to learn how to discern subtle differences of quality and the art of bargaining. To this day I still love to seek out these markets when I travel to new cities, especially foreign countries, because to me they represent the unadulterated lifeblood of the economy and the true fabric of the culture.

My real understanding of the enormity and complexity of the enterprise did not come until I was asked to work for a relatively small chicken producer in Maine. The output of this small "farm" was approximately 30,000 chickens per day, which meant there were almost three million chickens being fed at any moment. The amount of chicken feed needed to sustain these animals was prodigious, requiring over one hundred tons of feed per week. Scientifically formulated, the feed that was made up of over twenty ingredients, of which each price had to be constantly monitored. At that volume overall cost was very sensitive to even a small movement in market price for any constituent like Peruvian fish oil or marigolds (used to color the skin yellow).

The chicken farm hired me to improve their linear programming model, a mathematical technique that methodically balances trade-offs between variables, in this case cost and nutritive value. In addition to utilizing highly sophisticated techniques to monitor costs, there were also geneticists and nutritionists studying the most effective breeding techniques and nutrients to accelerate the chicken's growth. And this was considered a mom-and-pop operation, compared to Ralston Purina or Perdue.

To end this aside the latest data show that there were approximately nine billion chickens brought to market in the United States last year. Realizing that the same thought and effort goes into the production, delivery, promotion, and sale of almost every food item on any supermarket shelf demonstrates how central food is to the social organization of any country and to a large extent how much it is taken for granted. It is certainly a tribute to the efficiency and organization of the food industry that these processes are practically invisible. We would all like it to stay that way.

Recently the food supply chain has been in the press, and on the national consciousness, with the disturbing news of tainted food—beef with mad cow disease, spinach, tomatoes,

Chinese milk products. Remembering that "K is for Kosher," perhaps the most recent egregious violation has been reported at Agriprocessors, a kosher slaughterhouse in Iowa. The kosher laws (Kashrut) require that a kosher product be genuine by adhering to a strict code of behavior in its preparation. Not only were the ritual methods of slaughter compromised, but the working conditions and treatment of the plant workers were severely abused as well. The owners clearly did not accept, nor believe in, the old Hebrew National tagline, "We answer to a higher authority." The massiveness of the agricultural markets coupled with the routine movement of food across international borders has the potential to severely cripple the food system in ways similar to the sub-prime mortgage crisis if we don't remain extremely vigilant and enforce adequate inspection safeguards.

Ironically, another consulting engagement related to food changed my career and led me to spend the majority of my professional life working in the nonprofit arena. For my second job after MIT I worked as an Operations Research analyst for a consulting company that specialized in defense projects. One day I was assigned to a contract to resolve a dispute that centered on the efficacy of using wheat rust as a possible biological warfare agent. Wheat rust is a plant disease that kills wheat. Spores that are reddish in color are carried through the air, attach themselves to a stalk of wheat, and make it look like it has rusted, causing it to die. It was a major plant disease problem in early nineteenth-century America. Producing hybrid strains of wheat that are rust-resistant to the existing spores subsequently resolved the problem. But spores mutate and so new hybrids are constantly needed. The warfare argument, in short, was that we could produce a super virulent spore, blanket Russia's wheat crop with rust, threatening them with mass starvation, and then save them with our surplus stocks (once they "surrendered").

I spent a few months gathering data and becoming a plant disease maven. I decided that as part of my education I should visit Fort Detrick, the Army's biological warfare center (recently in the news because of the anthrax attack and the related suicide of one of their scientists). Fort Detrick had a stockpile of wheat rust spores in case they were needed and during my visit I was asked if I wanted to see them. Answering in the affirmative I was led through a series of greenhouses to see what amounted to a stack of cardboard boxes in a refrigerated vault. It was the walk that was significant. Every greenhouse was not full of blooming plants, but full of dead and dying plants. My hosts pointed these out with great pride and satisfaction, since their job was to kill plants not to grow them. The experience shook me to the core. Coupled with my belief that most of the work I had been assigned took the form of a thinking man's WPA, I decided to focus my professional interests on sustaining life, not killing it.

After a five-month "sabbatical" in Europe, I returned to the ranks of the employed through a connection I had made at Massachusetts General Hospital (MGH). When I was at MIT, I had volunteered for a battery of psychological tests on mental dexterity and aging at the hospital. One of the principal investigators of the study was Gardner Quarton—affectionately called Q by his friends—who was a major influence on my life. Through Q's introductions, John Knowles, the Hospital Director, Oliver Cope, the Chairman of the Research Committee, and others interviewed me and eventually I was hired with the title Assistant Mathematician in the Department of Psychiatry (Q's Department.). Computers were just emerging as a tool and there was a great deal of interest in how they could be applied to medical research and clinical care. It is only a slight exaggeration that John Knowles hired me because he had been told, this was 1961, that he would have an electronic medical record in six to twelve months. My job was to support researchers and clinicians interested in utilizing computers, statistics, and technology.

Although I was given a salary it was made very clear to me that I was responsible for my own support. In essence I was establishing and running an in-house service that launched my life-long career as an independent consultant. During my seven-year tenure at MGH I worked on a number of ground-breaking projects in neurophysiology, genetics, biomedical statistics, radiology, as well as clinical psychiatry (details to come in subsequent essays). In addition I was given a Harvard Medical School appointment to teach and mentor medical students in these disciplines. I had the good fortune to work with and support a number of students—Richard Friedman, Robert Greenes, and Stephen Pauker, among others—many of whom have gone on to have illustrious careers as physicians and researchers in medical informatics. My appointment/association at Harvard Medical spanned over forty rich and rewarding years, culminating with fifteen years as a consultant to Dan Tosteson, the Dean, and his executive team of David Bray and Jim Adelstein.

Karola could not have been more pleased with my career change. Although she constantly bemoaned the fact that she didn't know what I did (nor at times did I), my association with the medical and academic world was of great satisfaction to her. She was never one to push me into a given profession— "my son the doctor." Her overriding goal was to assure that I would grow up to be self-reliant and would be able to lead an independent life. That goal was often in conflict with her controlling nature, but always remained paramount.

As Rosh Hashanah approaches I know that wherever she is, she is planning to make her zwetschke kuchen and other special treats to share with her fellow angels. At the same time she is quietly checking in the pantry to make sure God is not overpaying for her Manna.

Shalom

שלום

Karola at her 97th Birthday Party in New York City

**Karola's Zwetschke Kuchen (Prune Plum Cake)**
—*New York Times* **Version**

12 Italian prune plums (pitted and cut in half)
1 stick unsalted butter (softened)
1 cup sugar
1 cup flour (sifted)
1 tsp baking powder
2 eggs
pinch of salt
cinnamon, sugar, or lemon juice for topping

1. Pre-heat the oven to 350 degrees Fahrenheit.
2. Cream the sugar and butter in a bowl (the butter will absorb all the sugar).
3. Add flour, baking powder, salt, beaten eggs, and mix well.
4. Spoon batter into a 9" cake pan with a removable bottom or a spring-form pan.
5. Place plums in concentric circles on the batter—skin-side up.
6. Sprinkle plums with lemon juice and/or sugar according to sweetness of plums.
7. Sprinkle with cinnamon depending on your taste (no more than 1 tsp).
8 Bake for an hour.
9. Remove and cool.

The plums will sink to the bottom.
Serve plain or with vanilla ice cream or whipped cream.
Can be refrigerated or frozen.

Enjoy!

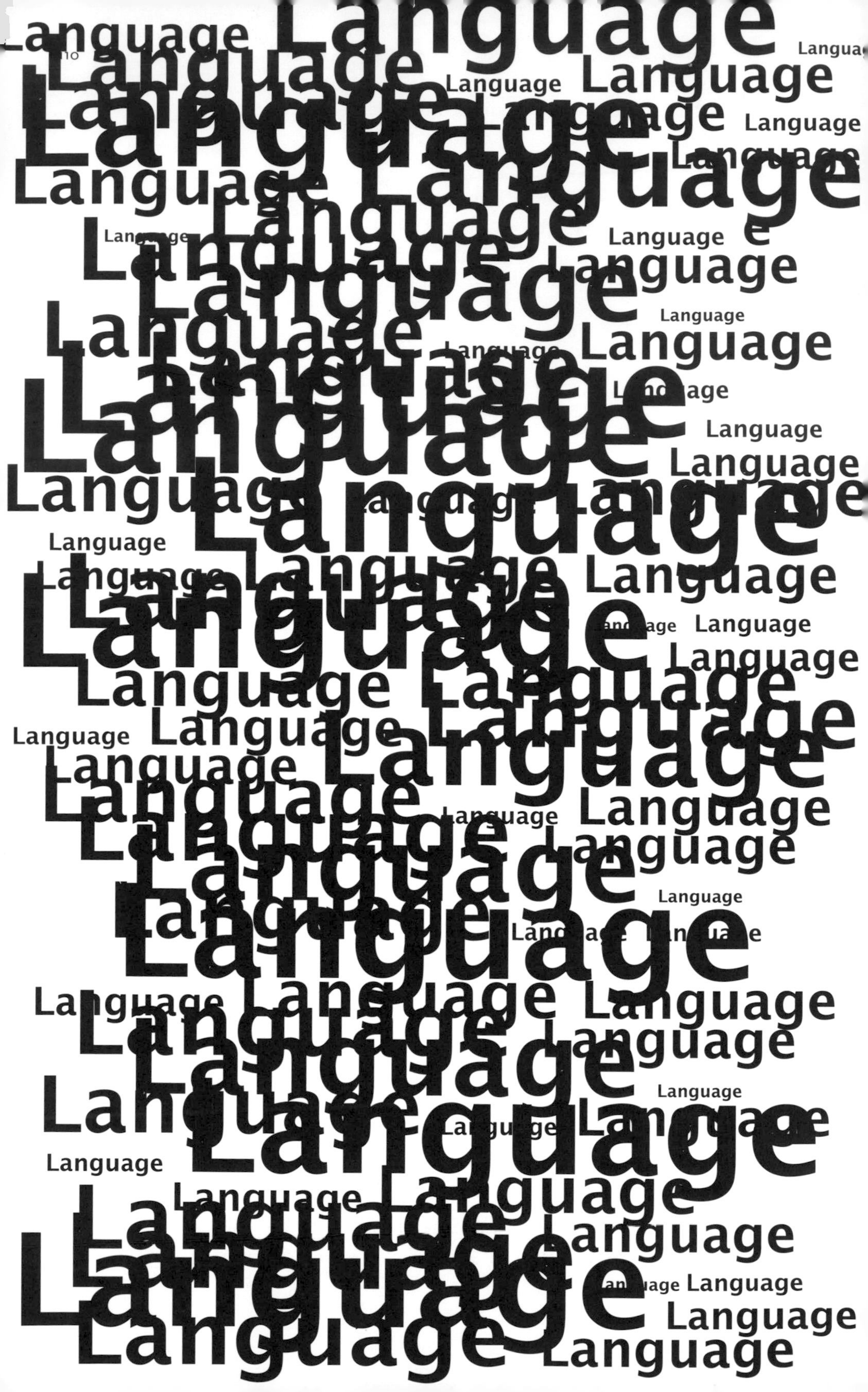
Language

# Lan·guage

A system of communication using words, written and spoken,
and particular ways of combining them
—OED

My imaginary friend Jack was always a closely kept secret. We
would race to the corner (I always won), talk about sports, or
just dream about the future together. He was always there when
I needed to speak to someone, although I would always carefully hide our *tête-à-têtes* from view. My constant inner dialogue
allowed me to express my hopes and fears as I sorted through
the experiences of daily life. Having someone to be supportive,
nonjudgmental, and adoring was very comforting. Jack is no
longer with me, but my inner dialogues have never gone away,
and, I hope, never will.

I think it is safe to say that the trait that almost everyone agrees sets humans apart from other animals is our facility to communicate with each other and ourselves through language. The art and act of using language guide our behavior. Language allows us to remember and learn from our past, assess our alternative actions in the present, and dream about our future. It lets us create our understanding of reality, that illusive construct we use to predict and explain the events. It is inordinately complicated and yet naturally acquired, almost without thought. In recent years, as a result of the thinking of Chomsky, Pinker, Dennett, and many others, attempts to understand the acquisition, usage, and storage of language have made linguistics, neurophysiology, and the cognitive sciences among the most heavily studied areas of science. Writing these essays has renewed and heightened my interest in the field and made me evermore sensitive to what a central role language plays in all our lives.

When it comes to reflections and memoirs, my hero is Lewis Thomas. While reading an article last week about the latest Nobel Prize in chemistry I could not help thinking how much Lewis Thomas would have enjoyed describing the importance of the prize-winning discovery: the isolation of a gene in certain jellyfish that makes them fluorescent, allowing researchers to visually track the deployment of proteins within a cell. Thomas, a renowned physician, wrote a series of essays for the *New England Journal of Medicine* called Notes of a Biology Watcher. These were ultimately collected in a series of books— the most famous being his first, *The Lives of a Cell*. Although his musings range over a wide variety of subjects, from punctuation, to music, to the state of modern medicine, most are reflections on the mechanisms of cellular behavior and the profound lessons we can learn from the complex workings within these tiniest bits of living matter. When I open one of his essays I picture him calling me over and saying, "Sit down a second and let me tell you what I have been thinking about. Don't you find it fascinating that . . . ?" Everything around you seems to get quiet and the ideas and the clarity with which they are presented enthrall me.

One of Thomas's major interests was language and how it differentiated humans from all other species.

It begins to look, more and more disturbingly, as if the gift of language is the single human trait that marks us all genetically, setting us apart from all the rest of life. Language is, like nest building or hive building, the universal and biologically specific activity of human beings. We engage in it communally, compulsively, and automatically. We cannot be human without it; if we were to be separated from it our minds would die, as surely as bees lost from the hive.
—*The Lives of a Cell*, Lewis Thomas

I concur that language is the defining trait of our species and yet outside the rarefied fields of linguistics, psychology, psychiatry, and literature, little time is spent understanding how this mechanism shapes how we think, act, or feel. Although language may seem central to our function it is far from the only signal-processing mechanism we employ. We are virtually flooded with other stimuli to be deciphered, absorbed, manipulated and acted upon. We take for granted that our physiological functions are constantly processing coded signals as complex and subtle as any aspect of language. The physiological signal processing is not extraordinary—every other living being on earth, simple or complex, does much the same thing. Breathing, digestion, reproduction, cell replacement—these are automatically processed in response to the unique signals. Domestic animals can learn behavior in response to pain or reward. But we have the additional capabilities of learning highly refined behaviors that may or may not be linguistically driven. Think of returning a one hundred mph-plus tennis serve, playing the Appassionata on the piano, or recognizing Ella after one or two notes. As we incorporate these phenomenal discernments and abilities within our bodies, their mastery belies the use of language to execute the performance of these feats in the moment. Language still plays an extraordinary role in prospectively anticipating, and/or retrospectively thinking about these actions.

Other animals are equally able to rapidly process the subtlest of signals in amazing ways. The echolocation ability of bats, the hovering of hummingbirds, the mating dances of insects, and the territorial display of colors across many species when understood in detail, inspires awe. Their ability to discern and process signals is on a par with anything we have to offer, and yet there is a significant difference. Animals, in almost every instance, are programmed to have one and only one response to a stimulus. There is no room or ability for interpretation. Our ability to consider alternative actions through the lens of language is the key difference.

Technological marvels such as telephones, televisions, and computers are most often what come to mind when we refer to living in "The Information Age." The underlying principles that ultimately drive these devices, that allow signals to be coded, transmitted, received, deciphered, and acted upon, are of small concern to the average citizen. Yet it is precisely the understanding of these most elemental building blocks, the underlying codes and how they are processed, that defines the information age and is of primary import. And the most important, the one we may know the least about, is language. How do we acquire, store, retrieve and utilize language and its properties to advance, or some may say degrade, our brief existence on the planet? I have chosen to highlight what I believe is the central uniqueness of language: ambiguity. You may think it is the precision of language that makes it useful; it is the vagueness of language that affords us the singular characteristic of being human—the fact that we have discretion. I again turn to Lewis Thomas:

Ambiguity seems to be an essential, indispensable element in the transfer of information from one place to another by words, where matters of real importance are concerned. It is often necessary for meaning to come through, that there be an almost vague sense of strangeness and askewness. Speechless animals cannot do this . . . Only the human mind is designed to work in this way, programmed to drift away in the presence of locked-on information, straying from each point in a hunt for a better, different point of view. If it were not for the capacity of ambiguity, for the sensing of strangeness, that words in all languages provide, we would have no way of recognizing the layers of counterpoint in meaning.
—*The Lives of a Cell*, Lewis Thomas

One of the defining features of any set of codes is the extent to which it is ambiguous. Some codes must be exact in order to work. You would not want a combination lock to allow sequences that were almost right. The same is true of telephone numbers and computer passwords. DNA and RNA, the universal genetic codes, must be precisely deciphered to produce the cells and proteins they are meant to generate, although mutations do occur.

Language is a very special type of coded signal and one of its singular properties is ambiguity. Sometimes "close" is good enough. Following a recipe requires set amounts, but a cup is not a cup down to the last drop. One of the clearest examples of ambiguity in language is the crossword puzzle. Without this quality, crossword puzzles could not exist. The easier the puzzle, the less ambiguous the clues that define the right answer; the more difficult, the more possibilities need to be considered. The gradation of the *New York Times* puzzles from easy to hard as the week goes on relies primarily on that premise.

As Thomas states, it is this lack of preciseness in language that affords us the ability to interpret events in a variety of ways. Special languages are sometimes innately ambiguous. Greater variation in allowable precision encourages individual readers or listeners to commute their meaning according to their own experience and knowledge. Poetry and music are examples of communications that invite highly variable levels of understanding; a Wallace Stevens or a Mahler doesn't necessarily preclude enjoyment or appreciation by those who haven't broken the code, but there are layers within layers that can be seen only with study.

Leonard Bernstein was a master at describing the underlying language of music. His Charles Eliot Norton lectures— *The Unanswered Question: Six Talks at Harvard*—(available on DVD and sold in book form) are a tour de force exploring how Chomsky's notions of generative grammar and syntax can be applied to music theory. Yet he felt that no amount of analysis could replace music itself. To illustrate, here is a short passage from his book *The Joy of Music*:

There have been more words written about (Beethoven's) the Eroica symphony than there are notes in it; in fact, I should imagine the proportion of words to notes, if anyone could get an accurate count, would be flabbergasting. And yet, has anyone ever successfully "explained" the Eroica? Can anyone explain in mere prose the wonder of one note following or coinciding with another so that we feel that it's exactly how those notes had to be? Of course not. No matter what rationalists we may profess to be, we are stopped cold at the border of the mystic area. It is not too much to say mystic or even magic: no art lover can be agnostic when the chips are down. If you love music, you are a believer, however dialectically you try to wriggle out of it.

On the other hand, mathematics, computer languages, and chemical formulas all utilize well-defined symbols, syntax, and operational rules that do not allow much, if any, interpretation. In every field of endeavor—scientific specialties, sports, medicine—a set of terms and concepts are especially named and used to give more precise meaning to facilitate communication and reduce the possibility of misunderstanding.

In some fields language is often wielded as a tool to maintain special status. Medicine is a good example. Body parts are named in Latin terms and pathologies are given specific names that have no other reference in the spoken language. Although necessary to assure specificity, it often seems, at least from this patient's point of view, that these names and terms are used to obscure communication to non-initiates, and protect members of the guild from challenges to their judgment. Thus when I, or anyone else, gets sick, a complete education in a foreign vocabulary is necessary to even hope to have a semblance of understanding of the condition, treatment, and prognosis. Even though physicians attempt to translate their diagnosis and knowledge to everyday speech, I certainly always feel that something is lost, or that I am purposely not being told the whole story. "Trust me" is not a wholly convincing message, whether it is delivered by doctors or lawyers, not to mention representatives of the Department of Homeland Security. The arcane nomenclature of medicine certainly precludes any transmission of emotion and empathy, dimensions that most patients and I crave to hear for reassurance.

Putting language in the context of general signal processing should help clarify the concepts of ambiguity and redundancy, which may initially seem counterintuitive. A brief and highly simplified explanation of the work of Claude Shannon will help.

Shannon became a seminal figure in the development of computers by demonstrating in his master's thesis that a special form of algebra, Boolean Algebra (named after George Boole) could represent all digital circuits. In the late '40s he devised a revolutionary qualitative and quantitative measure of communication, aptly called information theory. The opening sentence of his groundbreaking paper states, "The fundamental problem of communication is that of reproducing at one point, either exactly or approximately, a message selected at another point." Note this is a theory of sending messages (signals) over a channel, that may contain other signals (noise) and predicting how accurately they will be received. The signal may or may not be language. Based on the laws of thermodynamics, information theory states that information, like entropy, is actually a measure of disorganization. In Shannon's theory, the more predictable (organized) the code of a signal, the less information it carries; the less predictable (disorganized) the code of a signal, the more information it delivers. It is very important to emphasize that information and meaning are not the same. Taken to its logical conclusion, a perfectly predictable occurrence carries no information, and a completely unpredictable event carries the maximum amount of information. If we define a scale from 0 to 100 as an information scale, 0 represents no information and 100 stands for maximum information. As an example, getting a signal "AAAAAAAAAA" you would predict that A would be the next signal, and if it were, it would carry no information. On the other hand "2A$b∧m*t!" leaves you with no predictive capability and therefore the next signal will carry the most information. Notice that both the totally redundant signal and the completely random signal carry no meaning. Meaning lies somewhere near the middle of the scale. Highly encrypted codes, those that are designed with little redundancy, are near to the center and upper end of the scale. Language probably lies at about 20–30 on the scale. Language, therefore, is at least 20–30% redundant/ambiguous in the context of pure information as defined by Shannon and it is these properties that give it special value.

Language requires redundancy and ambiguity for several reasons. If there weren't any play, only one word would suffice for any meaning, which would make communicating difficult, if not impossible. The use of many words to mean the same thing gives language a richness and flexibility that it must have to convey textured and nuanced meaning. In addition we are only able to process so much information at any one time. In order to carry out a dialogue, the sentences that are uttered must be somewhat predictable in order for us to interact. Processing sentences with exact meanings would greatly slow up, if not make impossible, our ability to converse since our ability to decipher and understand would have to be precise.

At the most basic level, to speak a word we must access our memory for a phonetic sequence of sounds associated with a specific word. The word, in turn, represents an object or a concept we wish to identify, name, or describe. Stored electrochemically in part of our brain in a coded signal we as yet do not understand is not only the meaning of the word and its reference but the pattern of sounds necessary to convey the word and speak it. To utter the sound associated with the word, we retrieve this sound pattern and somehow decipher it to convert the stored electrochemical representation to a puff of air that we send past our vocal chords to make them vibrate and make sound. We then shape the resulting sound with our tongue and mouth into the pattern of our chosen word. The sound is transmitted in the form of an acoustical signal—or pressure wave—through the air to the ear of our listener. (The pressure of this wave is hardly discernable. Put your hand in front of your mouth as you speak and you will see that you feel next to nothing.) The fine hairlike receptors in the listener's ear vibrate sympathetically with the received signal and translate the acoustic signal back into an electrical signal that is then carried to the recipient's brain to be matched and recognized as the sound pattern of the word spoken. They then deliver the meaning that the sender wanted to convey by deciphering the coded message and retrieving the meaning in the user's brain.

The memory cells for the word not only carry its meaning and sound pattern, they also carry a host of related information—its symbolic representation in letters (to allow written deciphering, its smell where applicable, its emotional valence, its synonyms and antonyms, its part of speech, its strength, and its acceptable usage, to name just a few). Not only do we encode the word, but also the tone and emphasis of the speaker convey additional information about its intended use. This process may be repeated for every word but in actuality is shortened by a number of factors, including our ability to predict the word's meaning from the context of the dialogue and the structure (grammar/syntax) of the language. The words are then further processed into phrases, sentences, thoughts, or actions. All this material is accessed instantly from the thousands upon thousands of stored words and language rules, seemingly without much thought. As yet we really don't know how it is done. When broken up this way, speech is an outright miracle.

So how does this rudimentary breakdown of language processing help us in thinking about the everyday use of language? Consider our ability to have a conversation. In speaking to someone we need to listen to what they have to say, understand it, and formulate our own response, all in a reasonable amount of time. In order to accomplish this task the reliable processing of the incoming signal and encoding of our answer must be very fast—so fast that in order to perform these tasks at the required speed we cannot, and do not, execute all the functions described above for every word. In actuality we need not listen to everything that is being said because we can almost always predict the meaning of the utterance long before it is completed. Our ability is the result of the structural aspect of the language (syntax), our projection of what we think the speaker will say based on our experience from other conversations, and the relatively low level of information in each unit of the utterance. Thus there are a myriad of factors, beyond the individual words, that enable us to believe we understand the signal being sent. Consider *Windows Is Shutting Down* by Clive James:

Windows is shutting down, and grammar are
On their last leg. So what am we to do?
A letter of complaint go just so far,
Proving the only one in step are you.

Better, perhaps, to simply let it goes.
A sentence have to be screwed pretty bad

Before they gets to where you doesnt knows
The meaning what it must be meant to had.

The meteor have hit. Extinction spread,
But evolution do not stop for that.
A mutant languages rise from the dead
And all them rules is suddenly old hat.

Too bad for we, us what has had so long
The best seat from the only game in town.
But there it am, and whom can say its wrong?
Those are the break. Windows is shutting down.

The second stanza says it all. It is this redundancy/ambiguity inherent in language that allows for its rapid decoding and usage, but also for alternative interpretations. The fact is that we bring far more to any human interaction and conversation than our knowledge of natural language. The individual and cultural model of reality we project guides every one of our interactions with the world. Within that model is our assumed belief of who we think a person is, how we think that person will act, and what we believe they will say. This projection guides our interactions even when we meet them for the first time. Within specified limits we process what we expect to hear through our assumed model and match it to our expectations.

Take a look at the formality of diplomacy, in which discussion must be preceded by mutual knowledge of protocol, manners, and the shape of a negotiating table, as well as the subject at hand and the vocabulary to describe it. A crusade is one man's noble cause and another's genocidal invasion. Mistakes can be poisonous and fatal.

In more personal settings, we modify our view over time based on our actual experience, but it is extraordinarily difficult to dramatically change our initial beliefs once established. A good example is falling out of love. Once the break is made, interactions are reprocessed within the new belief structure and one often hears, "I should have known when s(he) said X that this wasn't going to work." The same reprocessing takes place in many other contexts. Paradigm shifts require that almost all prior explanations be reconsidered as the new world outlook replaces the old. Our innate tendency to hold tightly to our existing worldview drives us to make every interaction as predictable as possible. Information outside of these predictions (our comfort zone) is often registered but ignored.

An example of the predictive nature of language is the program ELIZA developed in the '60s by Joseph Weizenbaum of MIT. I along with Michael McGuire and Gardner Quarton had the privilege of working with Joe on the development of ELIZA (named for Eliza Doolittle of Pygmalion because we could make her look smart, but she was the same dumb program underneath). We ran a series of experiments to test her limitations. ELIZA was a program that used the pragmatics of language to emulate a conversation. It could recognize and respond to simple sentence structures with reasonable answers drawn from a script of modifiable answers. When it didn't "understand" it would simply say things to continue the conversation like, "hmm," "interesting," or "please go on." Although it was surprisingly responsive, it was often completely wrong. If someone typed, "What I mean to say is . . . " ELIZA might answer, "Mean is a strong word, do you often feel angry?" It was just these errors that were of interest to our study.

In our research we examined how individuals correct a misunderstanding. We ran the experiment at Massachusetts General Hospital. Subjects were told they would participate in a conversation over a Teletype (the machine Western Union uses). The illusion was that there was a person on the other end, but in fact ELIZA generated the answer. After an hour of typing the subject was debriefed. We expected to learn when in the course of the conversation subjects recognized they were "speaking" to our computer, and what inappropriate response triggered their change. To our great surprise no one changed his or her mind. The twenty subjects who thought it was a person at the outset were convinced it was a person at the end. In fact, most found it an interesting and enlightening dialogue.

The four subjects who thought it was a computer to start with still felt it was a computer at the end of the session, in spite of ELIZA's ability to randomly come up with some remarkable insights. Our experiments with ELIZA led us to examine more closely and publish on the nature of human-to-human and human-to-machine interactions. Our findings were highly relevant to the discussion above on the predictive nature of our conversations and how humans have a great deal of difficulty using evidence that disconfirms their existent view of reality. They also touched on much deeper questions related to the nature of intelligence, how smart can we make a machine?

Early in the history of computing Alan Turing proposed the Turing test as a measure of intelligent machine behavior. Turing proposed placing two Teletypes side by side. If a human interacting with them could not tell which a human answered and which a machine answered, the machine must be deemed intelligent. Turing test contests are held annually, and to my knowledge no one has as yet passed the Turing test. Yet the strides toward machine intelligence are significant.

The field of artificial intelligence and information processing has made great leaps into emulating and mimicking human behavior and presenting the results through synthesized language.

Although the development and refinement of these techniques now seems inevitable, many believe that these efforts can only meet with limited success and perhaps lead to disastrous consequences. Based partially on our work, Joe Weizenbaum went on to write a highly regarded book, *Computer Power and Human Reason*. One of his central arguments is that there are certain types of research into computing that ought not be undertaken.

The opposite view is eloquently and explicitly expressed by Ray Kurzweil in *The Singularity Is Near*. The Singularity is a time in the not-too-distant future when robots/automata will surpass the cognitive power of humans.

Clearly a radical transformation of our present reality and one that, if it comes to pass, is very disturbing. Put into Kurzweil's super-rational terms it is certainly a possibility. But are we really just rational signal decoders that can be replaced by next year's faster and more reliable computer models, generated no less by our own hands? I am not so sure. The ambiguity and predictability and inherent knowledge that I have lightly touched on in this essay make me feel otherwise. Our creativity and our obverse, sometimes self-defeating behavior is the result

of the unpredictable interpretations and constant transformations of the symbolic reality we ourselves create and must face.
Can that capricious, perhaps irrational behavior be replaced by
the machines produced by the Singularity?

To close let me return to my friend Jack. Although he is
no longer with me, I have many new virtual friends. Some of
them I have met, like "Julie" at Amtrak, and others are still to
be discovered. At the moment Julie can converse with me about
railroad schedules. As long as I have a straightforward request
she can expedite and meet my needs. If I have a unique need
her abilities are limited, but that is just a transitory issue. Soon
the Julies of the world will be more and more facile to interact
with you and me to the point that they may become indistin-
guishable from "real" people. It is now perfectly natural to
walk through a public place like an airport and observe people
seemingly speaking to themselves. A decade ago, observing a
constant verbal dialogue with no one would have caused alarm,
and might have led to a 911 call. Now, if one looks more closely,
hopefully a Bluetooth earpiece or wire is dangling from an ear and
we conclude that a cell phone conversation is in progress, but it
may in fact be with Julie. This shift of acceptable behavior may be
small, but it is not as insignificant and benign as it appears. As our
robotic "friends" are able to more closely emulate our language
behavior (and thought?), the world will become a very different
place. Will they ever be able to listen to and enjoy the Eroica?

Stay tuned!

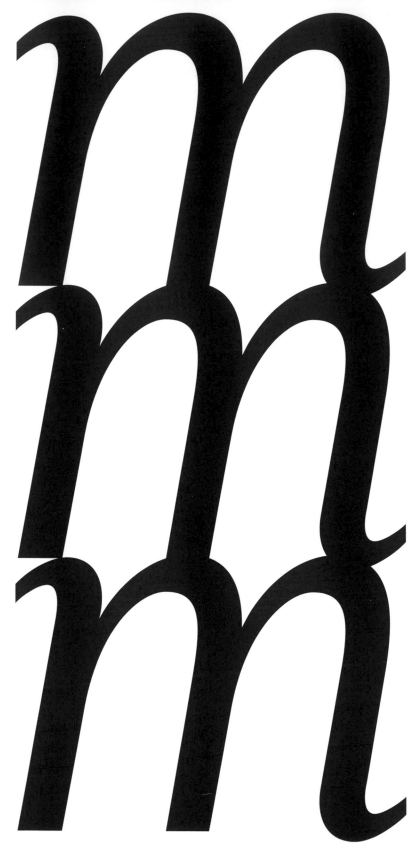

# *myths*

**Myth** A traditional story, either wholly or partially fictitious, providing an explanation for or embodying a popular idea concerning some natural or social phenomenon or some religious belief or ritual
—OED

# *memes and the*

**Meme** A cultural element or behavioral trait whose transmission and consequent persistence in a population, although occurring by non-genetic means (esp. imitation), is considered as analogous to the inheritance of a gene
—OED

# *marines*

**Marines** A branch of the U.S. armed forces forming a separate service within the Navy, raised in 1775 for service as landing forces with the fleet
—OED

The election of Barack Obama as the 44th president of the United States of America was accompanied by great celebration. The outpouring of joy went far beyond his supporters and far beyond the normal elation that comes with winning an election. There seemed to be a universal recognition that a historical event of significant proportions was taking place. John McCain in his congratulatory speech lauded the election of an African-American as unprecedented. Though many had tirelessly toiled in the vineyards of the campaign, even these "believers" had to admit they were moved and perhaps shocked beyond any expectations by Obama's accomplishment. What caused this great stirring of feeling?

My explanation is that his victory shattered a myth that has been part of American culture from its inception. Myths exist in every culture and are powerful determinants of how we see the world. They are the lenses through which every culture views, shapes, and believes its unique understanding of reality. Myths are often so deeply embedded in everyday thought that the average person would not think of questioning them. In the middle ages there was no doubt that the world was flat and the Earth the center of the universe. It takes a freethinking "outsider" or a crisis to provide a radical new perspective. The bases of these new ideas vary greatly, from philosophical/religious explanations accepted on faith, to new scientific theories that are amenable to quantitative testing and revision. The revolutionary alternative-reality explanations put forth by Christ, Luther, Copernicus, Marx, Darwin, and Einstein, to name a few, came from vastly different points of departure. They were all met with incredulity, anger, violent emotions, legal opposition, and at times war. Although their ideas are quite different, the response they evoked illustrates the devotion to and strength of investments in societal belief structures that are questioned. Acceptance requires an inordinate amount of rethinking and sheer energy to reorient the culture and the individuals within it. It often takes many generations. Old ideas have a stubborn life. Christ is still roiling the waters after millennia, and Marx and Darwin after centuries.

Claude Lévi-Strauss has written extensively on the role of myths in society and their inherent structure. With regard to form and purpose he writes:

Mythical thought always works from the awareness of oppositions towards their progressive mediation . . . the purpose of myth is to provide a logical model capable of overcoming a contradiction.
—"The Structural Study of Myth," *Journal of American Folklore*, Claude Lévi-Strauss

Joseph Campbell describes the classic pattern of a myth as a journey undertaken by a hero that causes him or her to encounter and overcome seemingly insurmountable obstacles. The object of the quest may be to meet with a divine being or obtain a magical/life-giving object (the Holy Grail, the Golden Fleece, the promised land).

In the American myth, the Lévi-Straussian opposition would be the dream of equality set against the truth of disparity. It is one of the issues at the core of Obama's heroic quest for the presidency. His victory represents to him and to millions of others throughout the world the attainment of the promised land. The promised land, an idea that resonates throughout Judaic and Christian culture, with special significance for black Americans, in this case is "the more perfect union" described in the Constitution where "all men are created equal." Although this is one of the fundamental tenets on which our country is based, it is an undeniable truth that in reality a large percentage of the population has not been treated equally.

On the one hand we have a land where we espouse "all men are created equal," juxtaposed with the undeniable truth that rampant discrimination has long completely negated this founding principle. Here is an excerpt from Obama's speech on race delivered on March 7, 2008:

Of course, the answer to the slavery question was already embedded within our Constitution—a Constitution that had at its very core the ideal of equal citizenship under the law; a Constitution that promised its people liberty, and justice, and a union that could be and should be perfected over time.

And yet words on a parchment would not be enough to deliver slaves from bondage, or provide men and women of every color and creed their full rights and obligations as citizens of the United States. What would be needed were Americans in successive generations who were willing to do their part—through protests and struggle, on the streets and in the courts, through a civil war and civil disobedience and always at great risk—to narrow that gap between the promise of our ideals and the reality of their time.

This was one of the tasks we set forth at the beginning of this campaign—to continue the long march of those who came before us, a march for a more just, more equal, more free, more caring and more prosperous America. I chose to run for the presidency at this moment in history because I believe deeply that we cannot solve the challenges of our time unless we solve them together, unless we perfect our union by understanding that we may have different stories, but we hold common hopes; that we may not look the same and we may not have come from the same place, but we all want to move in the same direction— towards a better future for our children and our grandchildren.

Our national prevailing myth has been that we are a land of personal freedom and opportunity and that we are slowly making progress in addressing inequality and eliminating these racial contradictions. The civil rights movement would no longer accept the pace and lack of resolution and set out to dramatically expose the myth as false, often precipitating the violent and forceful reactions that occur when the seeming inviolateness of myths are confronted—civil wars, lynchings, heresy trials, inquisitions, and burnings at the stake are just a few of the manifestations of these historic moments.

Although significant progress was made during the civil rights struggle through legislation and enlightenment toward greater opportunity, the underlying cultural values that underpin racial prejudice remained an abiding belief of many. Obama's victory has radically changed that worldview. For many, both his non-supporters and his true believers, a powerful fundamental myth of our society has been effectively shattered. There are reactionary elements on both sides of this change— some old guard civil rights leaders resent that Obama did not descend from the slave narrative, while whites expect that any day Obama will introduce legislation for reparations.

Some of the most compelling evidence of change (with a lower case letter *c*, not the upper case of the campaign) can be seen at the cusp of the old order and the new—the reports of canvassers at the doors of middle American homes being told, "We're voting for the nigger" and the tears in the eyes of Jesse Jackson in Grant Park as the Obama victory was announced.

I believe that a great deal of the unprecedented and unpredictable outpouring of emotion on election night and the following days resulted from the release of the energy needed to bind and maintain the disparity between the ideal of equality in opposition to the realities of discrimination.

To many, Obama's victory is seen in an even broader context. Quotes from the *New York Times* blog on the meaning of Obama's victory support and acknowledge that imagery:

Many of our citizens thought they would never live to see this day. This moment is especially uplifting for a generation of Americans who witnessed the struggle for civil rights with their own eyes—and four decades later see that dream fulfilled.

When Michelle Obama stated during the presidential campaign, "For the first time in my adult lifetime I'm really proud of my country," most open-minded people knew what she meant, especially now. I have never been prouder of America. Barack Obama's monumental presidential victory has inspired hope that America can live up to the egalitarian principles embedded in its constitution. This moment ranks with the Emancipation Proclamation, the ratification of the 13th Amendment, which ended slavery, and the Brown decision, as one of the most significant events in the history of U.S. race relations.

The exuberance of this moment parallels the 13th Amendment in many ways. There was euphoria among the slaves that were freed in 1865.

But no one seems to be more aware of the historic moment than Obama himself, nor more eloquent in describing it. During the campaign he drew a parallel to his journey toward the presidency and one of the dominant myths in the Western world—the exodus of the Jews from their slavery in Egypt and their goal of reaching the promised land. From a *New Yorker* article:

At the Brown Chapel A.M.E. Church, in Selma, Alabama, he joined older civil-rights leaders and churchmen in commemorating the voting-rights marches a generation ago. From the pulpit, Obama paid tribute to "the Moses generation"—to Martin Luther King and John Lewis, to Anna Cooper and the Reverend Joseph Lowery—the men and women of the movement, who marched and suffered but who, in many cases, "didn't cross over the river to see the Promised Land." He thanked them, praised their courage, honored their martyrdom. But he spent much of his speech on his own generation, "the Joshua generation," and tried to answer the question "What's called of us?" Life had improved for African-Americans, but "we shouldn't forget that better is not good enough." Discrimination still existed. History was being forgotten. Schools were under funded, citizens left uninsured, especially minorities. People were looking for "that Oprah money" but had forgotten the need for service, for discipline, for political will.

In Selma, Obama evoked a narrative for what lay ahead, and in that narrative Obama was not a patriarch and not a prophet but—the suggestion was distinct—the prophesied. "I'm here because somebody marched," he said. "I'm here because you all sacrificed for me. I stand on the shoulders of giants." He described the work that lay ahead for the Joshua generation and implicitly positioned himself at its head, as its standard-bearer.

—"The Joshua Generation," *The New Yorker*, November 17, 2008

Having shattered a myth in heroic fashion Obama now is subject to being the bearer of his own myth. Having completed a leg of his journey, he is now to be looked at and scrutinized with the expectation of extending his mythic qualities and performing miraculous acts to slay the evils of a shattered economy, wars without victory, and social justice denied. In spite of his pleas for realism and patience, the demands on him, because of his mythical heroic status, will be extraordinary.

Although the definition of a myth relates to a story, when myths are spoken of, referred to, or acknowledged in modern usage, more often than not it is in the negative. The threat of communism, the invincibility/integrity of public figures like movie stars or politicians, and the ever-increasing value of real estate are all referred to as myths once the illusions they evoked have proven false. We are of course subject to the enormous economic engines of advertising, PR, spin, and promotion that deliberately manufacture myths to serve the purposes of an individual, a product, or a movement. It is these myths, whose promoters often knew to be false at the outset, that provoke the negative responses.

In its more conventional and established meaning, myth plays an essential role as the repository of shared principles that govern behaviors by which a society functions. In relatively isolated traditional societies, myths and beliefs are relatively static and unchanging. They play a dominant and an often unbending role in every aspect of behavior from birth to rites of passage, communal living, and death. Modern societies are ever changing and fluid in their thinking, viewpoints, and adaptation to new ways of thought. Underlying myths are less well articulated, and have become more malleable and open to question. In these societies myths are complemented and propagated by the concept first introduced by Richard Dawkins in *The Selfish Gene*—the meme. (The use of the terms *meme* and *myth* can be and is confusing, especially in today's culture where whole enterprises are devoted to creating "buzz" about a product, or in which the news cycle can be set for the day by a rumor promulgated overnight by the likes of Matt Drudge. For the purpose of this essay I am using myth as a story and meme as a behavior or belief. The line between them is easily blurred.)

As communications become instantaneous (telephone, telegraph, the internet), global ideas, beliefs, and behaviors quickly become universal. Dawkins defined the word *meme* to express and capture the notion of how concepts and ideas are quickly replicated in modern society. Drawing a parallel to genes as biological replicators, memes are defined as cultural replicators.

What after all, is so special about genes? The answer is that they are replicators. . . . The gene, the DNA molecule happens to be the replicating entity that prevails on our planet. There may be others. . . . I think that a new kind of replicator has recently emerged on our planet. It is still in its infancy, still drifting clumsily around in its primeval soup, but already it is achieving evolutionary change at a rate that leaves the old gene pairing far behind.

The new soup is the soup of human culture. We need a name for the new replicator, a noun that conveys the idea of a unit of cultural transmission, or a unit of imitation. "Mimeme" comes from a suitable

Greek root, but I want a monosyllable that sounds a bit like "gene." I hope my classicist friends will forgive me if I abbreviate mimeme to meme. . . . It should be pronounced to rhyme with "cream."

Examples of memes are tunes, ideas, catch-phrases, clothes fashions, ways of making pots or of building arches. Just as genes propagate themselves in the gene pool by leaping from body to body via sperm or eggs, so memes propagate themselves in the meme pool by leaping from brain to brain via a process which, in the broad sense, is called imitation.

—*The Selfish Gene*, Richard Dawkins

From this definition first published in 1976 an entire new science of memetics has grown up to study how memes work. At the core of the studies of memetics is not only that memes are propagated by imitation, but that they "survive" in much the same way as genes, by natural selection. In contrast to genes that only propagate vertically, from generation to generation, memes can propagate horizontally (in real time) across cultures as well as vertically. As a result, behaviors and beliefs are changed across entire populations rather than in a single organism. Maintaining a Darwinian view of natural selection—that ultimately the stronger more robust memes best the weaker, less useful ones when they are so massively replicated—is a challenge that is not yet well understood and may prove to be fallacious. Memes can be very positive/benign (a new song, or wearing jeans and/or baseball caps askew), or they can be like viruses/parasites that propagate virulently and are negative/destructive (terrorism or genocide). Memes are the vehicles that communicate ideas without pronouncing them.

In her comprehensive and controversial book *The Meme Machine*, Susan Blackmore explores these issues at length. She goes further and suggests that the concept of self can be viewed as a collection of memes (the ultimate memeplex) that each individual employs to define their identity and beliefs. The concept of memes has been extended to technological replication—temes. Computer icons, spam, and viruses are examples of temes. There are an interesting number of TED talks on the subject.

There are no more powerful myths in any culture than those that relate to life and death. They define our perception of reality and shape our understanding of life's meaning. On a personal level, medicine and healing play an incredibly important role in mediating the conflict between life and death in every society. The practices and cures offered are based on an elaboration of the myths that mold the culture's worldview. In traditional societies, gods may be invoked through prayer, magical herbs may be used, or special rituals may be performed. In our culture the interventions are based on our ever-changing knowledge and insights of how the body functions. These explanations are based on discoveries and research that are constantly being tested and refined. At any point in time the prevailing beliefs are the basis for treatment and in many cases they have become highly effective. In many other instances the treatments are no more than best guesses. Often in retrospect these prescriptions are seen as ill-advised, at best, and at worst as ludicrous. Leeches and phrenology are examples of the latter, while ulcers, treated until recently as a stress-related rather than as a bacterial disease, are examples of the former. The explanations that lead to these medical practices are not unlike other myths. They are the acceptable formulations of medical reality at the time, and result in what is believed to be the most effective practices consistent with that understanding at that time. Unlike other sciences, the prevailing explanations have a direct effect on people. Since the stakes may be very high, when a person is ill and presents a symptom to a physician, they expect a cure. The proper treatment in many cases is not at all scientific, but simply results from a person with attributed knowledge, empathetically listening. In the words of Lewis Thomas:

The great secret of doctors, known only to their wives, but still hidden from the public, is that most things get better by themselves; most things, in fact, are better in the morning.
—*The New England Journal of Medicine*, October 12, 1972

Like any other myth, prevailing medical beliefs are difficult to change. While the adherence to a fallacious understanding of medical science may lead to questionable treatments, when viewed through the lens of more advanced knowledge the utilization of the practice, at the time, is understandable. As new knowledge becomes available its dissemination becomes critical.

Here is where memes come into play. I believe there are no more active promotions and communications of behaviors in our society than practices related to health. On a professional level, journals, meetings, continuous medical education (CME), Grand Rounds, and the internet are used to ensure the latest findings are available to the physician. There is no doubt that urging the public to adopt good health practices such as clean drinking water, exercise, safe sex, and so on result in highly effective improvements in everyday health. It is the active promotion of medical myths and memes to doctors, patients, and the general public through media, detail men, and the web that are suspect. Bad breath, acne, body odor, and erectile dysfunction are just a few of the medical/health problems that we are constantly told to worry about and to take action to cure. Although many of these messages relate to real symptoms and problems, most are manufactured in the name of good health/personal hygiene to promote specific products, prescription drugs included. As a result of these never-ending aggressive promotions the important problems are obscured and enormous amounts of resources are expended with little if any positive result. Rather than advancing our understanding of medical knowledge we are often left feeling confused and inadequate. This muddle of proven science and commercial interest is not unique to medicine. Perfected by the tobacco industry it is now pervasive on every major public policy issue from climate change to education to national defense.

While medicine deals primarily with life and death issues on an individual level, at a societal level these issues are at the root of defense of territory and ideas. At their core, myths and memes are the conveyance of ideas. Some ideas are literally so powerful that people are willing to die for them. "Give me liberty or give me death" is one of the most notable traditional illustrations in our culture. Suicide bombers are certainly a modern graphic example. Wars have been fought over any number of ideas, foolish and otherwise. Every country spends a huge amount of effort and funds in assuring it has the means to defend its core beliefs. If too threatened it is willing to ask its citizens to die in their defense. In the United States we have a vast military enterprise to realize that purpose, if needed. As with health conditions that are promoted in order to commercialize the cure, threats can also be manufactured or exaggerated to mobilize the cures for a nation's ills: the Spanish-American War ("You furnish the pictures, and I'll furnish the war," William Randolph Hearst) or the current exercise in Iraq (where are those WMDs?).

One of my most poignant examples of confronting a personal myth and its related memes was when I was working for the Center for Naval Analyses (CNA). I have worked for the defense establishment in a number of guises, the longest being my tenure as a consultant to the president of CNA, the think tank for the Navy and Marines. One of my assignments in the early '80s was to interview their "customers" to ensure they were working on the Navy and Marines' most salient problems. The study took the form of interviews with high-ranking officers in the service as well as renowned independent figures in the defense world. It was during my study of the Marines that I found myself confronting my own strongly held myths about the military in general and the Marines in particular.

The leader of the Marine Corps is the commandant. His schedule is published and managed with a precision you would expect from the Marines. A five-minute appointment with him was scheduled to alert the other officers I subsequently would interview of the high-level of importance and support for my study. They were even more impressed when the commandant, P.X. Kelley, and I had a lively exchange that in fact lasted forty-five minutes. At the conclusion of my appointment I promised to report my impressions back to him in addition to my final report. I believe these excerpts from the letter I wrote are self-explanatory:

During my career I had very little direct contact with the Marines. This lack of exposure, coupled with my liberal New York Jewish upbringing, biased me towards the Corps as a bunch of strong-willed, anti-intellectual, narrow individualists. What I found in my interviews, to my surprise, was just the opposite. Having been hardened to the bureaucratic mind-set, which gravitates towards low-risk, safe, and unimaginative action, I was taken aback by the introspective, broad-minded, sensitive, caring, and competent characteristics of the people I encountered.

It became clear during the discussions with your men that their high degree of discipline, their ability to assess risk and act decisively, their understanding of how to exercise independent thought in a consensus management environment contributes immeasurably toward the safety and security of our society. As a result all of us are afforded greater opportunity to realize our potential, both singly and collectively. I found myself thinking I would willingly accept the leadership of the officers I was interviewing if necessary. This trust grew out of my appreciation not only of their competence, but for the respect and importance they exhibited for the individual Marines under their command, while upholding the collective tradition of the Corps.

My experience radically changed my impression of the Marines. I learned that rather than being a gang of bloodthirsty warriors, they were, in fact, a group of highly trained and motivated men and women who were ready to die if necessary for the mythical American ideals of life, liberty, and the pursuit of happiness.

I learned something about myth and memes as well. Recruits to the Marines are attracted by the heroic myth the Corps carefully cultivates: "the few, the proud, the Marines." They are saying you too can be a hero and defend and even die for your country. The message and myth is appealing to a certain type of individual. The facts are that these individuals are not capable of performing these heroic tasks when first inducted. The skills and behaviors are intensely transmitted through training and memes to the extent that their lives are transformed. Not only are they made to be super self-reliant in order to answer the heroic call if needed, but they are also bonded together by a highly systemic organization that impresses on them how interdependent they are on each other and outside support services. They are in fact given the tools to be heroes and as a result perpetuate the Corps myth. They are also given a life-changing set of behaviors and discipline that never leave them.

Most recently I have witnessed the same devotion to country by my Rhode Island neighbor, Army Lieutenant Colonel Ron Tammaro. He volunteered to go to Afghanistan because he felt it was his patriotic duty. It is the devotion, belief, adherence, and ultimately the willingness and ability to act, like Ron and the Marines, that silently uphold the mythical underpinnings of the common good that our country is based upon. I believe that Barack Obama's victory reaffirmed many of these mythical beliefs in the common good in the minds of the many who poured out their emotions in the aftermath of the election. As I wrote at the end of my "Jackie" essay, it is my hope that Obama's achievement will eliminate the prejudicial stigmas associated with difference in our society in the same way Robinson's acceptance removed them from the sports world. We will then be able to take a giant step forward in realizing the myth articulated by Barack's hero Abraham Lincoln at Gettysburg:

That this nation, under God, shall have a new birth of freedom—and that government of the people, by the people, for the people, shall not perish from the earth.

Peace

# n3um8be2r

To compute, calculate, reckon, measure
—OED

On 01/12/09 at my address, 1501 Beacon St., Brookline,
Massachusetts 02446, my clock radio turns on at 6:15 a.m. to
WGBH 89.7 MHz and I am told that the temperature is 42
degrees Fahrenheit, that the Dow was up 45 points yesterday,
and that oil is $45 dollars a barrel. I get up, weigh myself at 152
pounds, and then shower at 94 degrees before I put on my size
15-30 shirt, 35-inch pants, and 11 shoes. I then eat my cereal with
3 ounces of milk and drink espresso brewed at 198 degrees. An
elevator takes me down 18 stories to level G3 where my 2001
Audi 2.7 liter A6 with 6 cylinders, 250 horsepower, 205/55R15
tires, and VIN #234Z678C189 will start when I crank the engine
with 12 volts from my battery. It will take me up the 5-degree
garage ramp to the streets where I will average 40 miles per
hour and 22 gallons per mile as I drive to Route 128 where I
have an appointment.

I could continue to bore you with this quantitative description of my day (or get even more precise), but I think you get the point. We live in a world dominated by numbers, whether we are consciously aware of them or not. Language may be the key link to differentiate us as a species, but our ability to quantify our thoughts with a myriad of numbers and their manipulation certainly may be the most important component of our thinking. Notice that almost every number I used above falls on a different value scale and yet I am sure that no one had any difficulty with these metrics. I think few of us are aware of how many metrics we know and use. Number systems are themselves an arbitrary construct. The set of assumptions we use to underpin the units of the systems make a huge difference in how well we experience the represented object or idea and how well we can utilize and manipulate them.

A simple example is the contrast between the Roman numeral system and the positional, or Arabic system in common use. Roman numbers are sufficient for naming small quantities of numbers. We are familiar with this system and it is still in decorative use today on clocks and other objects. The problem with the Roman system is that it does not lend itself to simple arithmetic computation. VI x III = XVIII is not a result that could be arrived at by the rules of arithmetic as we know them, nor as far as I know by any system. It could be learned by rote as our multiplication tables, but then every instance would need to be separately memorized. Somehow the Romans were able to make highly complex computations since they were incredibly industrious in building bridges, buildings, and viaducts. These structures must have required complex mathematical operations. I do not know how they were carried out. They certainly were not done with Roman numerals.

For any person to adequately function in modern society the ability to compute and manipulate numerical concepts is assumed as a basic need.

Reading, Riting, Rithmetic
All to the tune of a hickory stick

Attention to quantity goes back almost as far as any recorded history. Cave drawings have evidence of counting using simple strokes before 30,000 BC. In most cultures these strokes were only used to tally a small number of objects. Larger quantities were simply referred to as "many." Although various methods of computing were devised through the ages (finger counting, abacuses, counting boards), computational ability was viewed as magical and mystical. Often closely guarded by the priesthood, the existing skills were thought of as tantamount to a supernatural capability. In the Bible certain numbers have special significance and repeatedly appear. Six, seven, and forty are ominous numbers as represented by the six days of creation, the seven deadly sins, the forty days and nights of the flood, the forty days Moses conferred with God on Sinai, and the forty years the Jews wandered in the desert, etc. There was, and still is, a branch of study, known as Gematria, that is devoted to highly refined numerical analysis of scripture. Assigning numerical values to each letter and then summing up the value of words lends itself to quantitative analyses/interpretations of Biblical and other holy texts. The most striking example of this thinking is the obsession with the repeated appearance of the number 666 which stands for the devil/Antichrist. Its interpretation has been liberally applied to events from biblical sources such as the Book of Revelation to the writings of Martin Luther to the lyrics of the Beatles.

In spite of the intense interest and practical necessity for understanding the quantitative dimensions of everyday life, little or no progress was made in developing accessible computation in the western world for thousands of years until the introduction of the concept of zero about 1200 years ago.

The importance of the creation of the zero mark can never be exaggerated. This giving to airy nothing—not merely a local habitation and a name, a picture, a symbol—but helpful power, is the characteristic of the Hindu race from whence it sprang. . . . No single mathematical creation has been more potent for the general on-go of intelligence and power.
—On the Foundation and Technique of Arithmetic, G.B. Halsted

A profound and important idea, which appears so simple to us now that we ignore its true merit. But its very simplicity and the great ease, which it lent to all computations, put our arithmetic in the first rank of useful inventions.
—Pierre-Simon Laplace, quoted in Return to Mathematical Circles, H. Eves

The notion of nothing or a void was understood as far back as the Greeks. In spite of the extreme influence and sophistication of the Pythagoreans in developing geometry and their belief that only through numbers and form could one understand the universe, zero escaped them. Their thinking was too concrete to conceive of representing the void as a number and therefore creating a symbol to represent nothing or an empty class. Now easily grasped by the youngest of children the symbolic representation of nothing eluded or was rejected as meaningless in the Western world. In approximately the year 1000, Indian Hindu scholars introduced the concept to Europe. At about the same time the Arabic numbers were adopted. Their contribution was to make the symbols for quantities completely independent of the values they represented (*e.g.*, 4 is a completely abstract representation of four units, as opposed to IIII). It still took over five hundred years and the invention of printing for these two ideas—zero and abstract Arabic symbols—to gain full acceptance as the superior method of numerical representation and computation.

The introduction of zero made the positional number system in common use today possible. In a positional number system there is a base that is equal to the number of symbols that represent numerical quantities. In our digital system the base number is ten and thus we have ten symbols—0 1 2 3 4 5 6 7 8 9. Starting with the right column equaling one and moving to the left, each subsequent position or column assumes a value that is an increasing multiple value of the base. When a symbol appears in a column its value is multiplied by the value of that position and then added to the other numbers in the other columns to get the total. Thus $3657 = (3 \times 1000) + (6 \times 100) + (5 \times 10) + (7 \times 1)$. I have illustrated this seemingly trivial example because we are so ingrained to use the base ten that we often forget that not only are other bases possible, but they may be more desirable.

The common belief is that we use ten symbols because we have ten fingers (digits). The art of finger counting and computation was still in use as late as two hundred years ago.

A base of twelve (duodecimal) would be much more advantageous, for it would greatly simplify certain arithmetic operations since twelve has four divisors while a base of ten has only two. Mathematicians have argued that a base of a prime number (one only divisible by itself) such as seven or eleven also has unique computational advantages. The fact is that the most influential base in modern times is the base two or the binary system. It is at the underpinning of all modern computational equipment.

The great advance enabled by the acceptance of positional number systems was the use of a finite number of symbols and rules (arithmetic) that could be manipulated to compute things about the world. These systems allow a simple, but very significant shift in thinking—from counting to computation. Counting can only answer questions that ask "How many?" Computation enables answers to questions that ask "How much?" "How many?" only employs the integers (whole numbers). "How much?" requires the entire range of rational numbers (fractions) to be able to produce accurate results.

Positional systems made it possible to define the arithmetic operations that would provide consistent and useable results. Addition and multiplication, which is really repeated addition, caused no problem. Subtraction and division were another matter. Using the rules of arithmetic it was possible to subtract five from three resulting in a negative two. But like zero, a negative number is an abstraction. Positive numbers have a real world equivalent. Two pies, fourteen horses, even six ideas. You can count them. What is the real-world manifestation of a negative number? Clearly you can owe someone two dollars, but how is it "seen" except on a ledger. Even more difficult to grasp is division. Dividing twelve by seven results in an integer and a remainder we call a fraction. Negative numbers, fractions, and coordinates are just a few of the fascinating computational concepts that, although very difficult to initially accept and understand, have become part of our vocabulary. They have had profound mathematical as well as philosophical impact on our thinking.

The convention of using abstract graphical signs to represent numerical quantities was extended to further define special entities and operations. Symbols such as $\varpi$, $\sum$, $\infty$, $\int$, $\sqrt{}$, $\leq$, $\geq$ make the language of mathematics unique. Within any mathematical system the reference/meaning for these symbols is unambiguous. The mathematical syntax of operations is also rigidly defined. As a result mathematical "stories" or proofs must always meet highly specific criteria leading to results that have a singular meaning. There is only one way to interpret a mathematical statement, as opposed to natural language statements that are open for discussion and to interpretation. Part of the allure of mathematics to mathematicians is the beauty of its inherent logical consistency.

With the new tools of symbols that could be manipulated, mathematicians set out to explain the physical world in numbers, much as Euclid and the Pythagoreans had attempted to describe the world through geometry in ancient Greece. Ever since the Renaissance, mathematics has been used to reflect and explain the world as we observe and experience it. Even more importantly, its rigor often predicts what we should be looking for and guides us to observe the results its theoretical solutions proffer. Galileo in his book *The Assayer* was perhaps the first to state that the laws of the universe were mathematical. Newton's *Principia* stands as a monument of rational thought with his attempt to describe the world as a completely integrated system expressed in equations and numbers. The eighteenth and nineteenth centuries witnessed enormous progress made in mathematical thinking. In the early twentieth century Russell and Whitehead published their three-volume opus *Principia Mathematica* in an attempt to derive all mathematical truths from a well-defined set of axioms and inference rules using symbolic logic. (The standard joke is that only two people ever completely read the *Principia*—Russell and Whitehead.) With the publication of his incompleteness theorem in 1931, Kurt Gödel demonstrated that for any closed mathematical system, no set of axioms could be both consistent and complete. Essentially Gödel's theorem states that given any set of assumptions there is always a proposition within the system that cannot be proved. It is as great a philosophical insight as it is mathematical *tour de force*—the whole truth can never be known. Despite Gödel, our modern understandings of physical reality— electricity, relativity, quantum mechanics, the big bang—are the result of extensive abstract mathematical thought.

There is no more striking example of this thought exercise than the theory of relativity. The theory evolved as a result of Einstein's thinking about the concept of zero and how it relates to simultaneous observation. Einstein was concerned with how to simultaneously observe time in two places and assure that they were exactly the same. He worked across from the Bern railroad station where the simple, real-world problem was how to set all the railroad clocks to tell exactly the same time—a difference of zero. What he ultimately mathematically proved was that it couldn't be done, and there is no absolute, only relative, time. As we all know the solution was more than an interesting mathematical conjecture. It has led to a radical reformulation of how we understand the components of the physical world (time, space, matter, energy) and how they relate to each other. These insights are profound, including the surprising consequence that matter and energy are equivalent, related to each other by the square of the speed of light. The development of the simple equation $E=mc^2$ is perhaps one of the most striking examples of the use of mathematical thinking. It established the underlying principles that led to the understanding of atomic energy and all that it implies about the nature of our world.

Along with the evolution of these remarkable machines there has been an equally impressive development in that we are able to communicate with them and create algorithms (step-by-step instructions that instruct the machine's performance). Although the internal language of these machines is binary (not dissimilar to the on-off synapses in our brains), sophisticated means of communication that are understandable to humans are necessary for them to be useful and effective. As a result, special programming languages similar to mathematics in their rigor but with more natural language characteristics have been developed.

Everyday examples of user- (human) friendly devices from laptops to iPhones to ATMs are too numerous to mention. The speed of these devices coupled with concurrent achievements in communication technology is in its infancy. Witness the recent recognition of gesturing, as incorporated in the Wii system, as one harbinger of things to come. Currently, if you just think of receiving and watching a high-definition digital television picture that contains about ten megabytes of information in each transmitted frame, and that the frame is replicated thirty times per second, you get the picture (pun intended) that there is already a hell of a lot of work and accomplishment for our simple little zero, with much more to come.

Moving zero from machine capabilities to real-world constructs we find that zero is not always really zero. Witness the results of any downhill ski race or Michael Phelps's victory in the 100-meter butterfly at the 2008 Olympics. Without timing devices that measure in the thousandths of a second, these races would be declared a tie (zero difference between competitors). Another example is the measurement of temperature. Zero on the Fahrenheit and the Celsius scales is only a relative zero. Absolute zero, defined as the temperature where all motion ceases, is measured on the Kelvin scale. 0° Kelvin is equivalent to -459.67° Fahrenheit or -273.15° Celsius. Although these may seem simply a matter of arbitrary definition, 0° Kelvin has a physical basis with regard to all matter, while 0° Celsius is the temperature that water freezes to ice, and 0° Fahrenheit is just plain cold (as far as I know). Although absolute zero (0° Kelvin) cannot be attained, the properties that matter exhibits at these temperatures, super conductivity and super fluidity, are exceptional and have important computational applications. Working with matter at these practically zero extremes has become more or less commonplace. Integrated circuits drive almost all modern devices and the emergence of nanotechnology, where the unit of measure is in nanometers (one billionth of a meter), are beginning to and will continue to have dramatic effects on our lives as they evolve.

On the other end of the spectrum are the very large numbers that are formed with a plethora of zeros. We measure astronomical distances in light years (the distance light traveling 186,000 miles/sec transverses in a year). A light year is the equivalent of 5,878,630,000,000 miles. So when the nearest star to us after the sun is Proxima Centauri and is 4.2 light years away, it's a long way off, not to mention the diameter of the universe estimated at 20 billion light years. Recently every one has become familiar with the term "google." Google is derived from the mathematical term googol, which is defined as $10^{100}$, or 1 with one hundred zeros after it. I think you would agree that is a pretty big number (perhaps surpassed only by the multiple of earnings represented by Google's share price on the day it went public). What do you think of a googolplex $10^{googol}$ ? Carl Sagan once stated that it is impossible to write out a googolplex since the number of zeros would occupy more space then there is in the universe. So how about a googol$^{googol}$? That's a lot of zeros, but still less than infinity—but we won't go there. Suffice it to say, zero really does shape our worldly concepts and our relative place in it in most unexpected ways.

*Powers of Ten: About the Relative Size of Things in the Universe*, a movie and book by Phillip and Phylis Morrison and Charles and Ray Eames, affords us a dramatic visual presentation of our place in the world. Derived from Cosmic View, it progressively pictures the world starting from the edge of the universe to the inside of an atom. The first image has a scale of 1 cm = $10^{25}$ meters (~1 billion light years). Each subsequent image is reduced by a power of 10. At 1 cm = $10^0$ (1 cm = 1 meter) we are at a human scale showing a man sleeping on a blanket. The excursion continues and subsequently ends at 1 cm = $10^{-16}$ meters inside a carbon atom. That is the range of the universe as we know it, 40 jumps of magnitude from $10^{25}$ to $10^{-16}$. We reside in a very small band between the extremes of tiny atomic particles and the billions of galaxies measured in light years. At most we can see and directly experience only about six or seven of these orders of magnitude. We are equally limited as a species by the range of light we can see, the sounds we can hear, and the temperature we can tolerate. Through the wonders of science (electron microscopes, telescopes, infrared detectors, etc.) we have been able to extend our reality with remarkable results. By adding a number of zeros to the dimensions of the world we experience, every aspect of our being has been transformed. But as we journey further along these larger and smaller dimensions, important questions are raised with regard to our ability to understand and control our manipulations. On the small scale, atomic energy and the decoding of the genome are two striking examples of our ability to change not just our understanding of our environment and ourselves, but to alter their very nature. In a *New York Times Magazine* article, Steven Pinker wrote:

A firsthand familiarity with the code of life is bound to confront us with the emotional, moral and political baggage associated with the idea of our essential nature. People have long been familiar with tests for heritable diseases, and the use of genetics to trace ancestry—the new "Roots"—is becoming familiar as well. But we are only beginning to recognize that our genome also contains information about our temperaments and abilities. Affordable genotyping may offer new kinds of answers to the question "Who am I?"—to ruminations about our ancestry, our vulnerabilities, our character and our choices in life.

Dealing with large magnitudes is equally daunting. The amount of carbon we are spewing into the air is staggering. Can we really afford to keep operating at the scale of our present enterprises? The recent economic crisis is another case in point. Do we really understand how to manage the incredible numbers we are forced to confront. If the deficit and sums associated with it were written out as $1,000,000,000,000 dollars (that is a decimal not a binary number) rather than one trillion dollars, would we be as glibly confident in our abilities to rationally solve the problem? The facts are that we have ventured a far, far distance—many zeros away—from our natural instincts and capabilities. Senator Everett Dirksen's adage, "A billion here and a billion there and pretty soon you're talking about real money," now seems quaint. Let's hope we can find our way back without unraveling our social structure.

No aspect of our lives has been more affected by the advancement of quantitative thinking than modern medicine. When I was hired at Massachusetts General Hospital in 1961 to support researchers using computers, my title was assistant mathematician. The title was fitting, for in those days whether it was in the hospital or not, when I told anyone I worked with computers they would invariably reply they were never good at math. Although there was no lack of interest and exciting projects to work on back then, the use of computers and quantitative results was extremely limited. It is now impossible to have any significant medical interaction that does not employ some sort of number or sophisticated information processing. The difficulty is that there are so many tests and procedures offered that the patients and the physicians are often inundated with information that is hard to prioritize. It is certainly impossible to have any understanding of any major disease that affects you or your family without learning an entirely new language and set of measures that can rule your life. This drive to measure every conceivable physiological function that relates to a disease, either because it is available, recommended on TV, or as a hedge against the anticipated defense of a malpractice suit, has certainly driven the cost of care through the roof. Even without any affliction, keeping your blood pressure, cholesterol, caloric intake, and weight in check can be a major endeavor. Health insurance coverage requires an additional postgraduate course in deductibles, co-pays, and exclusions. The emergence of personal medicine afforded by the decoding of the human genome greatly amplifies the issue.

Like the early days of the internet, the dawn of personal genomics promises benefits and pitfalls that no one can foresee. . . . Depending on who has access to the information, personal genomics could bring about national health insurance, leapfrogging decades of debate, because piecemeal insurance is not viable in a world in which insurers can cherry-pick the most risk-free customers, or in which at-risk customers can load up on lavish insurance.

—*The New York Times Magazine*, Steven Pinker, January 11, 2009

Today's health care and medical treatments are predicated on the belief that the more precise the understanding of the problem the better the care. I have my doubts. Test results, decision trees, and productivity measures are often substituted for compassion and meaningful connection. It is a trend that is difficult if not impossible to reverse.

Whether you think you are a numbers person or not, I think you will agree our world is now inconceivable without an encounter with a number at almost any moment of the day. Most of us don't live our lives consciously aware of every number we encounter, as illustrated in the first paragraph, but our awareness is closer to the surface than many would like to admit. Perhaps if we were isolated on a desert island we could escape these encounters, but I suspect that it is so ingrained in our psyche that we could not escape forming some thoughts related to measurement even in that environment. So to end this piece I thought I would go back to a time when quantities were of import, but in a far more poetic, and, at least in retrospect, richer way. In his delightful book *An Exultation of Larks*, James Lipton expounds on the proper terms used to describe groups of things in medieval England. We are all still familiar with a number of these terms: a school of fish, a pride of lions, a bevy of beauties, a host of angels. What about an exclamation of larks, a rafter of turkeys, and a parliament of owls? The definitive list of these terms (one hundred and sixty-four) is found in *The Book of St. Albans*, published in 1486. William Blades in an 1881 introduction to a facsimile version wrote, "Those [terms] with which, at the period, every man claiming to be 'gentle' was expected to be familiar; while ignorance of their laws and language was to confess himself a 'churl.'"

And what could be worse than a churl (a rude ill-bred person)? Lipton bemoans, as do I, that we have not continued to extend our "gentle" ways, and continue with the identification and characterization of groups as an impatience of wives, a draught of bottlers, a drift of fisherman, a giggle of girls, a rascal of boys. But alas these poetic illusions must give way to the more precise measures we now employ. So when someone tells me, as they often do, "I'm not good with numbers," I can only think: yeah, tell me about it.

*Opera, Option, and Organization*

**Opera**  A dramatic musical work in which singing forms an essential part, consisting of recitatives, arias, and choruses, with orchestral accompaniment
—OED

**Option**  Something that is or may be chosen; an alternative, a choice
—OED

**Organization** An organized body of people with a particular purpose, as a business, government department, charity, etc.
—OFD

When I started working in the garment center as a billing clerk
in the shipping department in the summer of 1952 I would walk
four blocks every day from the IRT subway station at Times
Square to Korday Sportswear located at 1385 Broadway (38th
Street). On the way I would pass the old Metropolitan Opera
house at 39th and Broadway and read the posters of upcoming
events. They piqued my curiosity. The result was my subsequent
attendance the next fall at Saturday matinees as a standee for
the admission price of two dollars. (A twenty-five cent bribe to
an usher at intermission often landed the coveted outrageously
expensive empty $8 orchestra seat of a no-show subscriber.)
Prodded by my Aunt Jean, I had occasionally listened to the
Saturday Metropolitan Opera radio broadcasts sponsored by
Texaco and announced by Milton Cross. They did not prepare
me for the intensity of the actual performance. The scale and
grandeur of productions still being mounted by major companies are staggering even to initiates, and would astonish new-
comers who gave it a chance. Being exposed to them at the age
of fifteen along with the glorious singing of legends like Renata
Tebaldi, Jussi Björling, Jerome Hines, Leonard Warren, and
Zinka Milanov was an overwhelming, indelible experience.

I have little doubt that rock concerts, musical comedy, or for
that matter professional wrestling and religion as practiced in
mega-churches have similar power for their audiences. They are
the offspring of the production values that were first developed
and honed in the world of opera. Grand Opera is just that—
Grand (with a capital G). The scale and intensity of everything
is over the top. The theatres, scenery, plots, costumes, and singing are so boldly conceived and presented that they overwhelm
the senses.

An opera begins long before the curtain goes up and ends long after it
has come down. It starts in my imagination, it becomes my life, and it
stays part of my life long after I've left the opera house.
—Maria Callas

When properly done, it is hard to believe that what you are
seeing and hearing is real and taking place before your eyes.
Equally intense are the reactions of the audience. Arias were
greeted with tumultuous applause, or boos, and although I have

not seen it happen recently, in the old days the stage was often littered with bouquets during the performance. Curtain calls went on forever. (The world record was eighty minutes with 101 calls for Placido Domingo before being eclipsed by Pavarotti's final concert with 164 calls.) These fantastic performances have recently been made much more accessible through high-definition broadcasts into movie theatres, yet they cannot replicate, at least for me, the thrill of a live performance.

The interesting thing about going to the opera was how different it was from all my other experiences. A new work was presented at each Saturday matinee and I initially was indifferent to what was to be presented. In spite of the fact that I didn't know the plots and couldn't understand the dialogue (those were the days before subtitles) the music, singing, dancing, costumes, scenery, and lighting powerfully conveyed the essence of the story as well as the personality and motivation of the characters. I quickly learned that this was a world of emotion, not reason, and I had to just give myself up to and resonate to the outpouring of feelings that came from the stage and the orchestra via the music. Not being able to understand the spoken language also made me extremely sensitive to and aware of the richness of meaning that could be conveyed by gesture, mood, and inflection. Basses were invariably evil, tenors were heroic, and sopranos were meant to be beautiful (that often required some willing suspension of disbelief, a prerequisite for all theater). I came to realize that I, and the rest of the audience, were not only observers, but in a strange way participants in the performance as well. Our understanding of the actions, passions, conflicts, and resolutions resulted from directly experiencing the hopes, fears, triumphs and defeats the opera evoked in our hearts as opposed to our brains. In short, the opera taught me not only to see and hear with my eyes and ears, but also to observe, to listen with all my senses and faculties—a skill that has proven to be professionally invaluable.

Aside from its visceral impact, the world of opera also introduced me at an early age to life's great issues and dilemmas—good vs. evil, fate vs. free will, emotion vs. reason, authority vs. independence. Opera plots, although often rather fantastic, presented a set of stark alternative behaviors and realities to contemplate. Nowhere in my limited intellectual and emotional repertoire was I presented with the dramatic options that I experienced and pondered at the opera. Life could be led in many more ways than the limited alternatives presented by my parents and educators. The fact that a different opera was presented every week played a vital part in that realization as well. Although I entered the same building it was totally transformed for each performance. The framework and the magic that had been conveyed the previous time was totally replaced with a new set of realities and roles. The same singers took on different personas completely transformed by the new plot, music, and costumes. The different worlds that were so fluidly changed and represented had a marked effect on me, allowing me to contemplate a myriad of options that life could afford.

In many ways, although I didn't draw the parallel at the time, Korday Sportswear and the garment center in general, played out their own form of opera. Over my three summers at Korday, I took over everyone's job when they went on vacation. I knew the business from the inside out. Though I didn't realize it then, it was as full of drama, intrigue, and at times outright deception as any theatrical production. Garments were invariably promised with absolute assurance of delivery against impossible deadlines even though the goods were not ordered and the skirts were never cut. Histrionics and threats were the order of the day. The same scenes were played out with minor variations year after year. Everyone knew the sub-plots and played their parts. Once you understood the drill and your role in it, it became natural and routine.

At the time, the impact and lessons of my operatic and work experiences were not as apparent as they are now, but they, along with the diversity of New York City, made a marked difference in my *weltanschauung*. My lifeline was the New York City subway system that carried me all over the city. There were foreign movies like *The Bicycle Thief, Rashomon, La Strada*, and *The 400 Blows*. There were all the fabulous museums—the Met, the Natural History Museum, and the MOMA—along with free concerts, theaters and sporting events. For a kid with little or no money, the world was my oyster and the number of options seemed as limitless as the city was diverse.

Aside from greatly enhancing my sense of individuality, having the freedom to explore the city also made me acutely aware of the importance and influence of my surroundings. New York is often called a melting pot, but I found it to be more of a huge aggregation of different cultures that seemed to harmoniously coexist. Alistair Cooke called it "the biggest collection of villages in the world."

Another asset I was unknowingly developing was the use of mental maps. Each activity took place in a different part of the city. The stylized subway map was my high level guide, but once on the streets I needed a more intimate knowledge of the neighborhoods to successfully navigate to my destination. I am sure my interest in map collecting results from these early sojourns. I invariably use my mental mapping capabilities when visiting a new place, especially a large city. Whenever possible I put my feet on the street and walk around as much as I can and visualize where I am on the city's map. As a result I have found that upon revisiting a location I can instantly reorient myself and feel at home.

The maps I carried in my head did not just convey geographical information; they described the location's characteristics. Associated with each setting I also made mental notes regarding the different behaviors, options, and possibilities they afforded. Attendance at the opera was different from watching a ball game at Ebbets Field. Buying clothes at Gimbels was not the same as bargaining on Delancey Street. Working in the garment district demanded different behaviors than volunteering at New York Hospital. Navigating among these settings taught me lessons of observation and adaptive skills far beyond any intellectual proficiency my formal education offered.

The subway not only took me to all the venues described, it also brought me to Stuyvesant High School, as good an education as one could possibly receive anywhere. One of the specialized New York City schools, Stuyvesant was a gateway to higher education with fewer than twenty members of my graduating class of 870 opting not to go on to college. The only drawback was that at the time Stuyvesant was not coed. It was overcrowded and classes were taught in shifts. Freshmen and sophomores went from 12:30 until 5:00, while the juniors and seniors attended from 8:00 until 12:30. There were no study halls or lunch hour. The free time after school afforded me a degree of independence to explore what the city offered—this was no Dublin, where an Odyssey could be completed in twenty-four hours. Like the Greek version, it took years, and even that was not enough.

From Stuyvesant I went to Boston and MIT. Neither seemed to present the same degree of flexibility and opportunity as New York City and Stuyvesant. Boston was small and provincial and MIT was focused on engineering and science. The Department of Economics and the MIT Dramashop provided me an avenue to survive the "Institute."

Working on theatrical productions extended my fascination with performance art awakened by my earlier operatic interest. The ability to transform a space to convey different realities, especially unconventional presentations, broadened my understanding of the capability of the environment to enable and limit an individual.

Had I been in a liberal arts college I might well have decided to pursue a career in theater. The limitations of MIT reinforced my view of how strongly organizational structures influence individual options.

I considered many options upon graduation. Boston and Cambridge had grown on me and I decided to take advantage of their accessibility and charm over the variety and hustle of the Big Apple. I was interested in pursuing a career in psychology or publishing but finally succumbed to the budding fascinations of computer science, taking a position as a computer analyst. The late 1950s were the classical period of computing and I took the first programming course given at MIT. IBM had given MIT a 704, their top-of-the-line scientific machine carrying a price tag of over two million dollars. It literally took up an entire floor of a building and had all of 4,096 words of memory. Although I was not interested in a computing career, it was an extremely marketable skill and afforded a top salary. I ultimately took a position to work on SAGE, an air defense system to cope with the threat by Soviet bombers, which employed over fifty computer installations nationwide. Each site contained two 58,000 vacuum-tube machines, huge storage drums, and over one hundred interactive displays, which required half an acre of floor space. The conception and organization of SAGE (Semi-Automatic Ground Environment) was a tour de force, costing more than the Manhattan project—over eight billion (1960) dollars.

It is interesting to note the E in the project title—Environment. SAGE was possibly the largest project ever undertaken up to that time. The developers understood that only through the development of a unique *environment* that balanced the extraordinary capabilities of the computer with the expert judgment of humans could the endeavor be successful. As a result, during a mission, each action by every operator was recorded for study and then used to debrief the entire team on their reaction times and interactions with the system. These studies were used to improve the responsiveness of the system as well as provide invaluable lessons about human interactions with the machines.

The physical environment was also remarkable. The display rooms were bathed in blue light to make the one hundred displays more legible. The control panels looked like the most outlandish cartoons of massive computer installations ever conceived. SAGE set an example for large systems design, human-machine interaction studies, and project management for years to come. By the early 1960s, missiles replaced bombers as our primary threat, making SAGE obsolete by the time it was completed. However, just as all the early programming languages underpin subsequent languages, I believe the lessons learned from SAGE live on to this day.

After working two years on various aspects of defense systems I decided to quit and with the help of Dr. Gardner Quarton, I was able to create a position as the in-house technology consultant at MGH. My portfolio was very broad and although it was primarily meant to support the research community of the hospital, it also encompassed the clinical and teaching staffs. (I am fond of saying that John Knowles, the general director at the time, approved my hire because he was told that the shift to electronic medical records would be forthcoming within six months to a year—that was in 1961!) Needless to say, the opportunities at MGH were fascinating and endless. Among other things I was a broker between the investigators at the hospital who wanted to use the latest technology and the many technology firms and research institutes around Boston that wanted to explore the medical applications of their products. My group worked on brain mapping, DNA sequencing, statistical analysis, experimental design, radiation mapping (the forerunner of CT scans), and man-machine interactions, to name just a few projects. It was an ideal job that allowed me to combine my negotiating skills with my technological acumen to make things happen.

The most significant consequence of that experience, however, was the development of my clinical capabilities. Many of the projects were involved in the design of evaluation protocols for new clinical procedures. As a result I needed to learn the rudiments of clinical procedures such as patient interviewing, reading electro-cardiograms (EKGs), juvenile diabetic treatment, and radiation therapy. Toward that end I was approached by a psychiatrist, Dr. Peter Sifneos, to help develop an evaluation instrument for a new form of short-term psychotherapy he was introducing into MGH outpatient clinics. After six months of sitting in on meetings, I announced to Dr. Sifneos that I could not complete the task since no one on his team seemed to agree on any definitions and outcome measures. Much to my surprise he asked me whether I would be interested in seeing patients myself to gain firsthand knowledge. When I protested that I had no clinical training, he countered that he was convinced that I could do it under proper supervision.

Thus began my career as a psychotherapist. I saw patients in the MGH outpatient clinic for a number of years, eventually teaching the biweekly continuous case presentation of an ongoing therapy. My supervisor for my cases was Dr. Quarton. Q's knowledge of alternative models of behavior was vast, and case discussions ranged across multiple explanations of the patients' psycho-dynamics. I was afforded the opportunity to learn at the feet of a master. In addition to the clinical work we did together, we used the opportunity to develop a discipline of conceptually mapping the emotional state of each patient as he or she progressed through the treatment. The process delighted me since it called on the discipline of mapping I had developed during my New York explorations. Other aspects of my early experiences, especially opera, helped me more fully appreciate the discipline of listening and observing before acting. In my technological life I gained credibility by the quickness of my mind and the ability to offer solutions accurately and rapidly. Wasn't that the objective of computer science? My therapeutic training allowed me to be more patient and absorb more of the complexity and subtleties of the presented problems before offering a clarification or an interpretation. Letting people tell their story the way they saw the world enabled me to provide (with Q's help) much deeper and more nuanced options and relevant solutions.

I continued my interest in therapy after leaving MGH by being psychoanalyzed and receiving additional training as a group leader and a child therapist. These experiences coupled with my technological knowledge have shaped and are the basis of my subsequent career. During my tenure at MGH I developed an independent consulting practice that was initially based on my technological skills. Although I continued to work on projects and tutor at Harvard for many years, I steadily built my consulting practice until it became my full-time employment in the early 1980s. During my career I have watched as information technologies have emerged from more efficient and orderly ways to perform specific, well-understood, arithmetic tasks, to insinuating themselves into the mainstream culture to become the primary currency of almost all transactions. Earlier when I told people I worked with computers they would often respond by saying they were never good with numbers. Now it is difficult for many to understand how to live their lives without the utilization of an IT device, even for those who are no good with numbers. The Information Age has transformed our individual lives in a measured and very gradual manner, but the cumulative effects have been immense and dramatic.

In those early days of computing, organizations often found themselves acquiring information technologies at a pace they could not absorb or fully understand. Although I was initially engaged to solve problems thought to be primarily related to the introduction of new information systems, it became increasingly evident to me that these situations had their roots in managerial attitudes and behaviors related to the new technology. The same resistance to change and to adaptation of new modes of problem-solving I encountered and learned to help resolve in my therapeutic practice with individuals, slowly but surely became the basis for my work with senior managers as they struggled with the personal and organizational implications of adapting information systems. The discipline of organizational development (OD) as a management science was evolving in parallel. Over the years my engagements became more and more dependent on my interpersonal and OD skills, as opposed to my technological know-how, to solve problems.

My work with organizations has been primarily with large not-for-profits—hospitals, universities, museums, social service agencies, and think tanks. These values-driven organizations are inherently difficult to manage because their "product" is ill-defined and authority relationships are fluid and open to negotiation. (To whom does a tenured professor report?)

In many ways, understanding these organizations is like going to the opera. When the need for a consultant is identified there usually is a lot of drama and intrigue. Initially the institution's language is foreign, you only vaguely know the plot, and you are not sure who the important characters are or what role they play. Whoever hires you tries to explain all these elements, but it is often the equivalent of describing how a piece of music that you haven't yet heard sounds. It only makes sense after you have watched and listened and absorbed the parts being played out by the organization's actors in their chosen setting that you begin to get an idea of what the issues really are and what the options might be. Like the opera you have often seen similar performances, but you would be remiss if you believe that you can quickly formulate solutions based on your previous experience without intently listening to and observing what is really going on, as opposed to the versions you hear from the participants. Each production has its own unique character. The Houston Opera doesn't have to be like the Met to be great.

Every consultant brings his or her own set of tools to an assignment, guided by their personal history and personality. In my case, mapping, cultural anthropology, and psychodynamics are important dimensions of my practice. In my business practice, I construct parallel maps of the relationships between the relevant actors and how they interact with each other—organizationally, socially, and emotionally. The organizational map can be viewed as the equivalent of the corporate organizational chart, but in my experience the official public version bears little resemblance to how things are really put together. Of even more importance is how these relationships are played out behaviorally. Each organization has a history that drives its culture. The culture in turn implicitly sets the rules for behaviors that are acceptable and those that are frowned upon.

Without taking time as a cultural anthropologist to research and understand the history and roots of the organization's belief structure, it is very difficult to bring about significant and useable change. It takes time and patience to develop meaningful, practical, and acceptable solutions. Like individuals, organizations mature and develop. They must have enough capacity, skills, and insight to be able to incorporate different behaviors. Proposing alternatives that are beyond their capabilities or alien to their culture, even though theoretically correct, are destined for difficulty or outright failure. Organizational psychology and culture have a dramatic effect on individual behavior in enterprises of every stripe and scale. All the aspects of individual and family emotions—anxiety, aggression, authority, energy, envy, esteem, greed, rivalry—are evident in organizations. Understanding how these emotions are being allowed to play out is often the most important aspect of the work. Listening and observing with "a third ear" to how information is communicated, disagreements are handled, disappointment is expressed, authority wielded, aggression channeled, support given, and politics played, are critical parts of any intervention. How someone takes on and behaves in a role may be as much a function of the setting as it is their personality. It is like being cast in a play and/ or directing. Your role is predetermined and yet you are expected to bring new insights and energies to the part.

In our culture, with its premium on individuality, we strive for as much discretion as possible in choosing the roles we play and how we perform them. The constant struggles for equality and fairness—women's suffrage, affirmative action, gay rights — reflect our belief structure that everyone should have the right to choose the part they want to play. The facts are that circumstances and the environment are often as important in shaping one's options as in exerting one's own will.

Encounters with our health care system (some refer to it as our sickness care system) offer a good illustration of how organizations affect our options and behaviors. Seeking care is a rather unique experience since with few exceptions (e.g., annual physicals, vaccinations, plastic surgery) no one actively desires to avail himself or herself of a visit to the doctor or hospital. We often find ourselves in a position of uncomfortable dependence.

When we do get sick we expect the system to act and quickly meet our needs. A few of us are lucky enough to have a relationship with a personal physician to guide us through the care-giving maze. The majority must navigate without a map through terrain that is intellectually alien and are often oblivious to their cultural illness framework. These patients must be willing to put their faith in strangers and submit to questions and procedures that are more personal and invasive than ordinary encounters. Even those of us with a physician find ourselves in the same situation once referred to a specialist or admitted to the hospital.

In every case we find ourselves highly dependent on care-givers we do not know, in settings that are foreign and may even seem hostile. We must adhere to a set of rules and behaviors that would not otherwise be easily tolerated. Waiting times are often long, appointments are not well coordinated, visiting hours are restricted, procedures are performed and/or prescriptions are given without adequate explanation. To expedite their care, patients must often submit to the lapse in quality service because they are more concerned with their own welfare than the inefficiencies of the system that may sacrifice human interaction and the sharing of knowledge for action.

Many of these organizational and behavioral inefficiencies stem from historical neglect of organizational issues. The founding mission of hospitals was to serve the poor, who expected to wait and not be well served. Blue Cross and Blue Shield were primarily formed to ensure that hospitals and physicians were paid, as opposed to having a consumer focus. The exponential rise in heath care costs in recent years has focused attention on addressing the operations of all aspects of the system, including customer service. With the introduction of better management and information systems, these deficiencies are slowly being addressed. Many hospitals now provide valet parking, and concierge services, and they actively compete for patients with marketing campaigns. In addition the internet has provided a wealth of information, some of it good and some not, to support patient's in their encounters with health care providers. As the system becomes more transparent both medically and financially over the next decade, we will witness a radical change in how services are delivered by the system and in the expectations of the consumers. The dialogue between all the actors will become more comprehensible as the roles of all the actors change, hopefully leading to equitable and truly accessible care.

In the same way the internet and information systems have and will greatly affect the delivery of health care, the web environment has radically changed how we gather experience in our lives. A *New York Times* article compared the structure and experience of Wikipedia to the ambience and opportunities afforded by a city, calling the two analogous. Wikipedia can no more be completed than can New York City, which O. Henry predicted would be "a great place if they ever finish it." In fact, with its millions of visitors and hundreds of thousands of volunteers, its ever-expanding total of articles and languages spoken, Wikipedia may be the closest thing yet to a metropolis seen online.

In the same way I wandered about the city, users of Wikipedia, myself included, now wander through the hyperlinks embedded in articles. Rather than physically wandering from neighborhood to neighborhood, Wikipedia takes us on virtual journeys of undiscovered territories. Current excursions only take us on visual and auditory tours of the terrain. I have no doubt that we will soon be able to embark on expeditions that involve all our senses. How we will pursue our options in the future and what kind of organizations we will need to support our explorations is not yet known. As we substitute our fingers on the keyboard for our feet on the street, I hope we are able to preserve the powerful, meaningful, and life-affirming elements of surprise, delight, and awe that I felt when I first discovered opera.

Peace

The ability to act or affect something strongly; physical or
mental strength; might; vigor, energy; effectiveness
The capacity to direct or influence the behavior of others;
personal or social influence
—OED

Few words are used with more alacrity than *power*.

Nevertheless, its definitions and usage are endlessly varied, from the personal to the universal. At one extreme are the
physical manifestations—the muscle man, the steam engine,
the power grid, and wind power, to name a few. On the other
end are the behavioral and social aspects—knowledge, ideas,
authority, spirituality, religion, politics, economics, morality,
organization, personal. From cosmic, to nature, to governments,
to culture, to organizations, to neighborhoods, to individuals,
our feelings about and our exercise of power express themselves
in very different ways. Each form of power both produces and
requires significant amounts of energy. Each also carries its own
set of measures and infrastructure.

On the hard (physical) side of the spectrum, the structure, costs, strength, and measurement of power are well defined and closely monitored dimensions. On the soft (behavioral) end of the spectrum, the dimensions are subtler and much more difficult to quantify, yet of great significance. That the exercise of power is always multi-dimensional makes its study all the more intriguing.

I have tried to limit this discussion to individual and organizational power.

Understanding and exercising power has been a major preoccupation since the beginning of civilized time. Harnessing energy to enable and expand every aspect of human endeavor from agriculture, to war, to industrialization, to communications and information processing has been an unceasing endeavor. In parallel to the physical dimensions of power are the societal ones. We have struggled with the equally weighty distribution of power issues related to human rights from slavery, to suffrage, to racism, to sexual orientation. From the big bang, to flipping on a light switch, to getting a promotion, to deciding what school is best for Suzie, power plays a pervasive role in every aspect of our lives. The understanding of our identity, beliefs, relationships, abilities, and opportunities—all are defined and driven by how we assess our power to cope with the forces that are acting on us. The manner in which we address the issues and concerns in our lives is determined by that assessment. The weaker we are, or are made to feel, the fewer the options we believe are available to us to meet our needs and desires. Many of our determinations are based on reality. Externalities such as culture, law, and physical constraints, dictate the terms of how we lead our lives, in some countries more than others—the twentieth anniversary of Tiananmen Square is a pointed reminder.

The challenges we are willing to take on and how we approach them are highly correlated with our sense of our personal empowerment and the acceptable norms of behavior, as we understand them, in any culture. But it is often equally true that our assessments are flawed. We underestimate our abilities to act in certain situations. There are certainly avenues of empowerment that none of us adequately explore.

The undeniable fact that in modern times knowledge is power, and becoming more so with each passing day, makes exploring our potential and eliminating the obstacles to our personal power all the more important. The emergence of knowledge as the key commodity of our age, and the corollary acceleration of change, have made the ability to constantly transform ourselves, and maximize the power at our disposal, increasingly feasible, or, as people like Ken Robinson would argue, even necessary. In his book *The Element*, Robinson articulates and thoroughly explores the imperatives of finding our element:

Being in our Element depends on finding our own distinctive talents and passions. Why haven't most people found this? One of the most important reasons is that most people have a very limited conception of their own natural capacity. This is true in several ways.

The first limitation is in our understanding of the range of our capacities. We are all born with extraordinary powers of imagination, intelligence, feeling, intuition, spirituality, and of physical and sensory awareness. Many people have not found their Element because they don't understand their own powers.

The second limitation is in our understanding of how all of these capacities relate to each other holistically. For the most part we think that our minds, our bodies, and our feelings and relationships with others operate independent of each other, like separate systems. Most people have not found their Element because they don't understand their true organic nature.

The third limitation is in our understanding of how much potential we have for growth and change. For the most part, people seem to think life is linear, that our capacities decline as we grow older, and that opportunities we have missed are gone forever. Many people have not found their Element because they don't understand their constant potential for renewal.

Robinson convincingly argues that our current system of education and the philosophy that supports it actually creates obstacles and reinforces barriers to fulfillment. His thesis is that our antiquated system, targeted at addressing the power levers needed by the industrial age, stifles the creativity needed to effectively function in the information age. By emphasizing quantitative skills over artistic and creative expression we are disempowering future generations from leading interesting, productive, and innovative lives. He states that no one has a clue what job skills will be needed over the next half century, or what the organizational structures that sponsor these activities will look like. See his TED talk "Do Schools Kill Creativity?"

But we need not be futuristic thinkers like Ken Robinson to see how the nature of power and authority has already radically changed in the home and the workplace. As the result of television, telephones, and the internet, the power within households has been transformed from parents-know-best to growing self-determination by younger family members. The strict hierarchical delegation of authority that held the industrial workplace together has also rapidly matured to a much more collegial environment. Rather than the classic model of authority, with its reliance on downward power and subordination, modern businesses are adapting organizational designs that place emphasis on collegial settings where meaningful relationships and collateral networks provided for more productive venues to attain company objectives.

The power one needs comes of necessity, in many forms. It has multiple bases, including ones associated with information or knowledge, good working relationships, personal skills, intelligent agendas for action, resource networks, and a good track record.

The truism "knowledge is power" certainly applies to many jobs today. But the type of knowledge that is particularly important in leadership jobs is not the kind one finds in books or in educational programs. It is detailed information about the social reality in which the job is imbedded. . . . Good working relationships based on some combination of respect, admiration, perceived need, obligation, and friendship are a critical source of power in helping to get things done. Without these relationships even the best possible idea could be rejected or resisted in an environment where diversity breeds suspicion and interdependence precludes giving orders to the most relevant players. Furthermore, since these relationships serve as important information channels, without them one may never be able to establish the information base one needs to operate effectively.

—*Power and Influence: Beyond Formal Authority*, John Kotter

The challenge of creating and successfully sustaining a more egalitarian, cooperative, and productive environment in the home, workplace, or any setting demands a better and more sophisticated understanding of the sources of power. Where seniority and position were often the dominant determinants of power in the past, the ability to get things done now requires a combination of knowledge, charisma, organizational political savvy, access, listening skills, empathy, social networking capability, reputation, and credibility. How, and for whom, a leader exercises these attributes are the keys to power. There is a very delicate balance between the goals of the organization, the goals of the subordinates and the individual goals of the leader. Unless these are balanced and aligned, energy will be wasted on bar conversations and intrigue rather than putting it toward the stated goal. The trick for any leader is to work toward assuring, to the extent possible, that the group accepts that his or her actions and motives are maximizing the power needed to realize the common aspirations of all parties and not just his or her own.

I am not so naïve as to believe that power is not always exercised in a wholly transparent and above-board manner. There is a whole school of thought that cannot discuss the subject without addressing the degree of deception that is, and to some minds must be, employed to achieve power. In *The Prince*, Machiavelli (the *ne plus ultra* of power) is a staunch advocate for the need for deception. Being honest, open, compassionate, and generous may be important, but often deceit, cruelty, and secrecy are the rule of the day. Machiavelli's advice—be a lion and a fox—is widely practiced. It is certainly an aspect of human nature.

The consequences of this behavior cannot be ignored. The place where all the levers of power are worked unabashedly and with abandon are at any center of government and are further raised to a fine art in Washington, D.C. The currency of the city is measured in terms of access and influence. Elected officials, lobbyists, and staff members are forever embroiled in a constant high-stakes game of assessing tradeoffs to accomplish their objectives. The notion that one might totally act on principle to achieve one's ends is most often greeted with incredulity. My experiences in Washington have been that whenever I have been involved in a highly sensitive negotiation or issue, the newspaper description of the rationale and process has little or no correlation to what is actually taking place. This public-private power drama played out to embarrassing effect just recently when Israelis accused the new administration of reneging on the private understanding reached with the last administration as to the permissibility of settlements—an object lesson as to the dimension of time in any understanding of power.

The skills of vigilant analysis of all competing interests, selected disclosure of information, and the ability to compromise at key moments, are critical factors to success in this world of pure power brokerage.

Although I concur with Ken Robinson's assessments that we often restrict our options by the limited exercise of our personal power, I also believe that we as a society and as a species err on the other extreme. Often our inability to understand the extent of our power has consequences that are unpredictable, resulting in catastrophic consequences. Witness Chernobyl, the Exxon Valdez, and Hiroshima, to name a few. (We are equally inept, or in denial, at gauging the power of nature's force: tsunamis, hurricanes, earthquakes.)

The current economic crisis is a dramatic example. The belief that the power of the economy could keep sustaining expansive growth, which in turn enhanced corporate and personal power, led to just the opposite result. Many now find themselves in dire straits, without home or job. Almost all of us feel more chastened and concerned about our future prospects and the realization of our life objectives. In parts of the global economy, the auto industry and finance for example, an entirely new landscape is emerging with dramatically different repositories of power and influence. The ever-growing complexity of interrelationships in business, politics, technology, and public policy, some call it globalization, leaves us increasingly exposed to equivalent disruptive power shifts in the future.

The surprising and extraordinary changes and/or abuses of power are those that trigger most of us to directly address the issue. Without a wake-up call we are often too willing to accommodate the status quo. A sudden rise or fall in the stock market, a marriage, a divorce, a medical diagnosis, a scientific breakthrough, a natural disaster. These unexpected or highly unlikely events are the ones that force us to pause and reassess our status and feelings of control. It is in these moments that we tend to evaluate our situations and decide if, and how, we might change our lives or those of our peers. It may be as simple as deciding to quietly lose ten pounds. It might turn out to be as momentous as Rosa Parks not giving up her bus seat. In any case, life-altering decisions almost always have a component that is concerned with our assessment of power. Losing ten pounds requires that we muster willpower over time. Not giving up a bus seat may defy the establishment's power, and so change the world, but it can be done impulsively. Whether we explicitly identify such an event as a power issue, most meaningful decisions in our lives are related to a shift in our understanding of our power relationships.

Believing that power is a key driver of behavior, one of the first determinations I make in my role as an organizational consultant is assessing where the power in an organization really resides. The official power structure represented by the organization chart is rarely reflective of how things actually work. Organizations have distinct forms of acknowledging and tolerating the manifestations of power. Without a basic understanding of where the repositories are, and how the expressions of power are handled in different corporate cultures, understanding and constructively enabling meaningful change is difficult if not impossible. Charles Handy in *Gods of Management* categorizes corporate cultures by four personality types, each represented by an appropriate Greek god—Zeus, Apollo, Athena, and Dionysus. In the fall 2003 issue of *strategy + business*, Lawrence Fisher summarizes Handy's framework:

Cultures typified by a charismatic founder/leader Zeus are managed by sheer force of will, respect for the leader's outsized talent, and the pleasure of belonging to an inner circle. This culture works best in small startup organizations. The Apollo culture, which has dominated large corporate organizations for the past two decades or more, is one with clearly delineated rules, roles, and procedures, and management by hierarchy. This culture works best in stable, predictable markets and industries. The Athena culture is collaborative and task-based, drawing upon flexible teams of professionals who solve particular problems, and then move on to the next ones. Historically, the Athena culture has worked best in consulting firms, advertising agencies, and other fields where ideas are the product and where expertise can be applied in very specific ways. Finally, the culture of Dionysus, god of wine and song, is existential, typified by independent specialists who enter the organization only to achieve their own purposes. It works best where individual talent is at a premium and people are encouraged to work independently.

Conflicts inevitably arise when the cultures are mixed in inappropriate ways. Scrappy startups become more Apollonian as they grow, pitting Zeus and the founders' club against a middle management dedicated to preserving order. Athenian organizations also become more rules-based as they grow, alienating partners who would rather be judged by outcomes on specific projects than evaluated by formal appraisal procedures. Dionysians are often unmanageable by conventional means, such as perks, promotions, or the threat of dismissal; they also prefer to sell their services to a succession of highest bidders rather than accept the apparent security of a stable wage.

Handy's work illustrates how the locus of power in each of these organizations is entirely different, eliciting from participants very different behaviors with regard to authority. Working for Zeus, where all the power is held at the center, demands a very different set of behaviors than working for Dionysus, where any concentration of power is viewed with great suspicion. As individuals and educational systems take up the call voiced by Robinson and others for more creative and individualized expression, the structural core of organizations must also change to establish acceptable and workable occupational relationships.

Changes in education, the economy, and the values of people have not been mirrored by a corresponding change in corporate cultures. An emphasis on individual learning, growing affluence, and a market that prizes ideas and intellectual property above all else have prompted the population of Athenians and Dionysians to grow. These highly qualified individuals will not work for Apollo, or will do so only grudgingly, which undermines the goals of the traditional organization and limits workers' own opportunities. The resistance to Apollo and "bureaucratic corporatism" will only grow.
—Lawrence Fisher

John Isaacson, a renowned executive recruiter and close friend, describes me to others as one who speaks truth to power. I agree that is one of my characteristics, but when I start thinking about what truth and power really mean it causes me to respond with a variation of Merton Kahne's reply to my query—"How are you?" in my earlier essay of the same name—what kind of description is that to give a friend? We have already seen how the exercise of power, although pervasive, is very different and difficult to define in the thinking and social fabric and workings of organization. Since most of my professional life has been spent working in large nonprofit (Dionysian) institutions (universities, museums, hospitals, think tanks) identifying the locus of power, if one even exists, is challenging. Truth can often be equally ephemeral. We would like to assume certain truths to be self-evident, yet they rarely are (especially in academia). We spend much of our lives trying to discern the truth. Yet when we deeply probe our beliefs, or events we witness, we are often left with more questions than answers.

The most blatant and disturbing examples of power result from divergent acceptance or interpretation of the truth. Power in the name of truth is invoked on a massive scale with wars, crusades, jihads, genocides, and holocausts. Even more often power is exercised against new ideas in an attempt to maintain the status quo and instill the true message on the outlier. Galileo is a prime example of a person who is prosecuted for telling truth to power and suffering the consequences. No longer able to reconcile his astronomical observations with the prevailing truth that the Earth was the center of the universe, Galileo provided a new truth—that the Earth revolves about the sun, which challenged church dogma, undermining the entire premise of faith in the church. Galileo was prosecuted and silenced to preserve the existing beliefs.

Richard Goodwin in his play *Two Men of Florence* provides the audience with a textured and spirited exchange between the two men. Goodwin argues that the process of deduction behind the conclusion was equally as threatening to the church as the conclusion. His Pope is, pardon the pun, *agnostic* on the truth or falsehood of Galileo's findings, but explicitly concerned that if accepted they would demonstrate the triumph of reason over faith putting religion on a slippery slope from which it could not recover. Thus, Goodwin's Pope argues that the "truth" has to be denied, not because of the facts but because the process by which it is derived would undermine faith as the foundation of belief.

In our own age and culture, science has gained the upper hand over religion as the harbinger of truth (in spite of the

Inquisition), but that doesn't mean religion has lost the struggle. Indeed, the battles continue on an even wider scale. Every major issue—abortion, gay marriage, health care, national security, evolution, you name it—mobilizes passion and resources to strengthen and empower the campaigns to influence public opinion and public policy. It is often impossible to conduct a civil dialogue between opposing sides because of the strident tactics and rhetoric that each employs. The role of power in these "discussions" is manifested by the means groups will employ to meet their ends. The never-ending revelations of voter disenfranchisement and deceitful practices by individuals entrusted with the public good are testament to the importance and pervasiveness of concerns with power. Often the smaller the issue, the more heated the debate. That principle was long ago enshrined into Sayre's Law: "In any dispute the intensity of feeling is inversely proportional to the value of the stakes at issue." By way of corollary it adds, "That is why academic politics are so bitter."

Since issues of power are so pervasive, is it possible to harness the power expended on both sides of an individual issue to move the dialogue forward on a broader, more systemic level rather than continue fueling unproductive encounters that basically cancel each other out? The first step toward that objective is to acknowledge that the issues we address are part of a broad, encompassing system. Balancing and harnessing the system's power is the overarching issue. For over three decades Barry Oshry has been conducting a Power Lab on Cape Cod to teach productive and enlightened uses of system power:

We humans look with awe at the remarkable system accomplishments of such creatures as ants and bees and termites—thousands of such creatures working together, communicating, their differentiated responsibilities all coming together in the service of the Hill, the Hive. Yet their accomplishments, as amazing as they are, are dwarfed by our own. We humans are the most social of all creatures, and the accomplishments of our systems are truly astounding: the products they make, the services they provide, the food they produce, the art they create, the knowledge they generate, the technology they develop. Yet early on in my work I noticed a peculiar paradox. Human systems—organizations, families, nations—in addition to their amazing accomplishments persist in living out self-limiting and often destructive stories;

but members within these systems do not experience themselves as living out any familiar story. Members do not wake in the morning and say, "Hey gang, I've got a good idea, why don't we recreate the same old destructive story!" Instead, they simply rise, go about their business, do what they do—and then the familiar story happens. . . . We are system creatures. Our hearts and minds are shaped by the structure and processes of the whole system of which we are a part. Until we recognize and learn to work that reality of our existence, we are likely to continue to do needless damage to ourselves, to our systems, and to other systems. . . . When we ignore our systemic nature we fall into predictable, limiting, and destructive patterns of interaction. System leadership is about transforming systems, elevating them to new levels of possibility. The key ingredients of system power are: the belief that we can make a difference to our systems, deep knowledge of the processes of the whole, and the courage to act.

—*Leading Systems: Lessons from the Power Lab*, Barry Oshry

One of the best examples of the need to exert Oshry's "system power" is the endless debate about health care reform. Everyone acknowledges the urgent need for action, and yet for decades the problem has just gotten worse. The enormity of the problem and the myriad of entrenched interests have stymied any reform. It has been, and may be, impossible to rebalance the power in the system to everyone's satisfaction. There are so many entrenched interests—doctors, hospitals, insurers, government, pharmaceuticals, medical suppliers— –all trying to locally maximize their piece of the pie that no one has the power to manage the full complexity of medical care. They constitute yet another secular "church" intent on maintaining their grip on the system, reason be damned, complete with those martyrs, Harry and Louise. In his June 1, 2009, *New Yorker* article, "The Cost Conundrum," Atul Gawande raises this issue by contrasting the care delivered in McAllen, Texas, one of the most expensive health care markets in the country, with the Mayo Clinic and Grand Junction, Colorado, one of the lowest cost markets in the country. In McAllen every patient is treated episodically and seen as a profit center to be maximized. At Mayo or Grand Junction patient needs are systemically addressed to maximize quality of care. A corollary result is lower costs. Using McAllen and Mayo as opposite extremes Gawande writes:

In the war over whether our country's anchor model will be Mayo or McAllen—the Mayo model is losing. In the sharpest economic down-turn that our health care system has faced in a half a century, many people in medicine don't see why they should do the hard work of orga-nizing themselves in ways that reduce waste and improve quality if it means sacrificing revenue.

The lack of "systems power" is equally evident in practi-cally every other major human concern. As we have been able to unleash the power of the atom, crack the genetic code, and build internally programmed and self-replicating machines, that along with other innovations constantly and forever change how we live, we have not concurrently developed powerful gov-erning mechanisms to guide their deployment. Nuclear energy, global warming, and multi-national finance all require powerful orchestration that no one seems to have the power to conduct. The same can be said for non-technological issues: refugees, trafficking of human beings, genocide, and religious conflicts. These are uniquely human problems stemming from our extraordinary brainpower. Other species have little or no power to change their nature or their future. They and the planet are, however, subject to and victims of our actions.

Does the solitary ant comprehend the complex process of the Hill, the bee grasp the intricate workings of the Hive? It seems inconceivable, but who knows? What, then, do we make of ourselves? We human beings may be the most social of all creatures, given the vast array of human systems—families, organizations, sports teams, volunteer groups, religious institutions, schools, armies, small business. Can we comprehend the workings of these systems? Can we see the wholes of which we are a part? And if we are able to see systems, what new leadership and membership possibilities does that open up for us?. . . The development of system sight—and the possibilities such sight offers for creating sane, healthy, creative, and less destructive human systems—is a worthy challenge for us human beings and a step up the evolutionary ladder.
—*Leading Systems: Lessons from the Power Lab*, Barry Oshry

Power can be used to constrain or enable. We are the only species that has been able to extraordinarily leverage our innate power. Every other animal species conforms to a strict set of power rules within its ranks and with regard to its environment. Our future and the future of every species on Earth is dependent on our ability to judiciously use our ever-increasing ability to modify nature in a constructive, rather than a destructive, manner. Of course in the end we may still be overwhelmed by an act of nature that is not under our control. But for the events that we can control we must understand that power is not a dirty word. Goethe said, "Dream no small dreams for they have no power to move the hearts of men." In order to achieve these big dreams in the future requires that we embrace Oshry's concept of system power to bring about the critical systemic changes and the enlightened actions demanded by an ever-interdependent, technology-driven world. We must develop transformational leadership that will judiciously use its power to keep all forces, natural and man-made, in balance. Only by deploying our power thoughtfully and carefully will we be able to realize the dreams our power enables.

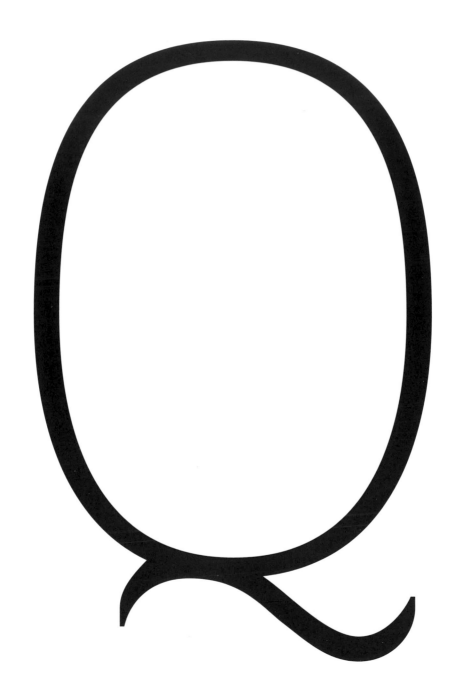

A sentence worded or expressed so as to elicit information;
a point or topic to be investigated or discussed; a problem,
or a matter forming the basis of a problem
—OED

When the rabbi was asked why he answered every question with a question, he replied "Why not?" Why not indeed! All humans spend their lives asking questions. We have the distinctive ability to question and envision alternatives. Why, when, where, what, who, how, if, are how we constantly try to make sense of the past, understand the present, and anticipate the future. Every other species can only respond to the present, and that reaction is invariably hard-wired and extremely practical. They can be conditioned to alter their responses, like Pavlov's dogs, but those responses are just as incurious as the old ones.

Like our fellow creatures, our survival also depends on honing our abilities to meet the ever-present challenges, but life for most humans goes well beyond immediate cause and effect. Our concerns range over a spectrum of queries from the most primitive and mundane—when and what will I eat next?—to the most abstruse and incomprehensible—what is the meaning of life?

question

As part of his satirical and very funny sermon in *Beyond the Fringe*, Alan Bennett succinctly addresses both the everyday dilemma of staying alive and the conundrum of life's meaning, metaphorically:

Life is rather like opening a tin of sardines.
We all of us are looking for the key.
Some of us think we have found the key—don't we?
We roll back the lid of the sardine tin of life.
We reveal the sardines—the riches of life therein.
We get them out.
We enjoy them.
But you know,
There is always a little piece in the corner you can't get out.
I wonder.
Is there a little piece in the corner of your life?
I know there is in mine.

His fellow Englishman William Shakespeare has Hamlet pose life's puzzle a little more seriously. (I know it's long and familiar, but take the time to read it slowly. It is amazing.)

To be, or not to be: that is the question:
Whether 'tis nobler in the mind to suffer
The slings and arrows of outrageous fortune,
Or to take arms against a sea of troubles,
And by opposing end them? To die: to sleep;
No more; and by a sleep to say we end
The heart-ache and the thousand natural shocks
That flesh is heir to, 'tis a consummation
Devoutly to be wish'd. To die, to sleep;
To sleep: perchance to dream: ay, there's the rub;
For in that sleep of death what dreams may come
When we have shuffled off this mortal coil,
Must give us pause: there's the respect
That makes calamity of so long life;
For who would bear the whips and scorns of time,
The oppressor's wrong, the proud man's contumely,
The pangs of despised love, the law's delay,
The insolence of office and the spurns

That patient merit of the unworthy takes,
When he himself might his quietus make
With a bare bodkin? who would fardels bear,
To grunt and sweat under a weary life,
But that the dread of something after death,
The undiscover'd country from whose bourn
No traveller returns, puzzles the will
And makes us rather bear those ills we have
Than fly to others that we know not of?
Thus conscience does make cowards of us all;
And thus the native hue of resolution
Is sicklied o'er with the pale cast of thought,
And enterprises of great pith and moment
With this regard their currents turn awry,
And lose the name of action.

The majority of us have opted *to be* and to focus on the questions that result from that decision. In our democracy we pride ourselves that we have the latitude and freedom to make *to be* choices. The option of *not to be* certainly may enter our mind at times, especially during old age or as a result of a catastrophe, but for most of us it is not a dominant concern. That does not mean *not to be* questions are absent, especially from the debate of societal issues. Suicide, abortion, euthanasia, genocide, war, torture, and capital punishment are all *not to be* issues that are highly visible, hotly debated, and extremely divisive. Corollary concerns of human rights, abuse of any kind, sexual exploitation, slavery, and oppression are also under constant scrutiny. The resolutions of these *not to be* existential issues are of paramount importance in shaping how we live. But we cannot spend our lives wrestling minute to minute with the rationale of our existence.

We all must come to some accommodation to these over-arching questions in life. Simplistically the question of the meaning of life can be arrayed on a spectrum of pure faith on one end and absolute reason on the other. There is a multiplicity of possible metrics for these arrays—religious belief vs. atheism, totalitarianism vs. democracy, fatalism vs. free will. Few of us find that we are at the extreme of these measures. Where we do find ourselves on these spectra, by choice or as a result of our environment, is a large determinant of how we approach everyday dilemmas, question and interpret the truth, what we can and do ask of ourselves, and the puzzles we choose or are able to solve.

In contrast to Mr. Shakespeare, Alan Bennett's formulation of life's puzzle is a more operational and realistic characterization of our everyday *to be* activities. We are all constantly looking for the key—whether it is the key to life, the key to the sardine tin, or the key to the car. Our understanding and desires for the right key change at every stage of our life, largely governed by our ability to navigate through a sequential set of maturational steps.

Stimulated by Freud's insights, a myriad of studies in the twentieth century have focused a great deal of attention on the consequences of developmental behavior and the questions that must be resolved. Jean Piaget in his renowned works on childhood dramatically demonstrated how our physical and psychological stage of development determines our ability to formulate questions and therefore understand and master the world around us. Erik Erikson and others extended the work into adulthood. In Erikson's eight stages of life, the resolution of a conflict is the key to successfully moving to the next level. The questions we ask ourselves as we move through these periods predominately revolve around the dominant conflict at that stage.

1. **Infant stage** Basic Trust vs. Mistrust—Are my caregivers reliable?
2. **Toddler stage** Autonomy vs. Shame and Doubt—Why? How does the world work?
3. **Kindergarten** Initiative vs. Guilt—Can I plan and do things on my own?
4. **Around age 6 to puberty** Industry vs. Inferiority—How do I compare to others?
5. **Teenager** Identity vs. Role Confusion—Who am I? How do I fit in? Where am I going in life?
6. **Young adult** Intimacy vs. Isolation—Who do I want to be? What am I going to do with my life? Will I settle down?
7. **Midlife crisis** Generatively vs. Stagnation—What are my accomplishments/failures. Am I satisfied or not?
8. **Old age** Ego Integrity vs. Despair—Did I do a good job? Was it worth it?

Shakespeare, in his infinite wisdom, anticipated much of modern psychosocial research with Jacque's famous monologue in *As You Like It*:

All the world's a stage,
And all the men and women merely players;
They have their exits and their entrances;
And one man in his time plays many parts,
His acts being seven ages. At first the infant,
Mewling and puking in the nurse's arms;
And then the whining school-boy, with his satchel
And shining morning face, creeping like snail
Unwillingly to school. And then the lover,
Sighing like furnace, with a woeful ballad
Made to his mistress' brow. Then a soldier,
Full of strange oaths, and bearded like the pard,
Jealous in honour, sudden and quick in quarrel,
Seeking the bubble reputation
Even in the cannon's mouth. And then the justice,
In fair round belly with good capon lin'd,
With eyes severe and beard of formal cut,
Full of wise saws and modern instances;
And so he plays his part. The sixth age shifts
Into the lean and slipper'd pantaloon,
With spectacles on nose and pouch on side;
His youthful hose, well sav'd, a world too wide
For his shrunk shank; and his big manly voice,
Turning again toward childish treble, pipes
And whistles in his sound. Last scene of all,
That ends this strange eventful history,
Is second childishness and mere oblivion;
Sans teeth, sans eyes, sans taste, sans everything.

The answers we seek and receive at every stage and age of our lives are highly dependent on our surroundings, culture, and caregivers. If, at an early age, we are encouraged to be curious, are taken seriously, and have access to a rich environment, our lifelong options are greatly expanded. If we live in a more traditional setting with defined expectations, be they class, cast, color, or gender, we may be relegated to a more limited set of perceived possibilities. In more open societies, curiosity is explicitly encouraged rather than stifled. How we experience and ultimately resolve each of life's stages can have a profound effect on our ability to successfully navigate through the subsequent challenges we all face. There must be a careful balance between support and discovery. Too much attention, to the extreme of smothering, can be as problematic as too much neglect.

As we grow and mature the questions we ask ourselves, and the answers we seek, become evermore complex, multidimensional, and hopefully more interesting. But the more refined the questions, the less straightforward the answers. We start to live in a number of different worlds. The dilemmas/decisions required by our professional, personal, interpersonal, religious, parenting, playful, sexual, learning, and teaching selves all pose questions for us to ponder that independently require different metrics, diverse frames of reference, and have varying impacts on our future.

The habit of asking questions and answering them is fundamental not only to the way we mature as individuals, but indeed to the way we mature as a civilization. Every culture and religion has rites of passage and rituals to assure understanding, and mastery of its critical knowledge and fundamental sets of belief. Jesuits, Muslims, Masons, African Bushmen, and Buddhists all have developed highly refined forms of inquiry to transmit their *weltanschauung*. Take the rabbi's "Why not?" It is derivative of the great value Judaism places on Talmudic reasoning—*pilpul*—a form of discourse that takes nothing for granted and disputes everything. One of the most significant rituals in Judaism, the Passover Seder, is built on four questions asked by the youngest child. That rite, like comparable rituals in other settings, has been the springboard for freewheeling discussions in families for centuries.

A good deal of our life experience is devoted to acquiring the skills to address the questions we ask ourselves or must confront, and clearly that experience begins before we start school. Formal education is designed to provide an even richer set of intellectual tools that will enable us to ask and frame salient questions to solve and answer cognitive questions. The better we are prepared to marshal the available resources to address diverse sets of queries, the richer and more diverse the opportunities life affords us. One of the oldest forms of pedagogy, the Socratic method, proceeds not by Question & Answer, but by Question & Question. Creating an environment that provides for constant questioning is essential to students developing the curiosity and acquiring the skills to become engaged and productive adults.

The recent emphasis on standardized testing and quantitative measures of achievement against arbitrarily prescribed norms are being implemented in a manner that in my mind defeats the purpose of a quality education. By teaching the test to produce the "right answers" the much more critical skill of posing the "right questions" and learning the right processes to find and/or derive the answer is almost entirely lost. You need a minimal set of skills and knowledge to function effectively in society. Assuring that students can answer a set of specific questions without any understanding of how these answers connect to the important tasks that everyday life will require of them not only seems counterproductive but also belies the principles that underlie any sound education. Life is not always true or false or even multiple choice.

But pedagogical skills are far from sufficient. Street smarts, ethical values, perceptual acuity, mechanical skills, political savvy, magic tricks, ability to dance, enjoy music, play sports, and resolve conflicts are just a few of the other abilities we need to acquire to navigate the world's shoals and lead a fruitful, satisfying, and meaningful life. All these experiences and capabilities are curiously intertwined. Maintaining emotional equilibrium and harmony between our internal personal goals and the objectives required to carry out our external more public objectives is often a major source of worry and discomfort. Receiving a promotion or job offer in a new city causing the family to uproot and leave a comfortable environment is a simple example of how opposing values may need to be resolved. We strive to generate our solutions using a consistent and unified set of principles and decision rules that are highly interdependent. To the extent we are successful, internal conflicts are minimized; we feel in control and effective. When new or unexpected circumstances demand we use multiple and perhaps conflicting decision criteria, anxiety, frustration, and sometimes helplessness result.

Events like the recent economic downturn with the fear of (or actual) job loss, the death of a loved one, or a catastrophic illness are dramatic examples. Feelings of vulnerability and loss of esteem raise deep questions that may cause wrenching reassessments and reformulation of our self-image and life plan. At such moments it is as if all the locks have been changed and all our keys no longer work. If our education and life experiences have given us the tools to develop alternative keys—keys that support the adoption of new or modified sets of skills—we hopefully can emerge with renewed energy and purpose.

It is at these moments in life that problem-solving skills are critical. Reading novels, solving puzzles, traveling, pursuing a hobby, playing an instrument and/or a sport, exercising. If we have remained curious, receptive to fresh ideas, and honed our understanding of alternative worldviews, we keep our facilities in tune to attack the unexpected events, good and bad, that may befall us.

Developing a deeper understanding of the impulses and psychological needs that make up our psychic nature is also a necessity. Thoughts about human nature in the twentieth century, especially in America, were greatly influenced by the work of Freud and his emphasis on the power of the unconscious, and the associated mechanisms of repression. Although his influence is now on the wane, the fundamental tenets of his work, that many of our actions result from unresolved childhood desires and urges, stymieing our ability to ask or face up to certain questions, has had a major influence on the understanding of everyday behavior. What we allow ourselves to ask of ourselves is central to constructively coping with our own needs as well as those of others. How well we address and reconcile our inner needs with the demands placed on us by external realities is of great importance in maintaining our physical and mental equilibrium.

The overlap and resolution of questions in our different real and inner worlds has been the subject of intensive inquiry. One of the most insightful studies on gaining personal satisfaction has been conducted by Mihaly Csikszentmihalyi (MC) at the University of Chicago. His classic research has resulted in a number of books on "flow"—the psychology of engagement in everyday life. Flow occurs when the challenge facing an individual is meaningful and requires a high degree of skill to overcome an issue or a challenge. Skiing a difficult mountain trail, cooking an excellent meal, and solving a difficult problem or puzzle all result in a feeling of flow by virtue of the intensity of the mental and/or physical effort to successfully navigate the difficulties that the task requires.

"Flow" is the way people describe their state of mind when consciousness is harmoniously ordered, and they want to pursue whatever they are doing for its own sake. . . . The optimal state of inner experience is one where there is order in consciousness. This happens when psychic energy—or attention—is invested in realistic goals, and when skills match the opportunities for action. The pursuit of a goal brings order to awareness because a person must concentrate attention on the task at hand and momentarily forget everything else. These periods of struggling to overcome challenges are what people find to be the most enjoyable times of their lives. A person who has achieved control of psychic energy and has invested it in consciously chosen goals cannot help but grow into a more complex being. By stretching skills, by reaching toward higher challenges, such a person becomes an increasingly extraordinary individual.
—*Flow: The Classic Work on How to Achieve Happiness,*
Mihaly Csikszentmihalyi

To attain flow, MC lists a set of criteria that include a loss of the feeling of self-consciousness—the merging of action and awareness, the integration of mind and body. Questions related to mind/body and their duality go back as far, if not further than, Plato and Aristotle. Some of the most precise exposition on the topic came from René Descartes (I think, therefore I am). Although still a topic of hot, pure, philosophical debate about the nature of man, the recent emergence of computers and information processing has added fuel to the fire of this discourse with the questions regarding whether machines think and therefore can have a mind (the field of artificial intelligence).

From the beginning computers could quickly manipulate symbols and achieve results (multiplication or retrieving information) that require what some call the mind in human beings. Since these operations were, and to a large extent still are, programmed into the machine by a human, these operations were considered rote mechanical manifestations by the machine of a human mind. As computers become faster and better, many of their computations can and do go beyond human insight. There is a belief, and in some a fear, that they will indeed develop the equivalent of a mind. Because computers will evolve in their own way, the odds are high they will develop a process of intelligence that is not the same as ours, or even understandable by us. Once accomplished, the "computer mind" will have the ability to pose questions and derive answers of their own choosing that cannot or may not be controlled or questioned by humans.

We are already witnessing the ubiquity and influence of computers in our daily lives. Less than a decade ago the terms search engine, browser, and bandwidth were as familiar to the average citizen as Sanskrit. Today, life without laptops, PDAs, and smart phones is impossible to an ever-growing portion of the population. Google has become the ultimate recipient of our questions and guide to our intellectual life. Computers with their vast memories and blinding speed allow us to ask questions, retrieve information, and solve problems at a mind-boggling pace. But it is important to remember that Google, Windows, MAC OS, and Facebook—whatever the program or operating system—are as much captives of their past as we are as individuals. They are designed to answer certain questions in very narrow ways. Although they open vast areas of capability, they too exhibit their own biases and restrictions imbued by their designers and programmers. Although they are constantly tweaked and improved they do not experience the vast array of maturational hurdles that we as humans must master. My dear old friend, recently deceased, Joe Weizenbaum brilliantly addressed these issues in his classic *Computer Power and Human Reason:*

And there precisely is a crucial difference between man and machine. Man, in order to become whole, must be forever an explorer of both his inner and outer realities. His life is full of risks, but risks he has the courage to accept because, like the explorer, he learns to trust his own capacities to endure, to overcome. What could it mean to speak of risk, courage, trust, endurance, and overcoming when one speaks of machines?

In the history of Western civilization man's ultimate goal has been to constantly strive to ask and attempt to answer the most insightful and meaningful questions possible, culminating with the development of a set of logical principles and the scientific method. For millennia, practitioners of Eastern thought such as Hinduism, Buddhism, and Taoism have honed a very different discipline of approaching the meaning of life and overcoming the duality of self and object. These practices employ a very dissimilar mode and set of questions than those asked in the Western world through the systematic rigor and hypothesis testing of modern science. Zen parables, known as koans, are one example. Often asked in the form of questions these queries are difficult or impossible to grasp, let alone be given a response. What is the sound of one hand clapping? Does a dog have Buddha nature or not? These are meant to evoke a state of mind, not an answer. The ultimate purpose of Eastern spiritual enlightenment is to lose all self-consciousness and become one with nature. To stop asking questions and just *to be*.

Whether we take up Hamlet's question *to be* in the Eastern or Western world, we will by our nature always be Weizenbaum's explorer, always be looking for Alan Bennett's key to the sardine can of life, Zen and information systems notwithstanding. But happiness, as Csikszentmihalyi has shown in his work on flow, lies in the journeys that the right questions initiate. Answers invariably lead to a new set of questions and challenges. Gertrude Stein got it right on her deathbed. When asked by her lifelong companion Alice B. Toklas, "Gertrude, What is the answer?" she responded without hesitation, "What is the Question?"

To hazard, endanger; to expose to the chance of injury or loss; to venture upon, take the chances of
—OED

Every day I get up and watch a movie. It's called my life. Some days are action-packed thrillers. Some are X-rated, although these are getting to be rarer than Westerns. Others are looking pretty formulaic. What makes them worth watching is that I get to produce, direct, and act in them as well. I think I know how things are going to turn out, but I am constantly surprised by unpredicted events and predicaments. New actors show up all the time and I need to figure out if I want to cast them in major roles or just as walk-ons. I also need to continually revise the script. Is it going to be a cliffhanger with lots of scary scenes, a mystery, a domestic comedy, or a reality show? It turns out to be all of these things. Although I think I get to decide everything, I am constantly forced to deal with unexpected changes. Some are minor and take little thought, while others are very dramatic and take the plot in an entirely different direction. Over the years I have gotten adept at understanding how well I can predict and handle unforeseen twists and how exciting I want the picture to be, but I am constantly surprised at some of my actions and their outcomes.

We are all telling ourselves the story of our lives and watching it at the same time. How the story unfolds is partly under our control and partly determined by the uncertainties that we must confront and how we cope with them. Some concerns—happiness, health, money, and job security—are constantly with us. Others appear from nowhere. Our marketing culture is very good at making sure we are kept on our toes with regard to possible (and for the most part improbable) situations. Until recently I never worried about what I should do if I had an erection lasting more than four hours. (I secretly crave the prospect of calling my doctor and telling him this is happening.) It's still not on the top of my list, especially since I don't take any drugs, but I now know it's a possibility to be considered along with a sudden drop in blood pressure, bad breath, double vision, and an infestation of creatures in my toilet bowl.

Like everyone else in this culture I am being bombarded with messages that offer solutions for risks that might befall me. In addition to the barrage of subtle and not-so-subtle fears raised by Madison Avenue, I am exposed to the uncertainty that surrounds the polar ice cap, the rice crop in the Philippines, the outcome of the corruption trial of Jacques Chirac, and the consequences of choosing trick rather than dispensing treats. My ability to thoughtfully sort, prioritize, and decide how to behave shapes the kind of person I am and the quality of the life I lead. My tolerance for uncertainty, my ability to gather and assimilate information, my subjective probability computations, along with my subsequent assessment of risk, affects almost every action and decision. In spite of the pervasive impact and power of these traits, it is often only in the most extreme and dire situations that I, and most of us, seriously attempt to understand how they influence behavior. In other words I often just watch my movie rather than script it.

It is important at the outset to distinguish between risk and uncertainty. They are not the same, although many people use the words interchangeably. They are in fact different, although related, concepts. Uncertainty is the possibility that there may be more than one outcome. Risk is about the effect, positive and negative, of a future event. Every living being has physiological mechanisms that take over when faced with the risk of physical danger. Each of us uniquely responds to these external threats based on our worldview:

We see a map of the world, not the world itself. But what kind of a map is the brain inclined to draw? The answer comes from the dictates of evolution, the survival of the fittest. Fundamentally, it is a map that has to do with our real survival: it evolved to provide, as a first priority, information on immediate dangers to life and limb, the ability to distinguish friend and foes, the wherewithal to find food, and the resources and opportunities for procreation. The world seems to be sorted and packaged in this way, substantially enriched by the categories of culture we live in, by learning, and by the meanings we form out of the unique journey each of us travels.

—The Art of Possibility, Rosamund Stone Zander and Benjamin Zander

Uncertainty is always with us; risk may or may not be. Although external risks are present, most risk results from our internal decisions and our actions. Every spin of a roulette wheel is uncertain. I am only at risk if I bet. Some risk is under our control and some is not. We all live with a degree of risk. How we tolerate and manage risk is a large determinant of how we live our lives.

Yet not many of us make a detailed assessment of our risk profile. It determines how we pick the sports we play, choose our mate, bring up our children, make investments, taste new foods, and share our experience with others. Over three hundred years ago, Benjamin Franklin wrote, "In this world nothing can be said to be certain, except death and taxes." If taxes and death are the only certain events, everything else we deal with must be uncertain. This is often called "the human condition." Our assessment of the uncertainties and the risk mechanisms we employ as a consequence are major determinants of our affairs.

Mankind seemed to have a shot at living in a world of certitude, but then Eve ate the apple and the rest is history. Richard DenUyl, the United Congregational minister in Little Compton, Rhode Island, asked in a recent sermon on the Garden of Eden, "Would we really want a world with perfect predictability?" His interpretation runs somewhat counter to most accepted theology. He argued that rather than look on the tasting of the forbidden fruit as the original sin that caused the woes of the human race, we should all be grateful for Eve's transgression that ushered in "the human condition"—the ability to choose. Without it life would be at best a bore, and at worst meaningless. If we were granted eternal happiness and immortality what challenges would we need to confront? "None" was his conclusion. The forbidden fruit enables us to experience the uncertainty that leads alternately to joys and rewards or the hardships and travails that result from the choices we make.

Although this interpretation of the religious story of the Garden of Eden emphasizes the ability of humans to choose, for much of human history religion and its stories were used as a counter to choice. The future was not determined by man but by the will of the gods.

With the Renaissance and the Enlightenment, a more rational approach rivaled faith to explain and govern the destiny of human affairs. Copernicus, Galileo, Leibniz, Newton, Descartes,

Hume, and Kant offered evermore sophisticated treatises on the nature of man and the world. In the twentieth century the determinate view of causation was replaced by relativity, the uncertainty principle, and quantum mechanics. Einstein, Bohr, Heisenberg, and Schrödinger gave us an even more detailed understanding of the physical world at the same time that they paradoxically made reality more uncertain. As man gains greater insight into his physical world, mystical explanations give way to scientific and rational views of the universe. The modern worldview enables us to believe we can understand and control our environment and our destiny. Yet despite the fact we have become the healthiest, wealthiest, and longest lived of anyone in history, we are increasingly concerned with the uncertainties and risks our scientific insights afford. Nuclear power, global warming, terrorism, epidemics, and carcinogens evoke our fear for the future. There is increasing concern that scientific progress and technology has outstripped our capabilities to control our destiny. In addition, "scientific evidence" is often cited and manipulated to emphasize and proselytize a particular bias with the same fervor as religious arguments. The recent financial meltdown, caused in large part by a failure to fully understand risk management, is a case in point. The future of institutions, nations, and species is largely determined by the accuracy and skillful employment of risk assessment.

Concurrently our subjective risk assessments in the context of these broader issues are often left unexplored. My choices are largely based on my past performance and my limited world experience. I am fairly certain that the sun will rise tomorrow, my furniture will be where I left it the night before, the Yankees will overpay their ball players, and any stock I invest in will eventually underperform the market. Then there are things about which I am not certain. My life expectancy, the happiness of my children, the performance of the Dow, the cleanliness of a public restroom—all represent uncertain future events that are of consequence. Some of them are manageable and some are not. The framework for most choices includes a set of costs and benefits. Decisions that fall in our comfort zone enable us to assess the cost and benefits with ease. In other instances, marriage, divorce, home buying, job change, and the elements are much more carefully weighed. Additional information is often collected, analyzed, and discussed with others to guide and shape the decision. The more possibilities we consider, the more opportunity for fulfillment and success for some, and for disappointment and failure for others.

Alice laughed. "There's no use trying," she said. "One can't believe impossible things."

"I daresay you haven't had much practice," said the Queen. "When I was your age, I always did it for half an hour a day. Why sometimes I've believed as many as six impossible things before breakfast.
—*Through the Looking-Glass*, Lewis Carroll

What we believe to be possible determines our world and our actions. Few of us are at the extreme of eternal optimism or pervasive pessimism. The quality of our life is largely governed by where between these two poles our belief structure lies. The future may be uncertain, but it is not unimaginable. What are the odds of an event occurring?

In all cases we try to limit our exposure to bad or disappointing outcomes and make the best possible decision. How can we shift the odds in our favor and assure that the assessments we are *constantly* making maximize the benefit to ourselves and those who are dependent on our judgment? In *The Art of Possibility* Rosamund and Benjamin Zander explore this theme and the observation of Lewis Carroll's Queen:

Our minds are designed to string events into storylines, whether or not there is any connection between the parts. In dreams we regularly weave sensations gathered over disparate parts of our lives into narratives. In wakefulness, we produce reasons for our actions, that are rational, plausible, and guided by the logic of cause and effect. Whether or not these "reasons" accurately portray any of the real motivational forces at work. . . . It is these sorts of phenomena that we are referring to when we use the catchphrase *it's all invented.* What we mean is, it's all invented anyway, so we might as well invent a story or a framework of meaning that enhances the quality of life and the life of those around us. . . . The frames our minds create define—and confine—what we perceive to be possible. Every problem, every dilemma, every dead end we find ourselves facing in life, only appears unsolvable inside a particular frame or point of view. . . . Create another frame around the data and problems vanish while new opportunities appear.

. . . When you bring to mind *it's all invented* you remember that it's all a story you tell—not just some of it, but all of it. And remember that every story you tell is founded on a network of hidden assumptions. If you learn to notice and distinguish these stories, you will be able to break through the barriers of any box that contains unwanted conditions and create other conditions that support the life you envision for yourself and those around you. We do not mean that you can just make anything up and have it magically appear. We mean that you can shift the framework to one whose underlying assumptions allow for the conditions you desire.

A memorable turning point in my career occurred thirty years ago when I resigned my position as director of a child welfare resource center for the New England states. Over a five-year span I had negotiated studies and provided support to more than twenty-five commissioners of welfare in the six states we served. Frustrated by the disruptions caused by these unceasing executive turnovers, I resigned thinking I would soon have a new job at MIT managing a health policy center. While I awaited the promised funding for the new program, which was constantly delayed, I temporarily expanded my modest consulting practice. For the first two years I constantly worried and thought of myself as unemployed even though I was highly successful at attracting engagements that kept me busy and well paid. Then one day I woke up and realized—this is what I do—that I was an independent management consultant. That reframing completely changed my self-image, my emotional state, and the structure of my subsequent professional and personal life.

The Zanders extol the virtues of reframing to stimulate creative problem solving. It can, however, have equally negative effects as witnessed by the alternative risk assessment frames employed on Wall Street that have precipitated the current state of the economy. Risk management is a term closely associated with the financial and corporate world. It has become a highly refined, sophisticated, and some say arcane specialty. Volumes on techniques and strategies of risk management abound. Hedging, leveraging, insuring, diversifying, charting, and a myriad of highly sophisticated mathematical models and computer simulations represent just a few of the practices employed by the army of risk managers. Organizations large and small, public or private, profit or nonprofit, all employ, to a greater or lesser degree, some form of risk management to formulate their plans and guide their actions. In our ever-changing world, failure to properly assess risk through myopia, complacency, and inertia are sure predictors of difficult times, if not outright failure. The recent demise or radical restructuring of major banks, corporations, and governments is a dramatic example of the consequences of not properly understanding and dealing with the nature of the risks they faced.

One of the most predominant risk managers in our society is government. When we choose a candidate, especially for president, we are expressing our belief in his/her ability to best manage the risks associated with the certain uncertainties of the modern world. The red phone ringing at three in the morning is a good example. Risk management is also at the core of the philosophies of the parties. In general, Republicans trust in the market and the private sector to be most effective, while Democrats are more prone to public-sector solutions. Whatever the party affiliation, there is agreement that terrorism, defense, global warming, public safety, human rights, employment, health care, addiction, immigration, etc., are all issues where the risks to the common good must be constantly monitored and managed.

The recent debate regarding health care insurance is at its heart a dialogue on risk management. Insurance is inherently a risk management strategy. Life insurance relies on a plethora of data allowing for actuarial computations that for all practical purposes minimize risk to the provider. Because the delivery of health care is subject to almost an infinite number of ever-changing conditions, the industry cannot employ the same actuarial skills to set the odds. New technologies, shifting demographics, and unpredictable demand, along with a myriad of other factors make the exposure and consequent computation of the risk and liabilities of coverage highly problematic. As the cost of providing health care becomes an ever-increasing percentage of our governmental and personal expenditures, the risks associated with the cost of its provision, and the subsequent bills, become frighteningly large. The advocates of government programs assert that only by spreading the risk across the whole population can they be properly managed and assessed. The opposition argues for the status quo. There are clearly no easy, quick, predictable, or even "right" solutions to this or any of the other major societal challenges facing our nation and the world.

The same is true in our private lives. Our personal risk management demands at least as much, and perhaps even more attention than the public and corporate world. We must constantly reassess our risk and tolerance for risk as our families and we grow older. Can Johnny cross the street by himself? Should Mother keep living alone? What is the proper ratio of stocks and bonds in my portfolio? Shall I tell my friend she has a speck of parsley between her teeth? These are all risks along with thousands of others that need repeated attention and re-evaluation.

Although we continually make these judgments, the instances when we openly examine and understand our risk profile are rare. Significant events that confront us with uncertainty—when we marry, change jobs, move, buy a house, have children—may cause us to closely examine and evaluate our tolerance for risk. But the self-awareness revealed in those instances when we need to make decisions that expose us to a high degree of risk is rarely used to examine our overall pattern of risk tolerance. Uncertainty is not ignorance, while unnecessary risk may be. Understanding how and why we take certain risks is key to knowing how we are likely to respond in uncertain situations. Our responses are instilled early in our lives by our culture, our family, our schooling and our personal experiences. Developing new tools and letting go of dysfunctional, ingrained patterns is one of the keys to a fulfilled life. Reading, psychotherapy, theater, as well as everyday life, all play a role in sharpening our discretion.

A major belief of modern society is that education is essential to understanding and resolving the uncertainties that are always with us and continue to become evermore complex. Yet there is little explicit attention paid to risk management in our educational system. Education does not reduce uncertainty. In fact in many cases it may increase it by giving us a broader range of understanding of the dimensions of the possible outcome of situations that face us. A person with one watch knows what time it is. A person with two watches can never be sure. A good education gives you at least two watches. Hopefully the result is expanded possibilities, independent thought, informed appreciation, and critical judgment. Perhaps the most important lesson we learn is that uncertainty is ever present. Uncertainty is seeing a range of possibilities and their relative chance of occurrence. Coupled with a set of analytic tools—comparative analysis, mathematics, the scientific method—we can better understand and cope with our environment and ourselves. Many worry, as do I, that our present system is failing to provide these discerning skills.

Equally important as a formal education (and the perspective and tools it provides us to acquire and apply knowledge) is the concurrent enlightenment from reflections based on our everyday experiences and actions. Experience, street smarts, and savvy, are all terms that capture the dominant component of our understanding of uncertainty and associated risks. Apprenticeships have long been the norm for learning practical skills and crafts. Most recently this more hands-on approach has been given more and more credence as a form of learning, especially in the professions.

One of my late mentors, Don Schön, writes in his seminal book *The Reflective Practitioner*:

Problem-solving within a broader context of reflective inquiry shows how reflection-in-action may be rigorous in its own right, and links the art of practice in uncertainty and uniqueness to the scientist's art of research.

The non-routine situations of practice are at least partly indeterminate and must somehow be made coherent. Skillful practitioners learn to conduct frame experiments in which they impose a kind of coherence on messy situations and thereby discover consequences and implications of their chosen frames. From time to time, their efforts to give order to a situation provoke unexpected outcomes—"back talk" that gives the situation a new meaning. They listen and reframe the problem. It is this . . . that constitutes a reflective conversation with the materials of a situation—the design like artistry of professional practice.

Schön's insights documented and sharpened the practices of professional schools of all kinds, particularly medical schools. The practice of medicine certainly has always required concerted, on-the-job clinical training in conjunction with basic science courses to produce effective, reflective doctors. The practice of starting the clinical experience earlier in the curriculum indicates the growing importance of this form of learning. It is an equally interesting exercise to think of the patient as a reflective practitioner. Even if death is a certitude that always governs the risks we are willing to take, most of us try to take our health for granted.

Once confronted with symptoms and/or a confirmed serious diagnosis, many of us become ardent learners and risk managers. Inquiries of friends, books, the internet, and others who have faced the same situation are quickly mobilized and studied. If we are given the choice of a procedure or prolonged course of therapy, our efforts are redoubled. Physicians require an informed consent from a patient or their surrogates for serious interventions. But is it possible to be thoroughly informed in a few days or weeks, if ever? Chemotherapy, radiation, and many drug therapies are measured methods of killing part of the body with the promise or hope of recovery before the results are fatal. The uncertainty of the outcome and the subsequent effects can often only be presented in statistical and theoretical ways. In the past, many physicians were as reluctant to present the risks and subsequent difficulties associated with an illness as the patient was to hearing about them. The availability of reliable information, especially on the internet, has changed that dynamic. Recent revisions to medical school curricula have been designed to place greater emphasis on doctor-patient interactions, especially with regard to discussing the psychological as well as the physical risks and consequences of treatment.

The evolution of the doctor/patient relationship reflects the adjustments that we, and society itself, constantly make as times and behaviors change. What once seemed absolutely unacceptable may just as quickly pass unnoticed. Cole Porter had it right when he wrote:

In olden days a glimpse of stockings
Was looked on as something shocking
Now Heaven Knows, anything goes
Good authors too who knew better words
Now only use four letter words
Writing prose, anything goes

Of course *anything* doesn't always go. Yet I, and I am sure you, can recount any number of currently acceptable social conventions that would have been deemed impossible and shocking even a decade ago. Many of the risks society and we believe in are invented and imaginary. That does not mean they do not have real consequences. Inter-marriage between races or religions may in fact carry no real threat or harm, but in certain societal contexts these acts may result in great danger and even death. If we insist on basing our social and business behaviors on assumptions rooted in the past and are shocked that at present anything goes, we are destined to become less and less relevant in the future. I am not advocating taking on more risk than your comfort level allows. I am arguing for a constant questioning of the assumptions and frames that underpin your assessment of risk.

As an example, I have witnessed a radical reassessment of the risks associated with employment since I became an independent consultant. Thirty years ago when I responded to the ubiquitous question "What do you do?" by stating that I worked for myself, most everyone inquired about the risks of job security, pensions, health insurance, etc. They clearly saw it as a high-wire act. Now the questions invariably focus on how they can replicate my practice. I believe this change reflects the radical shift that has taken place regarding the risks associated with institutional employment.

Risk is a great inhibitor of the possible. To return to my movie, the possibilities I allow my story to explore and live out are largely determined by my view of the risk these actions entail. My professional history cited above is a good example. I love the Zanders' line, "It's all invented—not just some of it, but all of it." It certainly puts uncertainty, risk, and life in a stark perspective. I have no trouble believing that the other venues where I observe and learn how others cope with the vicissitudes of life—*real* movies, novels, and plays—are all invented. But my movie, how can that be? My problem is I still don't know how it will all turn out. Søren Kierkegaard once said, "Life can only be understood backwards; but it must be lived forwards." Well, if it is all invented, I hope I can conjure up a happy ending, but of course I am not certain of that. Benjamin Franklin identified only two certainties—death and taxes. I would proffer a third—uncertainty, I think.

**Silence**  A condition of absence or void; a response
—OED

**Space**  A period of time; intervals separating things; regions of the universe; privacy
—OED

**System**  Functionally related events or actions, in dynamic equilibrium, to meet an objective
—OED

**Strategy**  A plan of action to achieve a goal; a guide to saying no
—OED

One of the great benefits and pleasures of writing these essays is the comments and observations I receive. They are thought-provoking and make me realize anew how simply I have treated the subject. Some readers connected to my personal anecdotes while others enjoy the more theoretical discussions. The length of each piece and the choice of words are other topics that engender comment. The feedback enriches me and constantly eggs me on.

I have been in a bit of a quandary about writing S. After some deliberation between silence, space, system, and strategy, I decided to explore the relationship between all four with silence and space as the overarching themes. The twist is that I would like to explore them silently and interactively with you—à la Harris Burdick.

Twenty-five years ago my friend Chris Van Allsburg, the renowned children's author, created a book called *The Mysteries of Harris Burdick*. According to Van Allsburg's introduction, Harris Burdick brought to his friend Peter Wenders an illustration for each of fourteen stories he had written. He gave Wenders the pictures, accompanied only by the title and a caption for each tale, promising to return with the stories if Wenders had an interest in them. Burdick then mysteriously disappeared, never to be heard from again. Each Burdick drawing shows a perturbation that breaks an otherwise tranquil environment. Over the years Wenders showed Burdick's work to his children and their friends, inspiring dozens of stories. Fascinated by the tale, Van Allsburg decided to reproduce the pictures as a book accompanied only by their title and captions "so other children would be inspired by them."

Here is my challenge. Inspired by Burdick, I have created illustrations of ten familiar systems we experience every day. The descriptive quotes, pictures, and "captions" that follow suggest a number of silent and spatial components that define and shape the chosen system and underpin the development of its strategic objectives. Following Van Allsburg's lead, I hope you will be inspired to take the time usually devoted to reading one of my essays and quietly gather your thoughts to reflect on the unique role played by silence and/or space in one or more of these contexts.

What do think are the most salient features of silence and space in these or any other environments? What might I write? What would your favorite teacher or mentor say?

I promise to return to my parochial broadcast mode of interaction anon.

Peace 和

## Architecture

Everyone who has thought even casually about the subject knows that
the specific property of architecture—the feature distinguishing it from
all other forms of art—consists in its working with a three-dimensional
vocabulary that includes man.

Painting functions in two dimensions, even if it can suggest three
or four. Sculpture works in three dimensions, but man remains apart,
looking on from the outside. Architecture, however, is like a great,
hollowed-out sculpture, which man enters and apprehends by moving
about within it. . . . It is interior space, the space that surrounds and
includes us which is the basis of our judgment of a building. . . . All
the rest is important or perhaps we should say can be important, but
always in a subordinate role to the spatial idea.
—*Architecture as Space,* Bruno Zevi

*Foundation, Structure, Space, Light, Height, Width, Length, Proportion,
Golden Mean, Enclosure, Shelter, Safety, Comfort, Scale, Awe*

MIT Chapel by Eero Saarinen

## Art & Vision

The aim of art is to represent not the outward appearance of things, but their inward significance.
—Aristotle

Everything you can imagine is real.
—Pablo Picasso

The most pathetic person in the world is someone who has sight but has no vision.
—Helen Keller

The most beautiful thing we can experience is the mysterious. It is the source of all true art and science. He to whom this emotion is a stranger, who can no longer pause to wonder and stand rapt in awe, is as good as dead: his eyes are closed.
—Albert Einstein

*Figure, Ground, Symmetry, Color, Texture, Line, Perspective, Rhythm, Abstraction, Representation*

## Communications

Saying nothing . . . sometimes says the most.
—Emily Dickinson

The single biggest problem in communication is the illusion that it has taken place.
—George Bernard Shaw

## Alphabets

## Braille

| a | b | c | d | e | f | g | h | i | j | k |
|---|---|---|---|---|---|---|---|---|---|---|

| l | m | n | o | p | q | r | s | t | u | v |
|---|---|---|---|---|---|---|---|---|---|---|

| w | x | y | z |
|---|---|---|---|

**Scott Kim's Reversible ABC**

*Signal, Noise, Syntax, Meaning, Order, Direction, Clarity, Codes, Language, Standards*

Native Americans using Smoke Signals, Frederic Remington

## Healing

Formerly, when religion was strong and science weak, men mistook magic for medicine; now, when science is strong and religion weak, men mistake medicine for magic.
—Thomas Szasz

The art of medicine consists in amusing the patient while nature cures the disease.
—Voltaire

Happiness is nothing more than good health and a bad memory.
—Albert Schweitzer

Practicing the art of medicine requires not only expert knowledge of disease, but an appreciation of the intimate details of a patient's emotional life.
—Bernard Lown

We need to give each other the space to grow, to be ourselves, to exercise our diversity. We need to give each other space so that we may both give and receive such beautiful things as ideas, openness, dignity, joy, healing, and inclusion.
—Max De Pree

*Care, Empathy, Compassion, History, Diagnosis, Science, Medicine*

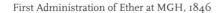

First Administration of Ether at MGH, 1846

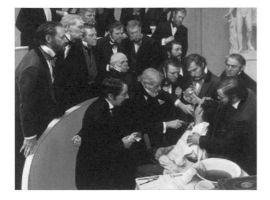

## Listening

To listen fully means to pay close attention to what is being said beneath the words. You listen not only to the "music," but to the essence of the person speaking. You listen not only for what someone knows, but for what he or she is. Ears operate at the speed of sound, which is far slower than the speed of light the eyes take in. Generative listening is the art of developing deeper silences in yourself, so you can slow your mind's hearing to your ears' natural speed, and hear beneath the words to their meaning.
—Peter Senge

One advantage of talking to yourself is that you know at least somebody is listening.
—Franklin P. Jones

Who speaks, sows; who listens, reaps.
—Argentine Proverb

The psychologist has to learn how one mind speaks to another beyond words and in silence. He must learn to listen "with the third ear."
—Theodor Reik

Through an understanding of nonverbal behavior, you will achieve a deeper, more meaningful view of the world around you—able to hear and see the two languages, spoken and silent, that combine to present the full, rich tapestry of human experience in all of its delightful complexity.
—*What Every BODY is Saying,* Joe Navarro

*Tone, Inflection, Hesitation, Eye Contact, Motivation, Empathy, Imagery, Logic*

Freud's Couch

## Music

Music is the effort we make to explain to ourselves how our brains work. We listen to Bach transfixed because this is listening to a human mind.
—Lewis Thomas

After silence, that which comes nearest to expressing the inexpressible is music.
—Aldous Huxley

You are the music while the music lasts.
—T.S. Eliot

*Notes, Rests, Scales, Melody, Harmony, Counterpoint, Dissonance, Rhythm, Pitch*

Pablo Casals, Yousuf Karsh, 1954

**Nature**

The best remedy for those who are afraid, lonely or unhappy is to go outside, somewhere where they can be quiet, alone with the heavens, nature and God. Because only then does one feel that all is as it should be and that God wishes to see people happy, amidst the simple beauty of nature.
—Anne Frank

We need to find God, and he cannot be found in noise and restlessness. God is the friend of silence. See how nature—trees, flowers, grass—grows in silence; see the stars, the moon, and the sun, how they move in silence . . . We need silence to be able to touch souls.
—Mother Teresa

Nature does not hurry, yet everything is accomplished.
—Lao Tse

The fog comes
on little cat feet.

It sits looking
over harbor and city
on silent haunches
and then moves on.

—Carl Sandburg

Two things are infinite: the universe and human stupidity; and I'm not sure about the universe.
—Albert Einstein

*Earth, Water, Air, Animals, Plants, Seasons, Sun, Stars, Black Holes, Gravity, Evolution, Reproduction, Photosynthesis, Climate*

## Philosophy

What we think, we become.
—Buddha

Cogito ergo sum
—Descartes

He who does not understand your silence will probably not understand your words.
—Elbert Hubbard

The point of philosophy is to start with something so simple as not to seem worth stating, and to end with something so paradoxical that no one will believe it.
—Bertrand Russell

Learn to get in touch with the silence within yourself, and know that everything in life has purpose. There are no mistakes, no coincidences, all events are blessings given to us to learn from.
—Elisabeth Kübler-Ross

```

```

Tabula Rasa

*Thought, Knowledge, Consciousness, Unconsciousness, Emotion, Free Will, Fate, Belief, Ethics, Morals*

## Poetry

Poetry is the chiseled marble of language; it's a paint-spattered canvas—
but the poet uses words instead of paint, and the canvas is you.
—Mark Flanagan

Silence is not silent.
Silence speaks.
It speaks most eloquently
Silence is not still.
Silence leads.
It leads most perfectly.
Silence is not silent.
—Sri Chinmoy

The waves of mind
demand so much of Silence.
But She does not talk back
does not give answers nor
arguments.
She is the hidden author of every
thought
every feeling
every moment.
Silence.
She speaks only one word.
And that word is this very existence.
—Adyashanti

The man bent over his guitar,
A shearsman of sorts. The day was green.
They said, "You have a blue guitar,
You do not play things as they are."
The man replied, "Things as they are
Are changed upon the blue guitar."
And they said then, "But play, you must,
A tune beyond us, yet ourselves,
A tune upon the blue guitar
Of things exactly as they are."
—Wallace Stevens

*Language, Sound, Voice, Image, Metaphor, Rhythm,*
*Experience, Accent, Verse, Rhyme, Structure*

## Religion

God's poet is silence! His song is unspoken,
And yet so profound, so loud, and so far,
It fills you, it thrills you with measures unbroken,
And as soft, and as fair, and as far as a star.
—Joaquin Miller

Let us be silent, that we may hear the whispers of the gods.
—Ralph Waldo Emerson

Meditation is silence, energizing and fulfilling. Silence is the eloquent expression of the inexpressible. When I pray, I talk and God listens. When I meditate, God talks and I listen.
—Sri Chinmoy

## Psalm 23 in English and Hebrew

The Lord is my shepherd; I shall not want.

He maketh me to lie down in green pastures: he leadeth me beside the still waters.

He restoreth my soul: he leadeth me in the paths of righteousness for his name's sake.

Yea, though I walk through the valley of the shadow of death, I will fear no evil:  for thou art with me; thy rod and thy staff they comfort me.

Thou preparest a table before me in the presence of mine enemies: thou anointest my head with oil; my cup runneth over.

Surely goodness and mercy shall follow me all the days of my life: and I will dwell in the house of the Lord forever.

23 · מִזְמוֹר לְדָוִד
יְהֹוָה רֹעִי לֹא אֶחְסָר:  ² בִּנְאוֹת דֶּשֶׁא יַרְבִּיצֵנִי
עַל־מֵי מְנֻחוֹת יְנַהֲלֵנִי:  ³ נַפְשִׁי יְשׁוֹבֵב
יַנְחֵנִי בְמַעְגְּלֵי־צֶדֶק לְמַעַן שְׁמוֹ:
⁴ גַּם כִּי־אֵלֵךְ בְּגֵיא צַלְמָוֶת לֹא־אִירָא רָע
כִּי־אַתָּה עִמָּדִי  שִׁבְטְךָ וּמִשְׁעַנְתֶּךָ הֵמָּה יְנַחֲמֻנִי:
⁵ תַּעֲרֹךְ לְפָנַי שֻׁלְחָן נֶגֶד צֹרְרָי
דִּשַּׁנְתָּ בַשֶּׁמֶן רֹאשִׁי  כּוֹסִי רְוָיָה:
⁶ אַךְ טוֹב וָחֶסֶד יִרְדְּפוּנִי כָּל־יְמֵי חַיָּי
וְשַׁבְתִּי בְּבֵית־יְהֹוָה לְאֹרֶךְ יָמִים:

*Soul, Faith, Prayer, Values, Grace, Bliss, Belief, Trust, Atonement, Morals, Credo*

The Creation of Adam, Michelangelo

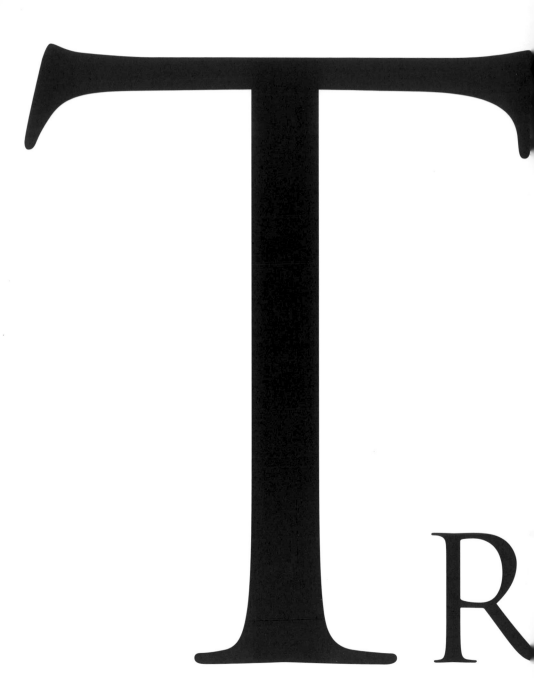

To have faith or confidence; to place reliance; to confide
—OED

"In God We Trust—All Others Pay Cash" read the sign next to
the register at Meyer's Candy Store, the social epicenter of my
neighborhood in Astoria, Queens, where I grew up. So when
Meyer did in fact trust you for a nickel candy or a two-cents
plain, you felt you were moving in pretty august circles. Those
were the days before credit cards, and every mom and pop
store, especially in the working class neighborhoods like mine,
extended credit to their known customers to allow them to make
ends meet until payday. The ability to put it on the tab went far
beyond the modest monetary transaction. It meant you were an
accepted and known member of the community—you knew the
rules and were trusted to follow them. These rules went far
beyond monetary transactions to include status, respect, expectations, and kept secrets. These formal and informal principles
of trust exist in all social settings, ethnic groups, tribes, and cultures. Often unspoken, they are determinants of expected behavior. Trust forms the basis for our most meaningful relationships,
be they familial, social, political, financial, or sexual. It serves as a
means of exchange and as our passport to acceptance, a sense of
security, and feelings of well-being and happiness.

# U S T

Not only did Meyer put his trust in God, so does everyone else to some degree. Whether or not you are a religious believer, the ethical and moral codes attributed to God (person or concept) guide the ubiquitous rules of acceptable conduct in every culture and every country. The Golden Rule, first attributed to Confucius, is an omnipresent underpinning to the teaching of every religious work from the Bible, to the Koran, to the Bhagavad Gita. Without trusting that other members of the culture adhere to the teachings of compassion, the ability to carry on a civilized society would not be possible. Interpretations and expressions of these basic principles range widely, resulting in very different forms of socially acceptable behavior. Christian fundamentalists put their trust in the literal "word" while brooking no argument about what the word means even after centuries of history and translation, while Judaic scholars may argue endlessly about the slightest nuance. No matter the spectrum of belief, the interplay between the expression of and the adherence to these ethical and moral principles in and between governments, industry, organizations, groups, and individuals determine how lives are led and what opportunities are afforded. Even in the United States where the doctrine of separation of church and state is a fundamental founding principle, one needs look no further than our currency to see our official national motto as of 1956—"In God We Trust." (Who knew? I always thought it was *E Pluribus Unum*.)

Biological necessity dictates trust in parents and caregivers to nurture and protect us from our first moment. Understanding and the underpinnings of social trust are quickly instilled as the basis of family relationships. As infants we learn the intricate dependency rules within our family and what behaviors are expected and acceptable in various social settings. As we grow older we earn more trust—he right to cross the street, stay over a friend's house, the keys to the car. We also learn a set of complex social, cultural, and religious rules associated with our family. Secrets and histories we are trusted to keep—Uncle Joe's alcoholism, Aunt Trudy's out-of-wedlock child. The rules and expected behaviors associated with these areas of trust may be stated explicitly, but most often they are implicit and absorbed by experience. In traditional families, tribes, and societies these norms are strictly followed and there is little leeway to deviate. In more modern societies, where traditions of many different cultures are accessible and the social and class boundaries are more permeable, trust relationships learned and accepted within our families and neighborhoods are constantly tested, modified, and redefined. Deliberate or unconscious transgressions of family mores become a rite of passage and are tolerated up to a point as we forge our own identities. Ultimately, how easily we are able to calibrate, apply, and invest the lessons learned in our familiar relationships to the societal trust relationships we must form and maintain has a great deal of impact on our social and financial acceptance and our success as individuals and organizations.

My own lessons in trust were quickly learned on the streets as well as in Meyer's candy store. Astoria was a tough, lower-middle-class neighborhood—the home of Archie Bunker. It had a diverse mix of people from many ethnic backgrounds and religions, although unlike today it was almost entirely Caucasian. We knew our neighbors and got along fairly well, although I cannot remember any extensive social interaction across ethnic and religious lines. My parents having escaped the Holocaust were part of a small German Jewish community in a predominately Catholic neighborhood. We knew well who we could and couldn't trust (or so we thought). While I don't recall experiencing any anti-Semitism or other overt prejudice, I do remember my Catholic friends who attended Our Most Precious Blood not being able to see a movie during Brotherhood week because it claimed that everyone was equal. That was a very different and exhilarating time. The prosperity experienced after the war really made me and everyone else feel that America was a land of opportunity. New York City in particular afforded a wealth of opportunities to grow and experience a huge variety of culture for free. The overall feeling of safety afforded by the city catalyzed my personal development. As a teen I would often leave the house early Saturday morning to visit museums and attend concerts. Riding the subway without fear I often returned home past midnight. I never thought I was in any danger, nor did my parents.

My most poignant memories of learning to engender trust are a consequence of my physical handicap. I was born with a severe curvature of my spine and a spastic right side. These deformities, and the fact I wore leg braces for many years (not to mention my flaming red hair), made my appearance remarkable, to say the least. At that time persons with physical handicaps were treated with special attention—discrimination is too strong a word—and quietly segregated from the mainstream. My mother was not about to let that happen to me and insisted I attend public school. This was certainly a long-term blessing, but it instantly required me to prove to my teachers and classmates I could be trusted to fit in. I did not want to be treated in any special way and worked hard to prove I was "normal" and an asset. I learned early that the protection of my personal interests on a daily basis was my own responsibility. I had to prove how trustworthy I could be with almost every individual or group with whom I interacted. In turn I had to assess how much I could trust them. On the streets that took the form of knowing all the baseball statistics and negotiating with the cops when they broke up a stick ball game because I couldn't run fast enough to get away. In school and on the playground it meant being seen as a strong academic contributor and clever strategist of prankish behavior. As I grew older and more confident I realized that everyone was worried about inclusion. The overriding concerns to prove myself slowly diminished, but sensitivity to the need to be accepted and trusted as a fundamental basis for lasting relationships did not.

I learned that trust is an integral part of all aspects of my life—social, psychological, financial, and sexual. It takes on many forms and has a variety of different dimensions. It ranges from the simple belief in my or someone else's competence to perform a specific task, to a moral conviction that a person holds the same values as I do, will reliably tell the truth, and keep important secrets. It usually involves another party, but trust can also be a concern with my own competence to perform a task, abjure from an addiction—drugs, alcohol, gambling—and act in a principled manner. I am always amused when I hear the phrase, "I absolutely trust her (or him)," since I am not sure I can always trust myself not to commit beyond my capabilities or act in an absolutely predictable way. I *of course* feel that my actions are always driven by a laudatory set of values, but as Dr. Freud and others have exquisitely demonstrated, our actions are not totally under our conscious control and often surprise us in unflattering ways.

These lessons in building trust are a key foundation of my professional career. I have spent the last thirty years of my working life as an independent management consultant and executive coach, primarily in the not-for-profit sector. My engagements have lasted over many years, in some cases decades. When I am asked what I do and how I have managed to sustain such long-term relationships, my answer that "the most important thing I offer is trust" comes as a great surprise to many. While it is true I must demonstrate other substantive skills to help solve the problems and clarify the situations that have led to my consideration for an assignment, without establishing trust I do not have much of a chance of being retained. That is especially true because I have chosen to be independent. The lack of a corporate umbrella of an established firm to vouchsafe for my competence makes the creation and belief in trust evermore important.

When closely examined, trust is the underlying currency of our social organization in much the same way money is the basis of our fiscal organization. As I start to write this essay on Martin Luther King Jr. Day, I remember that my first introduction to the notion of trust as a means of exchange came in hearing Dr. King's famous speech delivered on the steps of the Lincoln Memorial, remembered by us all as the *I Have a Dream* speech. Often overlooked, earlier in that oration King used the powerful analogy of money to graphically portray the misplaced trust that the people of color experienced in this country.

In a sense we've come to our nation's capital to cash a check. When the architects of our republic wrote the magnificent words of the Constitution and the Declaration of Independence, they were signing a promissory note to which every American was to fall heir. This note was a promise that all men, yes, black men as well as white men, would be guaranteed the "unalienable Rights" of "Life, Liberty and the pursuit of Happiness." It is obvious today that America has defaulted on this promissory note, insofar as her citizens of color are concerned. Instead of honoring this sacred obligation, America has given the Negro people a bad check; a check which has come back marked "insufficient funds."

But we refuse to believe that the bank of justice is bankrupt. We refuse to believe that there are insufficient funds in the great vaults of opportunity of this nation. And so, we've come to cash this check, a check that will give us upon demand the riches of freedom and the security of justice.

Trust, like currency, comes in many forms and has many dimensions. For the sake of brevity I will roughly characterize three forms of trust: strategic, organizational, and personal. Strategic trust as the belief in the goals and strategies of an individual or organization—will they do the right thing for themselves and for you? Organizational trust has more to do with the processes and decision-making utilized by organizations or individuals to reach their goals. Personal trust is just that—trust in the honesty, competence, reliability, integrity, and character of an individual or group.

The most abstract is the strategic trust that Dr. King cites. It reflects the belief that we can trust our government or any entity in our society to allow us to be free, to be treated fairly, and to feel secure. Democracy more than any other form of rule is built on strategic trust. We the people are trusted to choose who will represent us and how they shall govern. In turn we expect our elected officials to use the trust placed in them for the benefit of all. We all know it's not quite that simple. Special and personal interests abound. Nor is there a commonly held belief in what government should be doing, how it should be accomplished, or its overall capability (organizational trust). The "right" does not trust the workings of the bureaucracy and believes its role should be severely limited. The "left" does not trust the private sector to pay attention to the common good and thus believes in extensive public programs, regulations, and oversight. Each side gives examples of abuse and incompetence to prove their point. Although civil discourse is meant to air and resolve differences where possible, I think it is safe to say that the overall levels of trust needed for constructive dialogues to take place have been steadily eroding. Examples of mutual trust and personal respect for the opinions of the opposition are becoming evermore difficult as the suspicions and stridency of each side become increasingly harsh. I need only to observe the recent attempts to address any significant legislative issue, health care reform, immigration, and financial regulation to marvel at the lack of meaningful, trustworthy engagement.

Organizational trust relies on beliefs that the decision-making processes are consistent with the stated strategic goals and objectives. I and my fellow citizens are increasingly witnessing the erosion of our trust in government to protect us from harm and treat us fairly. Government is not the only institution whose inherent competence is incessantly questioned. Every major societal structure—banks, churches, hospitals, and professionals of all kinds—are viewed and judged with increasing skepticism.

The dramatic shift and erosion of trust in government, corporations, and organizations to assure steady and meaningful work is palpable and very real. The causes and implications of this change in attitude are highly complex. I believe they have dramatic consequences for the way we think about our society, how we relate to it, and how well it will allow us to compete in the future.

I am constantly revising my appraisals of trust with regard to family, friends, and all my other interpersonal relationships. At the same time I am also evaluating and modifying my understanding of my own competencies and belief structures. At the simplest level these assessments are made on two dimensions—competence and character. Trust in personal competence lends itself to metrics—skill level, quality of work, reliability, timeliness, and accuracy. These trust evaluations are simpler to quantify than the loftier ones of trust—openness, honesty, and integrity. Naturally the more experience I have had with a person or in a particular realm, the more comfortable I am in making a trust investment. Since I also assume I can trust family, friends, and highly regarded institutions to have my best interests at heart, their judgments often supplement my own evaluations. In most cases my expectations are met or exceeded. Hopefully when I am disappointed the impact is small. Making mistakes about competence may be disturbing but they are most often viewed as acceptable errors in judgment and, unless the consequent outcomes are disastrous, they are absorbed as a natural part of life and learning.

Yet when I examine intimate trust behavior more closely there is a paradox. The most trusted individuals are those I share or tell the most cherished and guarded details of my life. I expect that these will be kept in strictest confidence. They are among my most precious secrets. In turn I reciprocate with my most trusted friends. But keeping secrets can be interpreted as a form of betrayal or lack of trust. I am trusted because I can keep someone's secret. But at the same time I am not disclosing what I know to another trusted friend. How I walk that line can be tricky at best. I and everyone else have learned to carefully navigate that boundary. I trusted my parents and they in turn trusted me. Yet once I reached adolescence my mother knew full well that I was not completely open about all my activities. In the same manner there was not full disclosure on her part of her actions and history. To a large extent we both wanted it that way. Openness and transparency are major components of trust, but everyone is aware that in many instances total disclosure is unwarranted, unwise, and in extreme cases destructive. We are entitled to our secrets, even if it means a bit of obfuscation in our dealings with others. Small breaches of trust, little white lies, and selective omissions are tolerated because they help maintain social order. I think that everyone agrees that marriages and other life partnerships benefit by some degree of reticence. In fact, much of the allure in relationships often comes from the mystery associated with another person or situation. In certain instances we actually want to deceive or be deceived and we enjoy it. When the fans and feathers went out of striptease, something was undoubtedly lost.

Surprise parties, card tricks, optical illusions, and magic all fall into the category of artful deception. The stock in trade of magicians is deception. We expect them to lie to us. As I once heard the magician-philosopher Eugene Burger tell an audience, "I can tell you how I do these tricks, but would you believe me?"

These fungible boundaries have their limits. When they are breached, leading to a sense of betrayal, a whole different set of emotions is evoked. Divorce, embezzlement, cheating, bribery, and identity theft can all have dire ramifications on our physical and emotional health. Everyone has had instances in their lives where events have made them reassess their relationships with others and themselves.

We are also witness to shocking events in public life. Striking examples of betrayal of trust in the news abound— the financial crisis, Bernie Madoff, Tiger Woods, the Catholic Church, Toyota, etc. These are prime examples of how the hard-won currency of trust can be squandered on a scale far beyond our own personal and family disappointments. Our feelings of betrayal are compounded because we wanted to trust the people and institutions involved without examining the reality, even when the truth was hiding in plain sight.

Of these instances the most difficult one for me is the conduct of Catholic priests and their enablers in the church hierarchy. Trading on their position as the bulwarks and arbiters of moral behavior, individual priests not only betrayed their victims, but they foreclosed redress for their actions. Who could take the word of a child over the parish priest? Of even greater concern for me are the church's attempts to cover up and deny these acts and to justify their position by claiming these were just local aberrations.

In Madoff's case we see how greed and the potential for extraordinary gains clouded the judgment and common sense of highly intelligent analytical people. In retrospect and from the perspective of outside objective observers it is hard to fathom that Madoff's scheme could be perpetrated with such impunity and for so long a time. But by cleverly aligning himself with trusted institutions and individuals, in effect piggybacking on their positions of trust, he was able to perpetrate his scheme almost in perpetuity. Once he had enough trusted people involved in his scheme, bucking the crowd was tantamount to rebelling against societal norms, an action most people can't take.

Tiger Woods illustrates a different dimension of misplaced trust. He earned our trust for his extraordinary golfing skills and his competence under immense pressure. Corporate patrons rented his aura, hoping that their customers would believe that these same qualities would transfer to causes completely foreign to Tiger's competencies: consulting, nutrition, watchmaking. However, the underlying message in all celebrity endorsements is that extraordinary achievement in one realm maps directly to extraordinary competence in all others. The difficulty is when the trust in functional competence is transferred and overlaid on the more lofty dimensions of moral trust. The trust of competence is then transferred to the trust of truth. "I am not only a master of my craft, but I am a model of decorum as well." If true that is great. If not true, as it turns out in Woods's case, the whole house of cards falls. No one questions Woods's golf acumen even after the scandal. As he returns to his known competence, golf, the question is will he be able to again rebuild his lost moral trust.

Woods's case is a reminder of the paramount importance in contemporary society of establishing and maintaining a brand. The pervasive message of almost all advertising has always been targeted at building trust by establishing a brand. Every product is put forth as the most trustworthy of its kind for doing a specific job. A Mac/PC ad clearly demonstrates the underlying message of trust at the same time that it spoofs it. As Toyota has witnessed, years of building a brand, and the corollary trust in your product can practically vaporize in a matter of days.

Brand has transcended the boundaries of the corporate and entertainment spheres into the personal arena. Individuals increasingly are establishing their own brand identity through the internet via Facebook, YouTube, résumé writing, and video games. Major tools that individuals employ are openness and revelation along with putting "your best foot forward."

Transparency is the operative word. But supplying more information actually often results in less trust rather than more. Witness the reverse effect of the increasing call for transparency in the public sector. As David Brooks has pointed out in a *New York Times* op-ed on "The Power Elite," transparency can have the opposite of the intended outcome:

Since Watergate, we have tried to make government as open as possible. But as William Galston of the Brookings Institution jokes, government should sometimes be shrouded for the same reason that middle-aged people should be clothed. This isn't Galston's point, but I'd observe that the more government has become transparent, the less people are inclined to trust it.

Innovations like the internet force a change in our worldview and how we relate to each other. The introduction of any new technology is always met with apprehension. These fears are not new and are deeply rooted in our natural attempts to maintain the stability of our comfort zone. I once heard a lively discussion between two women on a bus in Edinburgh vowing never to ride the newly installed escalator in the city's largest department store. The same fears hold true for many travelers with regard to bridges, trains, and planes. As machines mediate more and more encounters, an interesting and increasingly disturbing wrinkle to the exchange of trust is emerging. The extent to which machines have become an integral, necessary, and trustworthy part of our daily lives is staggering. The World Wide Web is less than fifteen years old. Ten years ago few individuals had e-mail accounts. Now much of our daily correspondence and most personal records exist on a "cloud" computer somewhere in cyberspace. Every aspect of our everyday routine is increasingly dependent on an interaction with a device, be it an ATM, a supermarket scanner, a smart phone, a pacemaker, or an artificial hip. Nor will this trend abate. Information processing devices have raised the most critical concerns with regard to fiscal trust (ATMs), personal privacy (identity theft), and invasive procedures (robotic surgery). The adaptation and popularity of communicative networks (Facebook, Twitter), collaborative video games (World of Warcraft), virtual reality simulations (Second Life), and other forms of man-machine interaction most of us have not dreamed of have begun to completely rewrite the unspoken rules of trust. The assessment and granting of trust, already a highly subjective task, has been amplified to a highly developed art form in these interactive settings. We now routinely channel our communications through complex devices and networks, whose underlying rules are completely opaque to us as users and sometimes even to their developers. The unwritten guides used in the past based on our visceral experience, our reliance on trusted friends, our culture, and our intuition are largely being rewritten. Witness the sharing of intimate details in public forums that would have been unthinkable a decade ago. We have now reached the point where couples share information about their marriages on their Facebook pages before communicating with their spouses.

Often we are not sure if we're communicating with a real person or a made up persona. The following *New Yorker* cartoon says it all.

It has gotten to the point that the judicial system is in a quandary regarding the enforcement of child pornography and sex offender laws against teens who voluntarily share explicit images of themselves, known as sexting. How are we to reliably measure the trustworthiness of others when our interactions with them are evermore carried out in an accelerated timeframe over great virtual geographical, cultural, and generational distances?

*"On the Internet, nobody knows you're a dog."*

The importance of the future of trust deserves much more public attention than it has received up until now. We must learn to trust our own capacities as well as those of others to endure and overcome life's risks and adversities. The capabilities of machines have enormous potential to support our ability to lead more meaningful and productive lives, at the same time as they pose deep concerns over dependence, privacy, and loss of control. The impact and the increasing ubiquitous presence of these devices is a reality. They will continue to reconfigure all of our relationships—environmental, geographic, political, religious, interpersonal, familial, and even the relationship with ourselves. Like the subjects in our experiment we will have less and less ability to differentiate the real from the virtual—not in an experimental environment, but in everyday interactions. As our relationships are increasingly mediated by machine interactions, by virtue of the transcendence of geographical, cultural, temporal, and class boundaries, I believe the rules of assessing, offering, and receiving trust must be radically changed as well.

Over the past several years the underpinnings of happiness have become a major concentration of psychological and sociological inquiry. Of the myriad of factors measured, tested, and evaluated, the studies conclude that the depth, meaning, and longevity of a person's relationships are the best predictor of their perception of happiness. It is the hidden means of exchange, the meaningful currency of our important relationships. The richness of these relationships and the happiness of our lives are directly proportional to the amount of trust we can bank in each of our encounters. The good news is that our ability to amass this wealth is not dependent on the government, our employer, or even God. Our real net worth is a direct result of our ability to abide by a set of principles that guide our actions and engender a deep feeling of trust in us by others as well as in ourselves. Unlike Meyer, the sign in our candy store should read, "In ourselves we trust—All others take note."

# unity
## andUncertainty

**Unity** The fact, quality, or condition of being, comprising, or consisting of one in number; oneness, singleness
—OED

**Uncertainty** The quality of being uncertain in respect of duration, continuance, occurrence, etc.; liability to chance or accident; the quality of being indeterminate as to magnitude or value
—OED

"Schizophrenia beats eating alone" read my fortune cookie in an upscale Chinese restaurant, where else but in Cambridge, Massachusetts? Along with similar messages touching on existential angst and other weighty topics, this unusual, now defunct eatery (run by a Swiss National, serving a Cantonese version of Duck a l'Orange, and conveying the fortunes in rolled French pirouette cookies) prided itself on its ability to amuse and provoke.

I wonder whether even in our "normal state" we are ever really "alone." We are constantly in dialogue with multiple aspects of ourselves. Although we like to think we are a unitary being, it is clear that this sense of oneness is really an illusion.

Even though we may present a fairly constant, consistent, and predictable set of behaviors to the world, we are continually monitoring and balancing a wealth of senses from our body as well as our "mind" to decide how to respond or react in any given circumstance. The operative word here is *decide*. By virtue of our cognitive abilities we can choose our response to uncertainty. Some of these choices may be simple and unremarkable (shall I answer the telephone or let it ring?) to complicated and profound (will I say yes to her marriage proposal?). How we weigh, understand, evaluate, and react to these uncertainties determines our persona and our sense of self.

This ongoing dialogue is taking place on a number of different levels. Although many issues are resolved using our past experience and knowledge, many others are evaluated anew in light of more information and changing conditions. An illusion of constancy is useful and even necessary to maintain our sense of self and to bring order to our actions. But we all know that we are different people at different times and in different circumstances. The myriad of roles—teacher, student, mother, wife, shopper, gambler, leader—each of us plays in our daily lives causes us to be different people at different times. Except in the most severe cases, there is a common narrative, our true selves, that we internally believe underlies each persona. In its shortest form it is the elevator speech we tell ourselves of who we really are. In its more elaborated and introspective form it is a highly nuanced and complicated story. What that story is, how we understand it, how it changes over time, and how well it jibes with "reality" (whatever that is) in large part determines how we live our lives.

Understanding our essence has been an endless pursuit of mankind. "Is there a soul/mind/self that is independent of our body?" has certainly been central in formulating the answers given to the question "what is the meaning of life?" Our mind and its relationship to our body have preoccupied both Western and Eastern religious and secular scholars since the beginning of recorded philosophical thought. "The mind/body problem" has held a revered place in the discussions and writings of our greatest thinkers. The nature of consciousness, the idea of self, and how to understand the mind, are hotly debated topics, made even more salient in recent times by the emergence of the insights afforded by cognitive science, artificial intelligence, molecular biology, brain scans, and the mapping of neural functions. Every day brings us closer to understanding the encoding mechanisms employed by humans to store and retrieve memories and process thought. Once the mechanisms of storage and retrieval are deciphered it will be fascinating to see if the answers to the deeper existential issues will be clarified.

Since the computer is the reigning metaphor of the day it is not surprising that modern explanations of the way the mind works are often presented as information processing analogies. Dan Dennett in *Consciousness Explained* argues that human consciousness can be thought of as a virtual machine operating within the hardware of our brain. Hardware, moreover, that was not initially designed to accommodate any of the functional demands of its complex software functions. Francis Crick, the co-discoverer of the structure of DNA, puts it even more starkly in *The Astonishing Hypothesis*.

The Astonishing Hypothesis is that "You," your joys and sorrows, your memories and your ambitions, your sense of personal identity and free will, are in fact no more than the behavior of a vast assembly of nerve cells and their associated molecules. As Lewis Carroll's Alice might have phrased it, "You're nothing but a pack of neurons."

I certainly don't think I am just an assemblage of coordinated nerve cell impulses. What I do think is that I am a collection of an exquisitely diverse set of strengths, weaknesses, principles, and capabilities. I think that I know my traits and that I can describe them. I believe I understand how I have reacted and made decisions in the past and as a result I can predict how I will respond and will act in the future. Taken as a whole these perceptions of my physical and mental characteristics are what I call "myself."

In many ways these beliefs are an illusion. My characteristics are constantly changing and are subtly modified. My memory of past events and how I have acted or reacted are often flawed, and in many new situations my actions often come as a surprise. If someone asked me to quickly give a one-line elevator speech to describe myself, I would be tempted to say, *I am a crippled, liberal, New York Jew.* The facts are that I am extremely healthy, not physically impaired in any remarkable way, have second thoughts about the effective role of government programs, left New York City fifty-five years ago, and have regularly attended a Congregational Church for over twenty-five years. My penchant to use descriptors that are rooted in my past rather than ones that are more in keeping with "reality" results in part because I am constantly attempting, knowingly or not, to maintain a continuous and internally consistent story about who I am to myself—my core story. To be sure, my story gets constantly updated and modified, but it is this core story that I, and I believe everyone else, constantly attempts to unify. It is our story of our story.

In *Consciousness Explained*, Dan Dennett argues that though the self may seem to be at the heart of all these stories, it is a mythical place.

The strings or streams of narrative issue forth as if from a single source—not just in the physical sense of flowing from just one mouth, or one pencil or pen, but in a more subtle sense: their effect on any audience is to encourage them to (try to) posit a unified agent whose words they are, about whom they are: in short to posit a *center of narrative* gravity.

Growing up in a Western culture it is this *center of narrative* gravity that I think of as my unified self. The concept of a singular "soul," "spirit," and "self" are constructs that grow out of our Judeo-Christian tradition of monotheism. In Eastern religions the central goal of nirvana or enlightenment and discovery of one's true "self" is reached by striving to eliminate conscious egocentric thought as opposed to celebrating it.

God as the prime mover and creator symbolizes the ultimate unifying force. At the same time, by its very nature the concept of one God, responsible for all existence, represents the highest form of uncertainty, mystery, and the unknowable. Inexplicable events from the creation of the universe, life, after-life, proper behavior, rain, drought, good luck, bad luck—you name it—were and are attributed to the existence of a higher being. A being that is held to be unknowable and must be accepted on faith. Religious faith still holds an extraordinary central position in explaining the vicissitudes of life for millions.

At the same time there is a constant search for "the laws of nature" by scientific thought. Often seen in opposition to faith, these "rational" explanations have increasingly become the major organizing and explanatory frame through which we understand our world. At their root both approaches are dealing with the same quest in their own way: to find a unified purpose for existence. The paradox is that the discoveries and insights afforded by modern scientific thought have created *more*, not less, uncertainty. Each discovery seems to deepen our understanding of how much we *don't* know. Relativity, quantum mechanics, molecular biology, and dark energy have all led scientists to abandon determinism as an explanatory construct. As Dr. Heisenberg has taught us, no longer can we calculate a result with certainty. The best we can do is calculate the probability of a certain result.

Uncertainty has also increased in religious thinking with our realization that we are not the central players on Earth or in the universe. At the very root of Western religious belief and thought is the predominant place of man reflecting the image of God.

So God created human beings in his own image. In the image of God he created them; male and female he created them. Then God blessed them and said, "Be fruitful and multiply. Fill the earth and govern it. Reign over the fish in the sea, the birds in the sky, and all the animals that scurry along the ground."
—Genesis 1:27, 28

The Christian belief that God sent his own son to Earth to atone for human sins heightens the belief of centrality. Scientific thought until Copernicus also put man and the Earth at the hub of the universe. Progressively we have learned that we are not even close to the heart of the firmament. Not only are we not at the center of our solar system, our solar system is not at the center of our galaxy (estimated to contain 100 billion stars), and our galaxy is one of *billions* of similar galaxies. The magnitude of these numbers is staggering. An equal seismic shift has occurred in our understanding of our peripheral role in the development of life. Evolution has placed Homo sapiens into an equally humble position on a much grander scale of biological development. The elimination of a prime mover as a result of both realizations has had a profound effect on the conceptualization of our nature and our vulnerability.

The conceptualization of ourselves as a unified being still has credence, but it is undergoing a shift as radical as the reconstructions forced by the revolutions in astrophysics or evolutionary biology. The predominant form of communication has become electronic. Texting, e-mail, and streaming video have increasingly tied people to their iPhones, Blackberries, or computer terminals to constantly keep in touch. Our work life, leisure time, and routine daily activities progressively require the utilization of a machine to support or carry out any desired function. As a result the manner in which we interact with the world, including the formation and maintenance of relationships, is constantly moving away from physical contact to electronic encounters.

This shift has a profound behavioral effect on the nature of our identity, how we perceive ourselves, and how we are "seen" by others. A small example of this change is the e-mail elimination of body language in assessing the veracity of a conversational exchange. Joe Navarro, an ex-FBI interrogator, writes in his fascinating book, *What Every BODY Is Saying:*

Nonverbal behaviors comprise approximately 60 to 65 percent of all interpersonal communication and can reveal a person's true thoughts, feelings and intentions. For all these reasons, nonverbal behaviors are sometimes referred to as *tells* (they tell us about a person's true state of mind). Because people are not always aware they are communicating nonverbally, body language is more often more honest than an individual's verbal pronouncements, which are consciously crafted to accomplish the speaker's objectives.

The effect on our conceptualization of self and our understanding of others and ourselves can be even more profound.

Second Life is a fully developed virtual environment available for your exploration. In your Second Life (SL), as opposed to your Real Life (RL), you can define an entirely new virtual persona for yourself. You live in an environment you make up, and interact with a cadre of friends you create. You can realize and explore any set of experiences you wish, including meeting other participants in SL, buying land, traveling to real and imagined destinations, and/or participating in exciting adventures. If you can think of it you can do it. You are limited only by your imagination. But Second Life is not just for recreational purposes. Many corporations, universities, and other institutions are utilizing Second Life to conduct virtual meetings of their employees, virtual lectures or seminars, or foster community collaborations. Second Life affords a completely parallel set of virtual worlds where you can take on any number of distinct identities that allow you to explore and satisfy different aspects of your makeup in a safe, controllable, and acceptable space. How richly rewarding, creative, fulfilling, and lasting these virtual experiences are and will be, only time will tell. They certainly represent a marked departure from any interactive possibilities imagined a decade ago.

The speed of innovation has brought about equally startling changes in uncertainty. Charles Handy, another early visionary, wrote *The Age of Unreason* in 1989:

We are now entering the *Age of Unreason*, when the future, in so many areas is there to be shaped by us for us—a time when the only predictions that will hold true is that no predictions will hold true: a time therefore for bold imaginings in private life as well as public—for thinking the unlikely and doing the unreasonable. Changes are different this time: they are discontinuous and not part of a pattern. Such discontinuity happens from time to time in history. It is confusing and disturbing. . . . Little changes can make the biggest differences to our lives, even if they go unnoticed at the time. . . . It is the changes in the way our *work* is organized which will make the biggest differences in the way we will *live*. . . . Discontinuous change requires discontinuous upside-down thinking to deal with it, even if both thinkers and thoughts appear absurd at first sight.

The call for confronting the impact of the highly improbable has been echoed by Nassim Taleb in his provocative book *The Black Swan:*

A Black Swan is a highly improbable event with three principle characteristics: it is unpredictable; it carries a massive impact; and, after the fact we concoct an explanation that makes it appear less random, and more predictable, than it was. The astonishing success of Google was a black swan; so was 9/11 [and the recent Gulf Oil Spill]. Humans are hardwired to learn specifics when they should be focused on generalities. We concentrate on things we already know and fail to take into consideration what we don't know. We are, therefore too vulnerable to the impulse to simplify, narrate, and categorize, and not open enough to rewarding those who can imagine the "impossible." . . . We restrict our thinking to the irrelevant and inconsequential, while large events continue to surprise us and shape our world.

Every aspect of the rapidly expanding parallel virtual world is pushing the boundaries of my sensibilities. My identity and my place in the order of things are based on a stable and predictable world. My underlying assumption is that the world is there to be discovered. But more and more I and, I believe, others are coming to the realization that the world is in fact there to be constantly reinvented. The reality that I understand and that I assume should guide my actions still exists, but it has been supplanted by an entirely new set of capabilities and possibilities that could not have been imagined by myself, my teachers or my contemporaries. Our ability to successfully navigate in this new conceptual reconfigured space is still open to question.

In every realm of daily functions the rules of the game have dramatically changed. One has to look no further than the arena of combat, where we have moved far beyond electronic war games to electronic war, to understand the import of these issues. P.W. Singer's book *Wired for War: The Robotics Revolution and Conflict in the 21st Century* succinctly describes the behavioral and ethical concerns:

An amazing revolution is taking place on the battlefield. It is starting to change not just how wars are fought, but also the politics, economics, laws, and ethics that surround war itself. This upheaval is already afoot—remote-controlled drones take out terrorists in Afghanistan, while the number of unmanned systems on the ground in Iraq has gone from zero to 12,000 over the last five years. But it is only the start. Military officers quietly acknowledge that new prototypes will soon make human fighter pilots obsolete, while the Pentagon researches tiny robots the size of flies to carry out reconnaissance work now handled by elite Special Forces troops. . . .

New machines will profoundly alter warfare, from the frontlines to the home front. When planes can be flown into battle from an office 10,000 miles away (or even fly themselves, like the newest models), the experiences of war and the very profile of a warrior change dramatically.

Singer brings into sharp focus the disparities and difficulties associated with being simultaneously immersed in a virtual and in the real world. The ability to remotely wage war, by flying and bombing with a real drone located on the other side of the world and then going home to a suburban home for dinner with the wife and kids, is an unprecedented behavioral challenge. Yet similar juxtapositions are arising and are becoming equally accepted every day.

Remote/robotic surgery, computerized worldwide stock trading, realistic animation, and machine voice recognition all blur the boundaries of real and cyberspace. These innovations and many more that are still inconceivable will continue to challenge what we know and accept as reality. How do we prepare, reconcile, and adapt to productively function and reinvent ourselves as the world is transformed and confronts us with ever-new uncertainties?

Novels, movies, and theater provide venues to witness representations of other worlds, but they are for the most part objectively viewed and easily compartmentalized. Modern authors and especially playwrights led by Pirandello and Brecht have actively sought to obscure these lines. In plays like *Six Characters in Search of an Author* and *Mother Courage* the viewers are repeatedly asked to question the reality of the play they are watching and in turn their beliefs in their own reality. By constantly reminding us that the play is a representation of reality and not reality itself, they highlight the constructed nature of the theatrical events we are watching. Their objective is to communicate that our (the audience's) reality is equally a construction of our making as well as the playwright's and, as such, is changeable.

Until recently these may have been obscure, albeit interesting, hypothetical questions, more in the realm of philosophy than everyday existence. I no longer believe they are hypothetical. As we daily confront new realizations of unimagined worlds these are no longer ideal musings. How we harness this power in every realm of activity is indeed critical. The speed, magnitude and consequences of actions taken in an ever-increasing, highly interactive, richly interconnected environment are not easily predicted, nor easily undone. Paradoxically, the availability of enhanced communication and far-reaching networks has seemingly stifled our ability to carry on meaningful dialogues between opposing views. Rather than creating active public forums to productively work on differences, we have gravitated to the equivalent of homogenous, gated, electronic communities, seeking out and interacting with others of like opinion. Mirroring the physical gated communities that have sprung up around the world that purport to be functionally independent of the rest of society, these affinity groups have a similar effect on public discourse. Tony Judt assesses the consequences in *Ill Fares the Land:*

The contemporary impulse to live in private spaces with people like oneself is not confined to wealthy property owners. It is the same urge that drives African-Americans or Jewish students in colleges today to form separate "houses," to eat apart, and even to learn primarily about themselves by enrolling in identity studies majors. But in universities, like society at large, such self-protective undertakings not only starve their beneficiaries of access to a broader range of intellectual or public goods, they fragment and diminish the experience of everyone.

As a result the heterogeneity, respect for individuality, and the resulting productive dialogues that are the very basis and strength of democracy are, I believe, becoming increasingly threatened. The current backlash against government and the hot debate over its proper size and role directly results from this devaluation of the public space. Learning how to act responsibly and ensuring that we develop the proper forums, guidelines, controls, and balance in this ever-accelerating environment is a challenge we have yet to master.

So does schizophrenia beat eating alone? The answer might lie in the definition of terms. (Remember Bill Clinton? It matters what the meaning of "is" is.) Schizophrenia is a disease that does not allow a person to clearly grasp reality. A person hearing fantastic voices, communicating with imaginary beings, and often speaking in streams of consciousness characterizes it. How do we make that diagnosis in our age of information over-load, where we are subject to a barrage of unfiltered, unverified data, are fragmenting our attention into smaller and smaller cryptic snippets, and think nothing of seeing people seemingly speaking to themselves, assuming they are wearing an ear bud? Similarly, "alone" is a state of being by oneself. But it now takes a concerted effort to shut down our electronic appendages (there is a reason some call them crackberries) and stop our state of constant connectivity to attain a semblance of solitude. Many have turned to meditation, yoga, and mindfulness to deliber-ately seek the more natural tranquility of earlier times. I there-fore submit that as we all redefine ourselves and our reality, the wisdom of my Asian eatery's assertion becomes increasingly difficult to assess.

This seems a good place to end my musings. It was after all only a fortune cookie, not a madeleine.

# V
# IS
# ION

To show as in a vision; to display to the eye or mind
—OED

"Have you seen any interesting uses of light lately?" György
Kepes used to ask in his deep Hungarian accent whenever
we happened to meet. Kepes, a renowned photographer and
painter, was founder of the MIT Center of Advanced Visual
Studies—the forerunner of the renowned MIT Media Lab. He
profoundly influenced the visual arts, and those like myself who
were lucky enough to be his students.

In his seminal book *Language of Vision* he asserts:

Visual communication is universal and international; it knows no limits of tongue, vocabulary, or grammar, and it can be perceived by the illiterate as well as by the literate. Visual Language can convey facts and ideas in a wider and deeper range than almost any other means of communication. . . . It can interpret the new understanding of the physical world and social events . . . which are significant of every advanced scientific understanding of today . . . To perceive an image is to participate in a forming process: it is a creative act. Independent of what one "sees," every experience of a visual image is a dynamic process of integration, a "plastic" act. The word "plastic" is here used to designate the formative quality, the shaping of sensory images into unified, organic wholes.

Like most others, I take my vision for granted. On the simplest level I can describe how the visual system works: I detect, focus on, and project the light reflected off an object before me through the lenses in my eyes onto my retina. The light is transformed into electrical impulses that are transmitted along my optic nerves to the visual cortex area of my brain. There I somehow "see, understand, and store" an image that represents the object. In spite of years of research to unravel how the shower of light particles that enter the eyes and hit the retina are creatively formed to shape recognizable unified organic wholes, the process remains a mystery. As Kepes states, "To perceive an image is to participate in a forming process: it is a creative act" that goes far beyond the mechanics of sensing the light.

We are predisposed to recognize certain shapes and patterns to create mental pictures that make sense to us. We use a set of mental models to process images that are transparent and not easily articulated. Through the use of glasses, binoculars, microscopes and telescopes, x-rays, infrared, ultraviolet, we have been able to greatly improve and enhance our vision. As a result we perhaps know more about what we can't do under normal conditions than we know about what we can see.

Our capabilities are governed by our physiological structures that were developed by our evolutionary survival needs. In the same way the image captured by a camera is dependent on the type of film employed—black and white, color, infrared, Polaroid—the eye has an array of highly tuned sensors.

Lining the rear of the eyeball is a thin sheet, the retina, which includes
two sorts of photosensitive cells, rods and cones. We need two because
we live in the two worlds of darkness and light. A hundred and twenty
five million thin, straight rods construe the dimness, and report in
black and white. Seven million plump cones examine the bright, color-
packed day. There are three kinds of cones, specializing in blue, red
and green. Mixed together, the rods and cones allow the eye to respond
quickly to a changing scene. One place on the retina, where the optic
nerve enters the brain, has no rods and cones at all and as a result
does not perceive light, we refer to it as our "blind spot." Right in the
middle of the retina lies a small crater, the fovea, filled with highly concentrated cones, which we use for precision focusing when we want to
examine an object in bright light, to drag an object into sharp view and
grip it with our eyes. . . . The eyeball moves, subtly and continuously
to keep an object in front of the fovea. . . . When the retina observes
something, neurons pass the word onto the brain through a series of
electro-chemical handshakes. In about a tenth of a second, the message
reaches the visual cortex, which begins to make sense of it.
—*The Natural History of the Senses,* Diane Ackerman

The same is true of other animals; their capabilities are far
different from ours and equally fascinating. All animals are
equally highly selective in what they "see." In 1959 Jerry Lettvin
and his MIT colleagues published a seminal paper called "What
the Frog's Eye Tells the Frog's Brain." They reported that a frog
can only see very specific shapes and detect highly restricted
movements that allow it to catch certain bugs. Over the course
of my professional life I have been lucky enough to participate in a number of studies and endeavors that have tried to
unravel parts of these physiological mysteries. One of the first,
and perhaps the most unusual, resulted from housesitting in
Cambridge soon after graduating from MIT. The old Victorian
property had two unique features: a giant trampoline with elaborate harnesses to allow the owner to exercise his arthritic knees
(a great attraction to circus acrobats when they toured Boston),
and a bat house to support the research interests of the owner.

The intriguing and incredible characteristic of bats is that
although they can distinguish light and dark, they do not see
with light, but with sound, through echolocation. A bat can
navigate around string the width of human hair, as well as catch

miniscule bugs in pitch-blackness by listening to the reflection of sounds that it emits and that are reflected off its prey.
Amazing in its own right, this was of particular interest to the
Defense Department in the fifties and sixties as they worked to
refine and perfect radar. The electronics to operate and decipher
blips on radar screens filled rooms, if not buildings, while a bat
weighing about five grams and possessing a brain half the size
of a pencil eraser could easily out perform the existent equipment without any interference from the millions of other bats
that swarmed with it.

The bat house in the backyard consisted of a very large
room. It contained high-speed stroboscopic cameras designed
by "Doc" Edgerton specifically to take ultra slow-motion movies
of the bats as they located the mealworms or moths that we
shot into the air for them to catch. Bat sounds are normally well
above human hearing so there was also equipment to make
them audible and to record them to be analyzed in conjunction
with the film. The results were fantastic. The flying bats would
constantly scan at very high pitch until a target appeared. Then
a burst of sound would be sent out and the bat would maneuver
itself to catch the prey in its cupped tail. If it was out of position
it would often catch it on its wing or even somersault to change
direction. The belief is that these echolocating mechanisms are
so highly tuned that bats have not evolved for millions of years;
they didn't need anything more sophisticated than what they
already have.

My next encounter with the visual system resulted from
joining the staff of Massachusetts General Hospital as the
in-house technology consultant at the end of 1961. My sponsors
for the job were two psychiatrists/neurophysiologists Gardner
Quarton and Frank Ervin. They were staff members of the
Stanley Cobb Laboratories for Psychiatric Research, where I
was based. It was my good fortune that Stanley Cobb, one of
the great pioneers of psychiatric treatment and research (the
first Harvard Professor of Psychiatry), was still alive and working at the lab. Always a great naturalist he was spending his
retirement, in spite of suffering from severe arthritis, ardently
studying and prolifically publishing papers on the comparative
anatomy of bird brains. My conversations with him introduced

me to the anatomical differences in brain structure of different species and specifically to the extraordinary visual acuity that birds possess by virtue of their highly developed visual systems. An inscribed picture of Dr. Cobb has always had a prominent place on my desk and has inspired me throughout my career.

My job consisted of establishing a resource center to support the researchers in the hospital with technology and statistical design. Many of the projects I supported related to image processing utilizing computers, a nascent capability in the early sixties. Working with the radiologists at the hospital I facilitated the digitizing of x-rays utilizing the equipment that scanned photographs taken by the cameras on U2 spy planes. By producing a digital image of the x-rays we were able to manipulate the contrast, brightness, and sharpness of the image and to reveal structures that were hidden in the original analogue film.

One of the most fascinating and inventive undertakings I supported were the studies conducted by Frank Ervin. Transistorized mini-digital computers, like the Digital Equipment Corporation's PDP-1, with visual displays had just been introduced to the market. After some negotiation Frank and I were able to convince Ken Olsen, President of DEC, to give MGH a machine to demonstrate the usefulness of computers in conducting biological research. Frank was interested in replicating and extending the work of his Harvard Medical School colleagues David Hubel and Torsten Wiesel on the singular response of cells in the visual cortex. (Hubel and Wiesel went on to win the Nobel Prize in 1981.) Simply put, they postulated that the visual cortex was made up of sections of cells that responded only to very specific stimuli; some cells only fired upon "seeing" vertical lines, others to horizontal lines, and still others to diagonals or movement. The brain then integrated these neuronal firings into an image to be processed and understood. Using our new computer, Frank designed an experiment that utilized the visual display to generate lines with different orientations and then map the response of individual cells in the visual cortex of cats to the different line orientations. Since our machine had very limited memory, and no high-level computer language, this extremely inventive closed-loop system required expert programming. Stephen Packer, a student at Harvard, who subsequently became a physician and a world-class authority in medical decision-making, carried out that task.

I tell these stories not only because they still captivate me but also to dramatically point out how specific the capabilities to "see" are attuned to each species' specific needs. Understanding how the eye works is only a small part of the story since seeing really happens in the brain. It is how the brain makes sense of the electro-chemical handshake that takes place in the optic nerves that still eludes us. Advances in brain scanning are starting to give us insight into these miraculous processes, but they are still a mystery. Adding to the conundrum is the fact that we do not need our eyes to see. Without difficulty we can vividly recall images from years earlier and see them in our mind's eye. With equal alacrity we can construct scenes that are described to us by others or we can conjure up imaginary events. Our dreams are surprisingly real; they often depict events that we have never witnessed, and are capable of stirring intense emotions as we witness our conjured reality. Equally fascinating is how we teach our brain to see better and better, and to make incredible rapid and finely tuned discriminations.

The ability of the brain to learn to tune its visual acuity has lately been shown to be even more profound than previously imagined. Despite our inability to fully understand how we physiologically process images, we have developed incredible capabilities to see, process, and store images in a host of inorganic media. The earliest records of human existence are cave drawings dating back to 32,000 BC. Man's ability to render visual images steadily improved, especially with the introduction of writing, printing, and perspective drawing in the Renaissance. But nothing compares with the impact on our modern sensibility of the visual world as the discoveries and rapid adaptation of the technologies in the nineteenth century. The railroad, evolution, geology, photography, and telegraphy annihilated the conceptual understanding of time and space that had governed man's relationship to nature. The result was a transformation in the way we observe, record, and remember what we see.

Of all these technologies photography is the most insidious. It does not impose itself on the world in the same manner as the factory or the railroad by changing the manner in which we work or move. Rather it transforms the way we view and see the world by dramatically expanding our visual horizons and our sense of self. Until the Industrial Revolution most everyone's vision was primarily focused on reading the signs of nature for changes of weather and the seasons to determine when best to harvest crops and when to migrate. Although images always existed, until the advent of photography they were suspect and not to be trusted to the same degree as direct experience. Photography changed all that.

In her brilliant essays in *On Photography* Susan Sontag captures the impact of this dramatic change on our sensibilities and its implications.

In teaching us a new visual code, photographs alter and enlarge our notions of what is worth looking at and what we have a right to observe. They are a grammar and, even more importantly, an ethics of seeing. Finally, the most grandiose result of the photographic enterprise is to give us the sense that we can hold the whole world in our heads—as an anthology of images. . . .

Photographs are perhaps the most mysterious of all the objects that make up, and thicken, the environment we recognize as modern. Photographs really are experience captured, and the camera is the ideal arm of consciousness in its acquisitive mood. . . . To photograph is to appropriate the thing photographed. It means putting oneself into a certain relation to the world that feels like knowledge and, therefore, like power. . . .

Photographic images now provide most of the knowledge people have about the look of the past and the reach of the present. What is written about a person or an event is frankly an interpretation, as are handmade visual statements, like paintings and drawings. Photographed images do not seem to be statements about the world so much as pieces of it, miniatures of reality that anyone can make or acquire. . . . Reality has come to seem more and more like what we are shown by cameras. It is common now for people to insist upon their experience of a violent event in which they were caught up—a plane crash, a shoot-out, a terrorist bombing—that "it seemed like a movie." This is said, other descriptions seeming insufficient, in order to explain how real it was.

My own example is my experience of showing the night sky to urbanites visiting me in Little Compton, Rhode Island. An isolated farm community, without streetlights, it was little affected by light pollution until a few years ago. When someone looked to the heavens on a dark starry night, the response was invariably one of awe, followed by the phrase "It is just like a planetarium." The real world mirrored the image rather than the image representing the real.

The true impact of photography did not reach the masses until the introduction of the Kodak Brownie and the movies early in the twentieth century. Since then images increasingly mediate our interaction with the world. Every aspect of personal and professional life is constantly transformed with the introduction of technologies with extended visual reach. Medicine is a prime example. Without MRIs, EKGs, EEGs, and laparoscopic instruments the modern physician could not function. In the past each of these displays uniquely processed specific analogue signals and were especially built to process these signals. As the world becomes digital many of these unique machines are being consolidated, often blurring the boundaries of specialization as we know it. The dramatic shift in the practice of medicine is reflected in every aspect of human endeavor, from the simplest entry-level position to the most arcane and rarified research.

As we become increasingly dependent on the recall, processing, and display of visual data we must also become increasingly sensitive to its and our own limitations. We know and accept that images are malleable, and can be manipulated, enhanced, or retouched. Yet in most cases, unless there is an evident distortion, we accept them as accurate reflections of the objects and truths they are meant to represent. (Insightful examples of how different image presentations change our understanding of data can be found in the books of Edward Tufte.) Our acceptance is an extension of the trust we place in images and events we witness directly. But a number of studies have shown that eyewitness accounts (think Rashomon effect) are often open to question. What I tried to demonstrate in my naïvely simple discussion of the neuroanatomy and neurophysiology of the visual system, is how uniquely attuned each system is to the biological/survival needs of the particular organism.

These capabilities serve the creature well in activities that are critical for its survival, but invariably restrict them in other areas of behavior. Understanding these limitations is even more important in humans because of the highly sophisticated pattern recognition processing the image undergoes in our brain.

The emergence of images as a major explanatory lens through which we understand the world and our place within it reflects a long succession of information processing transformations. As visual processing becomes the primary representation of reality, its impact has sparked the increasing interest of scientists, humanists and philosophers. In *After Thought: The Computer Challenge to Human Intelligence*, James Bailey defines and describes three overriding information epochs—Place, Pace, and Pattern—that have shaped scientific thought and dominated our understanding and utilization of information. Our fundamental understanding of nature was transformed as the issues of *place* were addressed and mastered. Our relationship with nature was then radically altered by the change brought about by *pace* innovations. Bailey believes that the new parallel processing computational methods will foster equally seismic shifts in our *Weltanschauung* by enhancing the ability to recognize, identify and analyze *pattern*. Although it is difficult to compare the power and capacities of the human mind and computational devices, I have seen estimates that by certain measures all the computing power now existent can be thought of as having the capacity of one human brain. Extrapolating, using the same measures, that capability will increase to ten thousand human brains within ten years. How that will affect our relationship with our environment and with ourselves is anyone's guess. I believe one thing is certain; images will be the major mode of discourse.

When technology shifts it bends the culture. Once, long ago, culture revolved around the spoken word. The oral skills of memorization, recitation and rhetoric instilled in societies a reverence for the past, the ambiguous, the ornate and the subjective. Then about 500 years ago, orality was overthrown by technology. Gutenberg's invention of metallic moveable type elevated writing into a central position in the culture. By the means of cheap and perfect copies, text became the engine of change and the foundation of stability. From printing came journalism, science, and the mathematics of libraries and the law. The distribution and display device that we call printing instilled in society a reverence for precision (black ink on paper), an appreciation for linear logic (in a sentence), a passion for objectivity (of printed fact) and allegiance to authority (via authors) whose truth was as fixed and final as a book. In the West, we became people of the book.

Now invention is again overthrowing the dominant media. A new distribution and display technology is nudging the book aside and catapulting images, and especially moving images, to the center of the culture. We are becoming people of the screen. The fluid and fleeting symbols on a screen pull us away from the classic notions of the monumental authors and authority. On the screen the subjective trumps the objective. . . . Truth is something you assemble yourself on your own screen as you jump from link to link. We are now in the middle of a second Gutenberg shift—from book fluency to screen fluency, from literacy to visuality.

—"*Becoming Screen Literate*," Kevin Kelly, *The New York Times Magazine*, November 21, 2008

Kelly's progressive stages of orality, literacy, and visuality are reflective of similar frames that appear in the writings of a host of futurists and modern philosophers musing about the current predominant ideas that shape the way we structure our world view. W.J.T. Mitchell has written several fascinating books attempting to grapple with the issue.

Although we have thousands of words about pictures, we do not yet have a satisfactory theory of them. . . . Perhaps the problem is not just the pictures, but with theory, and more specifically, with a certain picture of theory. The very notion of a theory of pictures suggests an attempt to master the field of visual representation with a verbal discourse.

—*Picture Theory*, W.J.T. Mitchell

He then goes on to quote the philosopher Richard Rorty who has characterized the history of philosophy as a series of "turns" in which "a new set of problems emerges and the old ones begin to fade away."

Ancient and medieval philosophy was concerned with *things*, the seventeenth to the nineteenth century with *ideas*, and contemporary philosophy with *words*.

The final stage in Rorty's history of philosophy is what he calls "the linguistic turn," a development that has complex resonances in other disciplines in the human sciences. Linguistics, semiotics, rhetoric and various models of "textuality" have become the lingua franca for critical reflection on the arts, the media and cultural forms. Society is a text. Nature and its scientific representations are "discourses.". . . . It is clear that another shift in what philosophers talk about is happening. . . . I want to call this shift "the pictorial turn."

—*Picture Theory,* W.J.T. Mitchell

Although images have radically affected the way we think, work, and relate to each other the cultural transition to their increasingly dominant position has been rather seamless. (Except when I watch friends agonize over the purchase of a Kindle.) In part that may be due to the historic existence of images side by side with more linear forms of communication like text. It also results from the sensitivity of industrial design and marketing. A colleague recently told me, "I can't wait to see the next Apple product, so I will know what I didn't know I needed."

We are all in the midst of this extraordinary dynamic reality—individuals, businesses, and society as a whole. We are living in a time when almost any visionary idea seems plausible. In the past a visionary was defined as someone who imagined things that were unreal or unachievable. Visionaries were people who "have seen the light" not seen by others. They were most often dismissed because they were too far ahead of their time, or they offered dreams of unrealistic utopias or the imminent end of the world. At the same time visionaries who saw their predictions come true were hailed for their great insights, often posthumously. Every business strives to have a visionary leader to guide it into the future and constantly outthink the competition. It is not an accident that we call this trait **imagin**ation. Only a rarified few possess this extraordinary gift. Thomas Edison, the Wright Brothers, and Steve Jobs come to mind. Many others have equally profound insights but go unheralded. Max De Pree tells one of my favorite stories exemplifying visionary thinking in the epilogue to his lovely little book, *Leadership Jazz.*

In the late fourteenth century, the members of New College in Oxford moved into their quadrangle, the first structure of its kind, intended to provide the residents all they needed. On the north side of the quadrangle sit the chapel and the great hall, beautiful buildings and, as you might imagine, the focus of the life of the college.

In the middle of the nineteenth century, almost five hundred years later, the college hired architect Sir Gilbert Scott to restore the roof of the hall. The roof and the great oak beams that supported it had badly rotted. And so representatives from the college and Sir Gilbert visited Great Hall Woods, in Berkshire, where they expected to find trees for replacement beams. Sure enough, the replacements were standing there, waiting to be hewn out of the living oak trees planted a century before for just that purpose.

We are now all becoming visionaries in a different way. Constantly bombarded by images from every angle, we must become increasingly cognizant of the quality, relevance, and reliability of what we see. Kevin Kelly identifies the need to develop screen fluency, a new language and set of tools to allow us to navigate through and comprehend images with the same alacrity that our current capabilities enable us to understand text.

If text literacy meant being able to parse and manipulate texts, then the new screen fluency means being able to parse and manipulate moving images with the same ease. But so far, these "reader" tools of visuality have not made their way to the masses. . . . With full-blown visuality, I should be able to annotate any object, frame or scene in a motion picture with any other object, frame or motion-picture clip. I should be able to search the visual index of a film, or peruse a visual table of contents, or scan a visual abstract of its full length. But how do you do all these things? How can we browse a film the way we browse a book? It took several hundred years for the consumer tools of text literacy to crystallize after the invention of printing, but the first visual-literacy tools are already emerging in research labs and on the margins of digital culture. . . . With the assistance of screen fluency tools we might even be able to summon up realistic fantasies spontaneously. Standing before a screen, we could create the visual image of a turquoise rose, glistening with dew, poised in a trim ruby vase, as fast as we could write these words. If we were truly screen literate, maybe even faster. And that is just the opening scene.

We already possess some screen literacy even though most of us cannot describe it. When we watch a movie we know that certain fades mean we are moving forward or backward in time. We take for granted that we can zoom in or out when viewing a digital image. Programs like Photoshop or iMovie teach us and offer us seemingly limitless capabilities to create, enhance, and edit images that would have been deemed impossible a decade ago. But we are still at the nascent stage of our understanding of the communicative power of images. Marshall McLuhan's famous phrase "the medium is the message" is even more relevant today as we undergo "the pictorial turn" to pattern recognition and visuality. Whether we realize it or not, to comprehend and fully participate in the world, we are all enrolled in a process of learning to become more fluent in a new language, the *Language of Vision*.

Have **you** seen any interesting uses of light lately?

Shalom

# the six w's

A formula for getting the "full" story: **What** happened? **Who** is it about? **Where** did it take place? **When** did it take place? **Why** did it happen? **How** did it happen?

I disliked my eighth grade English teacher Miss Hanna with a passion. A strict disciplinarian she was the quintessential old-fashioned school marm; a fossil my classmates and I had to endure. Her insistence on teaching grammar, making me parse sentences, and in my compositions adhere to the rule of six W's—what, when, who, where, why and how—drove my friends and me nuts. (She steadfastly held that *how* counted as a sixth W because it had a W at the end.) I now realize that Miss Hanna was determined to make us critical thinkers and clear communicators by pounding her seemingly old-fashioned notions into our highly resistant adolescent skulls. Her insistence that I look for and understand the hidden grammatical structures that shaped my thoughts, and then clearly communicate them had an undeniable effect on my ability to think critically, to effectively frame and solve problems, to understand the underlying meanings associated with the story of my life, and to appreciate the multi-dimensional complexity of the world.

I had not thought about Miss Hanna and her obsession with parsing and the W's for 60 years until I read my dear friend Harry Davis's convocation speech given to graduates at the Booth School of Business at the University of Chicago, "Why Are You Here and Not Somewhere Else." Like Miss Hanna and every other great teacher, Harry has an undeniable effect on his students, albeit in a subtle and gentle manner. When students enroll in a professional post-graduate school knowingly or unknowingly they are seeking answers to the six W's associated with their chosen interest or discipline.

Harry's specialty is innovation and strategy, befitting of the title of his professorship—creative management. But unlike most instructors he does not only teach his students the disciplines they will need to creatively manage their future place of employment. Among his great talents is his ability to stimulate their imaginations through story telling, especially theatrical role-playing. Using a variety of techniques he extends their thinking a step beyond the advertised subject matter of the class. As they are about to embark on the new professional career of managing an enterprise, Harry's ultimate aim is to make each person better understand the one enterprise they will need to manage throughout their lives no matter who employs them, namely themselves. Thus the closing assignment in his strategy class is to write a realistic personal strategy. The result is an exploration, an examination, a rethinking, a refining, and often a revelation of the beliefs and underlying structures that are driving each student's unique life story. A rather daunting, often exhausting, but extremely valuable exercise.

Rudyard Kipling made the six W's famous in a poem that appears in the *Just So Stories:*

I keep six honest serving-men
(They taught me all I knew);
Their names are What and Why and When
And How and Where and Who.

Once considered the bedrock of good journalism, the discipline of answering the six W's makes a narrative logically consistent and understandable. Answering what, where, who, when, why, how ensures that the action (what), the actors (who), the location (where), the time (when), the motivation (why), and the mechanism (how) are included in any story.

Our ability and need to tell stories is central to our existence as conscious beings. In *Consciousness Explained,* Dan Dennett states that as beavers build dams and as spiders make webs, humans tell stories.

Our fundamental tactic of self protection, self control, and self definition is not spinning webs or building dams, but telling stories, and more particularly connecting and controlling the story we tell others—and ourselves—about who we are.

The neurologist Antonio Damasio takes the notion of story one step further.

Telling stories, in the sense of registering what happens in the form of brain maps, is probably a brain obsession and probably begins relatively early both in terms of evolution and in terms of the neural structures required to create narratives. Telling stories precedes language, since it is, in fact, a condition for language, and is not just based in the cerebral cortex but elsewhere in the brain and in the right hemisphere as well as the left.

Philosophers often puzzle about the problem of so-called intentionality, the intriguing fact that mental contents are "about" things outside the mind. I believe that the mind's pervasive "aboutness" is rooted in the brain's storytelling attitude. The brain inherently represents the structures and states of the organism, and in the course of regulating the organism as it is mandated to do, the brain naturally weaves wordless stories about what happens to an organism immersed in an environment.

—*The Feeling of What Happens,* Damasio

The question for philosophers like Dennett and neurologists like Damsio is, how real are these mental maps we generate? Dennett claims that all stories, including our sense of self, are illusions that we make up to satisfy our need to understand our world. There is no doubt that we think they are real and that we, in fact, project a similar reality on to the thought processes of others, even though we have no direct experience with anyone except ourselves.

In the age of the sound bite, elevator speech, tweet, and text, exhaustively detailed accounts are not as highly prized as quick, salient, and often superficial descriptions. Yet at the same time the role played by the story as a tool for making sense of the world, for understanding ourselves, for leading and for convincing others, is increasingly gaining popularity. Bookshelves and university curricula are full of offerings that develop and enhance story-telling techniques. In each of our lives we generate and are witness to a unique set of stories. Stories that we are constantly telling and revising to explain ourselves to ourselves, to help us understand, relate to, and function within our world.

Our ability to ask and answer questions of ourselves about ourselves is one of the defining attributes of human beings. Our story is one of the most interesting stories we know. But rarely do we explicitly, methodically, and comprehensively take stock of ourselves the way Harry asks of his students. Aside from participation in some form of psychotherapy I suspect most inner narratives are similar to mine: well-honed responses that are incrementally and often imperceptively updated. Except when faced with a major life-changing event—marriage, divorce, job change, death—systemic examination for most of us is rare, and some would say it is impossible. The task is so complicated because of the multiplicity of stories that describe each of us. Every dimension of our being—chronological, educational, professional, medical, familial, financial, relational, political, recreational—has an incredibly rich tapestry of events and an almost infinite number of asides and nuances to explore, revise, explain, and describe. In addition each of these dimensions has a past, present, and future and is played out in the context of a myriad of different relationships and settings. Yet despite all of these difficulties we do produce a narrative that is believable by others and ourselves.

People often experience themselves, at any given moment, as containing or being a "self" that is complete in the present: a "sense of self" often comes with a feeling of substantiality, presence, integrity, and fullness. Yet selves change and are transformed continually over time; no version of self is fully present at any instant, and a single life is composed of many selves. An experience of self takes place necessarily in a moment of time; it fills one's psychic space, and other alternative versions of self fade into the background. A river can be represented in a photograph, which fixes its flow and makes it possible for it to be viewed and grasped. Yet the movement of the river, in its larger course, cannot be grasped in a moment. Rivers and selves, like music and narrative, take time to happen.
—*Hope and Dread in Psychoanalysis,* Stephen Mitchell

Of the many narratives I am constantly producing none is more central than my resolve to Miss Hanna's question about myself, who am I? As reflected in the Mitchell quote, the roles and behaviors that govern my life cause my response to be highly dependent on the time, place, context, task to be addressed, and mood I am in at the moment. Yet somehow I integrate these many fragments to produce an overarching story that in general, but certainly not always, guides my actions in a consistent and predictable manner. In a somewhat paradoxical manner I am constantly observing myself as if from the outside to learn who I am. At times I don't know how I will behave or what I think until I actually perform an action or hear myself articulate a position. While some of my behavior is unique, a good deal of *who* I think I am is determined by other forces: my culture, my job, my religion, my marital status. How I balance these inner and outer forces uniquely defines me to others and to myself.

In our society a key component of any story is how we obtain the resources to support ourselves. As a result *What do you do?* is often the most asked question after, *How are you?* It can be a straightforward attempt to learn someone's occupation. It also can be a loaded question. Even if I just name an occupation my response to some extent reflects my background, my education, my social status, and perhaps my political outlook. In our supposedly classless society it can often be a subtle way to ascertain "class." Even in a long established relationship there is often a felt need to answer the question. Whenever I get together with my beloved friend "Mac" Brown she will invariably say, "Steve I have known you for over 40 years and I still don't know what you do. . . . What *do* you do?" Because in part I like to tease her, but mostly because I feel it is irrelevant to our relationship, I smile and change the subject.

I have always looked upon "What do you do?" as an opportunity to engage in a meaningful dialogue. To that end, I purposely deflect or dodge the question. Often I just hand an inquiring person my business card, a card that contains only my name and address. When the recipient fails to find a job title, he usually points out that it does not answer his question and asks me again "What do you do?" I simply respond, "What do *you* want me to do?" My longtime friend Mike Joroff, a world-renowned expert on work, often uses my response in his lectures as an example of breaking the parochial attitudes associated with defining a person by their work and opening up a richer and more personalized interchange. I find that to be true. By giving an oblique answer I am attempting to go beyond the niceties of social convention and present my interests and activities in a manner that is more tailored and aware of the characteristics of the person I have just met. My motive is to establish a richer, more connected relationship than a simple acceptable response would foster.

"What do you do?" with all its implications is a profound and extremely important part of our culture. How work is created, distributed, acquired, rewarded, and regulated within our society determines the economic climate that governs our lives and our ability to prosper and develop our full potential. In spite of the pervasiveness of work, in this and every other setting its meaning spans a spectrum of activity that makes it a very difficult word or concept to define.

I've never worked a day in my life. With the trivial exceptions of some teenage summers, I've never worked with my hands or shoulders or legs. I never stood on the line in Flint among the clangor and stench of embryonic Buicks for ten hours of small operations repeated on a large machine. . . . Doubtless my grandfather Hall, my father and I made a stereotypical three generations: My father's father grew up without school, doing muscle work, and built a successful business; so he sent my father to college who worked out his life at a desk adding columns of figures among blond-wood cubicles where properly dressed men and women worked with numbers five days a week and half a day on Saturday. Then there's me: I stay home and write poems—and essays, stories, textbooks, children's books, biography. . . . Work?
—*Life Work,* Donald Hall

In contrast to Donald Hall, those who have stood on an assembly line in Flint find their work demeaning, repetitive, and boring. They sharply delineate their work-life and often view it, albeit necessary, as evil. Their attitude is starkly reflected in Studs Terkel's introduction to his book *Working:*

This book, being about work, is by its very nature, about violence—to the spirit as well as the body. It is about ulcers, as well as accidents, about shouting matches, as well as fistfights, about nervous breakdowns as well as kicking the dog around. It is above all (or beneath all) about daily humiliations. To survive the day is triumph enough for the walking wounded among the great many of us. . . . It is about a search too, for daily meaning as well as daily bread, for recognition as well as cash, for astonishment as well as torpor; in short for a sort of life rather than a Monday to Friday sort of dying. Perhaps immortality too, is part of the quest. To be remembered was the wish, spoken and unspoken, of the heroes and heroines of this book.

As both Hall and Terkel make clear, the role and meaning of work goes far beyond the specific activities and economic remuneration. Work is the vehicle that makes many of us feel we are making a contribution to the world and a difference to those around us. It is a major basis for accomplishment and for giving our lives meaning. The time spent at, the energy expended for, and the meaning of work are pivotal concerns for all but a privileged few. How we choose, understand, perform, and derive fulfillment from its execution is a large determinant of our satisfaction with our lot in life.

We spend over one-third of our lives actually in the workplace, and one of the loneliest things you can find is somebody who is in the wrong kind of work, who shouldn't be doing what they are doing but should be doing something else and haven't the courage to get up and leave it and make a new possibility for themselves. But it's lovely when you find someone at work who's doing exactly what they dreamed they should be doing and whose work is an expression of their inner gift. And in witnessing to that gift and in bringing it out they actually provide an incredible service to us all. And I think you see that the gifts that are given to us as individuals are not for us alone, or for our own self-improvement, but they are actually for the community and to be offered.
—An interview with John O'Donohue, *On Being* with Krista Tippett

Those who find what they do challenging, rewarding, and gratifying often do not make a distinction between their work life and the rest of their time. They, like Donald Hall, often do not call their daily activities work. But even when work is difficult, repetitive, and exhausting it can bring great satisfaction and dignity for a job well done and a paycheck well earned. The complexity of the tasks and the sophisticated thoughts required to execute them are often overlooked.

Many testaments have been written, both fiction and memoir, about the physical labor of our forbears: from accounts of the prairie farm, mills, and the mines to tales of immigrant life—the Lower East Side to the agricultural fields of Central and Southern California. One of the most stirring moments in Mario Cuomo's keynote speech to the 1984 Democratic National Convention is the memory of his father working long and hard hours in the family grocery store, teaching the young Mario "all I needed to know about faith and hard work by the simple eloquence of his example." Such invocation speaks powerfully to Americans, stirs things deep in our culture and personal histories. How interesting it is, though, that our testaments to physical work are so often focused on values such work exhibits rather than on the thought it requires. It is a subtle but pervasive omission. . . . It is as though in our cultural iconography we are given the muscled arm, sleeve rolled tight against the biceps, but no thought behind the eye, no image that links hand and brain. I find myself here wondering about Cuomo's father. I imagine the many decisions he had to make, the alternatives large and small he weighed, the moments when he had to think quickly through his fatigue.

—*The Mind at Work: Valuing the Intelligence of the American Worker*, Mike Rose

The centrality of the work ethic described by Cuomo and Rose is an important part of everyone's core story in our culture. My father's invariable question when he came upon a store that he viewed as performing an unnecessary task or service like selling party balloons or tarot readings would be: From this you can make a living? Brought up in the highly organized German system of apprenticeship he had very definitive notions of what constituted a legitimate form of employment. Work was the center of his world and in many ways he lived to work as opposed to working to live. In my father's world occupations were well delineated, had specific educational requirements, and rites of passage. When you said you were a butcher, baker, or candlestick maker your activities were self-evident. Today things are not that simple, if they ever were. New jobs and professions—executive coach, robotics engineer, MRI operator—seemingly spring up overnight to meet needs that did not exist a generation ago.

The paradox of technological innovation is that the increased capabilities that transform our lives and enable us to perform feats that a previous generation would consider miraculous carry with them unintended consequences. We must ponder the implications of the hidden costs derived from the new world of enhanced information processing and constant connection. Like previous paradigm shifts, these new innovations radically alter our relationship to the world and to each other; they also transform our inner landscape of how we think about our possibilities and ourselves. As the world has become more fluid and more dynamic, our exposure and hopefully tolerance for other lifestyles, values, outlooks, and behavior also evolves. As a society and as individuals we are more and more open to a multiplicity of interpretations and to understanding a wider range of behavior that we witness around us and within us.

In the midst of all this change most of us look to the past to anchor who we are. The stories of our nation, our culture, our religious tradition all provide a context with which to explain our view of the world and our beliefs. Every holiday, secular or religious, affords an opportunity to retell a story that defines how we got to be who we think we are. These events serve as an important reminder of our unique relationship with our forefathers, our loved ones, and our surroundings. They heighten our sense of belonging to a greater whole and lessen our feelings of being alone.

Our hunger to belong is the longing to find a bridge across the distance from isolation to intimacy. Everyone longs for intimacy and dreams of a nest of belonging in which one is embraced, seen, and loved. Something within each of us cries out for belonging. We can have all the world has to offer in terms of status, achievement, and possessions. Yet without a sense of belonging it all seems empty and pointless.
—*Eternal Echoes: Celtic Reflections on Our Yearning to Belong*, John O'Donohue

A shining example of defining belonging is the Seder dinner on Passover. The bible commands the Jews to retell the story of the flight from slavery in Egypt to assure that they do not take themselves or their freedom for granted. The admonishment in the Bible to narrate the Exodus is so strong it is as if the events happen in order that the story can be told. Not only are the Jews directed to tell the story but they are told to be able to respond appropriately to the questions of four different personalities— the wise, the wicked, the simple, and the one that does not know how to ask. These multiple versions are meant to ensure that the story is understood by the recipient and is responsive to the times, place, and temperament of the listener.

Where O'Donohue finds intimacy in belonging and establishing relationships in the physical world, Sherry Turkle finds that in the electronic realm belonging can lead more and more to isolation. As we find ourselves tethered to "the network" that increasingly dominates modern life, our story, our sense of self becomes increasingly difficult to tell, even to ourselves.

Online life reshapes the self. I acknowledge the many positive things that the network has to offer—enhancing friendship, family connections, education, commerce, and recreation. The triumphalist narrative of the Web is the reassuring story that people want to hear and that technologists want to tell. But the heroic story is not the whole story. In virtual worlds and computer games people are flattened into personae. On social networks, people are reduced to profiles. On our mobile devices we often talk to each other on the move and with little disposable time—so little in fact that we communicate in a new language of abbreviation in which letters stand for words and emoticons stand for feelings. We don't ask the open ended "How are you?" Instead we ask the more limited "Where are you?" and "What's up?" These are good questions for getting someone's location and making a simple plan. They are not so good for opening a dialogue, about complexity of feeling. We are increasingly connected to each other but oddly alone in intimacy, new solitude.

—*Alone Together: Why We Expect More from Technology and Less from Each Other*, Sherry Turkle

Where O'Donohue finds intimacy in belonging and establishing relationships in the physical world, Turkle finds that in the electronic realm belonging can lead more and more to isolation. Being in constant contact seemingly reduces and even negates the need to get "the full story." Our communications become abbreviated at the same time that we find ourselves relating with greater frequency to an ever-expanding group of people. As a result, time, place, and even reality actually fall by the wayside. We no longer need a physical presence at a particular place or time to form a relationship. We can take on, develop, and explore multiple personae without difficulty and often without consequence. How these trends play themselves out and how they will ultimately change who we consider ourselves to be is an open, and to many, worrisome question.

In her conclusion to *Alone Together*, Turkle reminds us that the Net, because it has become so pervasive, is thought of as all grown up, when in fact it is still in its infancy. As it has amply demonstrated it has the power to change our lives and the way we live them. The exponential rate of change it represents, coupled with other equally dramatic technological advances, make it exceedingly difficult for me to comprehensively frame the story of our time and how it affects me. I find myself challenged, at times unknowingly, to examine and redefine who I am, what am I doing, why am I doing it, where will it lead me, when will it happen, and how can I incorporate and embrace any change. What metrics can I use to understand and relate my story in the comprehensive manner of the six W's? Can I put together a story that would pass muster with dear old Miss Hanna and satisfy my own needs? The challenge for me, and I suspect for you as well, is to find an adequate set of metrics to meaningfully answer Harry's question: why are you here and not somewhere else?

Recently I was able to greatly clarify my answer. I had the wonderful privilege of toasting "Mac" Brown at her 85th birthday party. In a room full of family and friends I told her I would finally give her the answer to her eternal quest to learn what I do. "Mac, I do what everyone else does in this room—I adore you!" In that moment I realized what I had always known: that our heartfelt feelings for each other are truly the most meaningful dimension of our lifetime together. Nothing else really matters. Dan Dennett may be right that what I understand to be my reality is just a set of stories that I am constantly telling myself. Even so, I must govern my behavior with a set of principles that are constructive and affirming of my worldview. Toward that end a quote commonly attributed to Philo of Alexandria is key for me: "Be kind, for everyone you meet is fighting a hard battle." Each battle is unique, including mine, but recognizing the universality of the struggle defines what is important to me and teaches me to be tolerant, understanding empathic, and loving. Invariably, when I am feeling unhappy, confined, and find myself questioning my life's purpose, I am most often concerned with my economics and my material assets. When I reflect on what most heightens my feelings of joy, satisfies my longings, and confirms my sense of belonging—when my unalienable rights of life, liberty, and the pursuit of happiness are most realized—my wellbeing and strength comes from the depth and meaningfulness of my relationships. My adoration for my family, friends, neighbors, and the beauty of the world around me are the central and most significant themes in my life story. The ability to express those feelings to others and myself is really the essence of what I *should* do.

What *should* you do?

## X = The Unknown

In algebra and higher mathematics used as the symbol
for an unknown or variable quantity
—OED

Of all the letters in the alphabet I have always thought of X as
the most interesting. It is the most rare—the fewest number of
words start with X—the most mysterious, the most salacious,
and perhaps the most important. X-rated, x-rays, X marks the
spot, Generation X. When you really want to get someone's
attention X is often the letter of choice.

A sign of affection, a symbol of the unknown, a locator of treasure, a mark of identity, a veil of the forbidden, a symbol of the divine, an identifier of the profane, and a call to the extraordinary: X really gets around. In spite of its very selective use, when it does appear it really packs a punch. If you were to lead your life as a letter, X might not be a bad choice. It has a *je ne sais quoi* for me that is unmatched by any other letter.

My affection for X stems back to my first memorable encounter in algebra class. I was always good with numbers, but with the introduction to algebra, the whole exciting real world of mathematics was laid out before me, and X led the way. Every equation, every new topic, every intriguing problem presented had the unknown mysterious X at its core daring me to discover what it really represented. To be presented first with a seemingly impossible task, and then to be shown how to solve the conundrum with a few deft maneuvers was a truly heady experience. No matter how devilish and devious X became it spurred my passion to methodically track it down and expose it for who it really was. X is truly a worthy opponent. It is not just lurking around the dark corners of algebra, but continually resurfaces in geometry, trigonometry, calculus, chemistry, physics, genetics, and in life. X is everywhere and it is indefatigable. To this day, even though I know many of its clever and devious tricks to avoid discovery, it still appears in new guises to tease, provoke, and sometimes haunt me.

To me X's challenge is always present. It basically says, *You like things to be balanced and known. It is my job to represent the unknown—the uncertainty you abhor. Can you solve the riddle you face and find the balance you crave, or must you live with my presence until you find better and sharper tools to uncover my secret?*

In many ways solving for X lies at the very heart of human nature. By virtue of our oversized brains we, as a species, have the ability not only to experience the present, but uniquely relive the past as well as contemplate the future. How the human mind got to be what it is and how it functions, our consciousness, continues to be a monumental unknown. My consciousness is what sets me apart from other animals and other humans. It gives me the ability to construct my unique reality, and the reflective ability to solve for any number of unknown Xs. The X of consciousness is perhaps the greatest challenge.

No aspect of the human mind is easy to investigate, and for those who understand the biological underpinnings of the mind, consciousness is generally regarded as the towering problem. . . . If elucidating mind is the last frontier of the life sciences, consciousness often seems like the last mystery. . . . Some regard it as insoluble.

Yet it is difficult to think of a more seductive challenge for reflection and investigation. The matter of mind, in general, and of consciousness in particular, allow humans to exercise, to the vanishing point, the desire for understanding and the appetite for wonderment at their own nature that Aristotle recognized as so distinctively human. What could be more difficult to know than how we know? What could be more dizzying than to realize that it is our having consciousness which makes possible and even inevitable our questions about consciousness?

Consciousness is, in effect, the key to a life examined, for better and for worse, our beginner's permit into knowing all about the hunger, the thirst, the sex, the tears, the laughter, the kicks, the punches, the flow of images we call thought, the feelings, the words, the stories, the beliefs, the music and the poetry, the happiness and the ecstasy. At its simplest and most basic level, consciousness lets us recognize an irresistible urge to stay alive and develop a concern for self. At its most complex and elaborate level, consciousness helps us develop a concern for other selves and improve the art of life.

—*The Feeling of What Happens,* Antonio Damasio

The most fundamental way I, and I believe others, experience reality is through the senses, which includes the sense extensions developed over the years: instruments like telescopes, microscopes, telephones, MRIs, and a host of other amazing devices and machines. Beyond what I can see, feel, hear, touch and smell are the unseen aspects of our reality: love, jealousy, happiness, pain—the gamut of emotions. But these, like consciousness, are dependent for their reality on the functioning of my brain and ultimately how it enables me to sense and process my experiences. It is paradoxical that the very thing, my consciousness, that gives me the ability to experience the "real world" and explore and solve for unknowns may, as Damasio states, be unknowable.

The concept that something is unknowable is extremely difficult, if not impossible, to accept. Humans are not willing to live with a high degree of uncertainty. All aspects of the natural world—reality—have been a source of wonder, speculation, elucidation, and explanation since the beginning of recorded time.

The attempts to reduce uncertainty, to understand the laws of nature, have taken on many forms.

Early on the predominant form was to believe in supernatural forces. Our existence, natural phenomena—earthquakes, floods, rain—were attributed to unseen forces in the universe that are beyond our understanding. As Western culture developed the Greek philosophers believed and taught that it was possible for man to understand the workings of the world through logic/rational thought. Coupled with Judaism, where the belief that one supreme being brought about the order in the universe according to a specific plan, the ubiquitous quest to understand, explain, predict, and to some extent control nature —to solve for the X of the laws of nature—began to dominate human thought.

This search for knowledge has evolved along two major dimensions: religious and scientific. Religious thinking attempts to uncover the workings of the world and to read the mind of God—the creator—through close readings of holy texts. The scientific approach assumes the workings of nature, our physical world, are governed by a set of laws that can be methodically uncovered and documented with acute observation, experimentation, and sophisticated mathematics.

The capability to generate any of these explanations is dependent on our linguistic ability. This unique human trait gives us an organized method of communication that enables our ability to understand, store, manipulate, recall, and predict the events we experience. Without the use of language to consciously record, organize, and remember our experiences, our capability to solve problems would not exist.

To support the necessary rigor and objectivity of its disciplines, science utilizes not only "natural languages," but relies heavily on the languages of mathematics. Written and spoken language is highly imprecise, and the quest for clarity often leads to redundancy. In mathematics the symbols are uniquely defined, and the syntax is highly specified. Its beauty, what I responded to in algebra class, is its clarity, consistency, universality, and resolvability. In an equation, there are no superfluous prepositional phrases or dangling modifiers. As a result of these qualities it has played a pivotal role at the center of scientific dialogue throughout the history of human inquiry.

The miracle of the appropriateness of the language of mathematics to the formulation of the laws of physics is a wonderful gift which we neither understand nor deserve. We should be grateful for it and hope that it will remain valid in future research and that it will extend for better or worse, to our pleasure, even though perhaps also to our bafflement, to wide branches of learning.
—"The Unreasonable Effectiveness of Mathematics in the Natural Sciences," E.P. Wigner, *Communications in Pure and Applied Mathematics*, February 1960

The "miracle" of language, both natural and mathematical, leads to a fundamental question regarding our understanding and conception of reality. Are we *discovering* the world through the lens of language in the same manner that astronomers discover new galaxies through the lens of a telescope, or are we *inventing* the world by utilizing our linguistic facilities to construct mental maps that satisfy our thirst for rational explanations? This is a critical distinction in our conception of how the world works.

Religious thinking is devoted to the *discovery* of God's intent and thinking and deciphering its meaning through an unshakeable belief in the initial intentional molding of the universe by a superior being. Every culture has creation myths that attribute reality to the work of a supernatural prime mover. The dominant Western belief of an almighty being is most famously told in Genesis:

In the beginning God created the heaven and the earth. The earth was without form, and void, and darkness was upon the face of the deep; and the winds of God moved upon the face of the waters. Then God said, "Let there be light." And there was light. God saw that the light was good, and he divided the light from the darkness. God called the light Day, and the darkness he called Night.
—Genesis 1:1

These religious beliefs in the supernatural, in a host of forms, are the fundamental underpinning to the laws of nature for the majority of the world's population. At their core they depend on a set of assumptions (faith) that cannot be proven but must be accepted. These assumptions then become the predominate window through which the world is viewed, questioned, and comprehended. The nuanced interpretation of the meaning and effect of faith on everyday behavior is profound. The moral and ethical guidelines by which all of us, even the most die-hard atheists, process, address, and resolve the concerns that face us are derived from these traditional beliefs. The complexity of Talmudic reasoning and ecclesiastical thinking that explicates and buttresses these beliefs is equal to the most arcane mathematical formulations. But no matter how insightful the analysis, the boundaries of knowledge are readily accepted. Although one can become increasingly aware of God's will and desires there is an inherent limit to understanding. There will always be aspects of the universe and its workings— God's plan—that will remain a mystery.

The religious and scientific accounts of creation differ radically in their metrics. In scientific thinking the universe is estimated to be 14 billion years old, with human-like creatures evolving approximately 50 to 200 thousand years ago. Measured in thousands of years, religion focuses on the behavior of human beings, the earth, and the solar system, an infinitesimal part of the universe from a scientific point of view. Science sees the entire universe as its purview, ranging from the oscillating strings of string theory that are $10^{-31}$ meters in length (that's 31 zeros after the decimal point), to the edge of the constantly expanding universe at $10^{26}$ meters. In contrast to religious beliefs, science does not recognize inherent limits to its quest for knowledge. At its core it deems that the laws of nature can ultimately be fully understood through acute observations that are organized into rational theoretical formulations.

Modern science does much more than demand that it shall be left in undisturbed possession of what the theologian and metaphysician please to term its "legitimate field." It claims that the whole range of phenomena, mental as well as physical—the entire universe—is its

field. It asserts that the scientific method is the sole gateway to the whole region of knowledge.
—*The Grammar of Science*, Karl Pearson

Certainly science is a form of discovery, but at its heart the scientific method is one of *invention*. When a theory no longer is sufficient to explain observations that contradict its predictions, a new theory must be invented. For some scientists and philosophers these new explanations are just better stories, invented to comfort our uneasiness of not knowing how the world works. The universe may indeed follow a set of laws but they are not the work of a prime mover. They are the result of ancient geographical phenomena, natural selection, the survival of the fittest, and adaptation. For others the constant refinements are keys to the puzzle of the laws of nature that may have an underlying coherence.

Perhaps most notably Albert Einstein spent the majority of his life searching for a set of equations to explain the unified laws of nature. Although not religious in the common understanding he did show reverence for the great mystery of life.

The most beautiful experience we can have is the mysterious. It is the fundamental emotion which stands at the cradle of true art and true science. Whoever does not know it and can no longer wonder, no longer marvel, is as good as dead, and his eyes are dimmed." It was the experience of mystery, even if mixed with fear that engendered religion. A knowledge of something we cannot penetrate, of the manifestation of the profoundest of reason, and the most radiant beauty. It is this knowledge, and this emotion that constitute the truly religious attitude. In this sense, and this alone I am a deeply religious man. I cannot conceive of a God who rewards and punishes his creatures, or who has a will of the type of which we are conscious in ourselves. Enough for me, the mystery of the eternity of life and the inkling of the marvelous structure of reality, together with the single-hearted endeavor to comprehend a portion, be it ever so tiny, of the reason that manifests itself in nature.
—*The World as I See It*, Albert Einstein

In our scientific age we are increasingly of the belief that a rational explanation can eventually be found for any natural phenomena by developing the proper framework and intellectual insight.

Yet the great unknowns that have intrigued mankind from the beginning of thought are still as salient as they were centuries ago. How was the universe formed? How did we as a species come to exist? Does life have meaning? Is there an existence beyond life on Earth? Are there other forms of "life" in the universe? These are timeless questions that have generated a myriad of explanations. We have developed evermore sophisticated tools to expand our understanding of these fundamental queries, but nevertheless at every turn we are confronted with a view of reality that is more complex and alien to our existing modes of thought than the last. In spite of, and perhaps because of, these incredible advances in mathematical methodology and computational capability the Xs that confound us now are more profound and more perplexing than ever.

Science is founded on uncertainty. Each time we learn something new and surprising, the astonishment comes with the realization that we were wrong before. . . . I do not understand modern physics at all, but my colleagues who know a lot about the physics of very small things, like the particles in atoms, or very large things, like the universe, seem to be running into one queerness after another, from puzzle to puzzle. . . . The greatest achievements in the science of this [twentieth] century are themselves the sources of more puzzlement than human beings have ever experienced. Indeed, it is likely that the twentieth century will be looked back at as the time when science provided the first close glimpse of the profundity of human ignorance. We have not reached solutions; we have only begun to discover how to ask questions.

—"On Science and Certainty," Lewis Thomas, *Discover,* October 1980

The space-time continuum, quantum mechanics, the unconscious, black holes, and dark matter completely belie our intuitive understanding of our surroundings and our actions. With every new discovery/insight our knowledge is expanded and yet our uncertainty seems undiminished, if not amplified. As our knowledge has gotten deeper and more refined we have constantly been confronted with the realization that explanations we were sure to be true, were in fact dead wrong. We

have made great progress in understanding and harnessing
the unseen energy that engulfs us—electromagnetism, gravity,
nuclear forces, information—and yet often the more we know,
the less we seem to understand.

In the quantum world, *relationship* is the key determiner of everything.
Subatomic particles come into form and are observed only as they are
in relationship to something else. They do not exist as independent
"things." There are no basic "building blocks." Quantum physics paints
a strange yet enticing view of the world that, as Heisenberg characterized it, "appears as a complicated tissue of events, in which the connections of different kinds alternate or overlap or combine and thereby
determine the whole." These unseen *connections* between what we previously thought to be separate entities are the fundamental ingredient
of creation.
—*Leadership and the New Science,* Margaret Wheatley

It is ironic that in the information age, an era that allows us
to instantly gather a seemingly endless amount of data, we often
do not or cannot discern the relevant and central questions that
need to be addressed. Freud famously pioneered the powerful
idea that our thoughts and subsequent actions are primarily
dependent not on our rationality but on the more primitive
emotional drives of our unconscious. His theories and those
of his disciples dominated the psychological teachings of the
mid-twentieth century.

Properly speaking, the unconscious is the real psychic; its inner nature
is just as unknown to us as the reality of the external world, and it is
just as imperfectly reported to us through the data of consciousness, as
is the external world through the indications of our sensory organs.
—*Dream Psychology: Psychoanalysis for Beginners,* Sigmund Freud

With advances such as PET scans and psychoactive drugs,
psychological thinking has become more interested in the
functioning of the brain rather than the workings of the mind.
Leon Eisenberg summarized this shift in his famous quote:
"In the first half of the 20th century, American psychiatry was
virtually 'brainless.' . . . In the second half of the 20th century,
psychiatry became virtually 'mindless.'" Now new technologies,

unexpected random events, and the increasing evidence that our perception of reality is guided more by the subjectivity of our emotions than by our objectivity, demand that the cognitive maps that drive our decisions and problem-solving capabilities need constant attention and revision.

In *The Black Swan*, Nassim Nicholas Taleb preaches that our inherent bias to exclude and not consider the real probability of dramatic unlikely events (black swans) dooms us to constantly make very bad decisions. "Black swan logic" makes *what you don't know* much more relevant than what you do know." In *The Folly of Fools* Robert Trivers explores the effect of deceit and self-deception on humans through the discipline of evolutionary biology. Animals, even plants, lie to each other all the time. What are the consequences of the inherent traits that enable certain flowers to resemble insects, opossums to play dead, fireflies to send false signals etc. on human decision-making, actions, and behavior? And lastly the possible negative impacts of information technology are explored in Sherry Turkle's *Alone Together*. She saliently observes that as we become tethered to our "smart" devices, we rely more and more on technology, and less and less upon our relationships and ourselves. Our inability to meaningfully interact directly with each other dampens and diminishes us.

As the magnitude and complexity of our insights have exponentially expanded it is a testament to the human mind and spirit that we have been able to absorb the vastly more intricate formulations that these new concepts pose, and have developed new problem-solving methods to engage them. In evolutionary time we have just come on the scene. Civilized society is at best only 5,000 years old in a lineage of 14 billion years of development. The "modern" conception of the universe is only 100 years new, at best. We have a long way to go and many more scientific revolutions before we even come close to comprehending the true nature of our reality, if ever. The danger is that these recent advances have brought us ever closer to deciphering the basic biological codes of life (the genome) and the ability to alter the energy relationships that underlie our nature and our world. The ability to unleash the power of the atom and the capability to modify our genetic code offers us the potential to radically change the process and the progress of our destiny. Without further understanding and insight into the consequences of our ability to reshape our evolutionary path we could easily be sowing the seeds of our destruction. The assumptions, and in some cases the axioms that are the basis of our understanding of the world, are often outdated or just wrong. Coupled with the bombardment of information from a plethora of sources, often unsubstantiated, rooted in false assumptions, or carrying unspoken biases we are in constant danger of making decisions that are incorrect and potentially irreversibly harmful.

Although I resonate with these concerns I must admit they rarely occupy my everyday thoughts. My X's are much more immediate and seemingly consequential even though, in the larger scheme of things, they are rather mundane. Over the years I have mapped my reality from lessons and events drawn and distilled from my senses, education, readings, and experience. But no matter how facile and wise I become, my X-solving abilities are too often severely challenged by needless difficulties. Any interaction with a bureaucracy, no matter how simple, demands my most advanced problem-solving capabilities. Whether it is the taxman, the Registry of Motor Vehicles, or the health care system, my seemingly logical objectives are thwarted as I attempt to navigate their mindless maize of procedures. Perhaps the finest and most famous example of convoluted thinking, honed to perfection, is reflected in the following passage:

There was only one catch and that was Catch-22, which specified that a concern for one's own safety in the face of dangers that were real and immediate was the process of a rational mind. Orr was crazy and could be grounded. All he had to do was ask; and as soon as he did, he would no longer be crazy and would have to fly more missions. Orr would be crazy to fly more missions and sane if he didn't, but if he was sane he had to fly them. If he flew them he was crazy and didn't have to; but if he didn't want to he was sane and had to. Yossarian was moved very deeply by the absolute simplicity of this clause of Catch-22 and let out a respectful whistle.

"That some catch, that Catch 22," he observed.

"It's the best there is," Doc Daneeka agreed.

—*Catch-22,* Joseph Heller

Luckily the world is not dominated by Catch-22s. In spite of all the difficulties in solving the X's that confront us, whether they are cosmic, theological, technological, bureaucratic, or mundane most of us muddle through and take pride in our X resolution capabilities. Although problems of existence may be too esoteric, technological challenges beyond our reach, bureaucratic obstacles too frustrating, and everyday issues a bit prosaic, many of us seek out additional problems for recreation. Crossword puzzles, board games, jigsaws, Sudoku, reading mysteries, etc., occupy a significant portion of our discretionary time. When I was a teen I waited for the next issue of *Scientific American* in order to devour Martin Gardner's column on Mathematical Games with as much anticipation as the current generation awaits the announcement of the winner of *American Idol* or *Dancing with the Stars.*

I believe our relentless solving for X is at the core of the human condition. I further believe that the most important of all the X's is the X of ourselves. In all our various guises we struggle to understand, define, and redefine who we are, what we believe, why we are here, how we relate to our world, and what will become of us in old age and at death. It is not an accident that Polonius' advice is so often quoted:

This above all: to thine own self be true,
And it must follow, as the night the day,
Thou canst not then be false to any man.
—*Hamlet,* Act 1 Scene 3, William Shakespeare

Without clear insights into our own mystery it is difficult to fathom any other. It is no secret that the essence of human happiness is almost wholly dependent on the quality of relationships. Without an in-depth knowledge of ourselves the ability to genuinely empathize with others and understand their "real world" along with our own is greatly limited. Without in-depth scrutiny of our own proclivities, needs, and desires we are hard-pressed to understand, accept, and solve the most critical X we confront: us.

Know then thyself, presume not God to scan,
The proper study of mankind is man.
Plac'd on this isthmus of a middle state,
A being darkly wise, and rudely great:
With too much knowledge for the sceptic side,
With too much weakness for the Stoic's pride,
He hangs between; in doubt to act, or rest;
In doubt to deem himself a God, or beast;
In doubt his mind or body to prefer;
Born but to die, and reas'ning but to err;
Alike in ignorance, his reason such,
Whether he thinks too little or too much:
Chaos of thought and passion, all confus'd;
Still by himself abus'd or disabus'd;
Created half to rise, and half to fall;
Great lord of all things, yet a prey to all;
Sole judge of truth, in endless error hurl'd:
The glory, jest, and riddle of the world!
—*The Essay on Man*, ii, 1-18, Alexander Pope


XXX

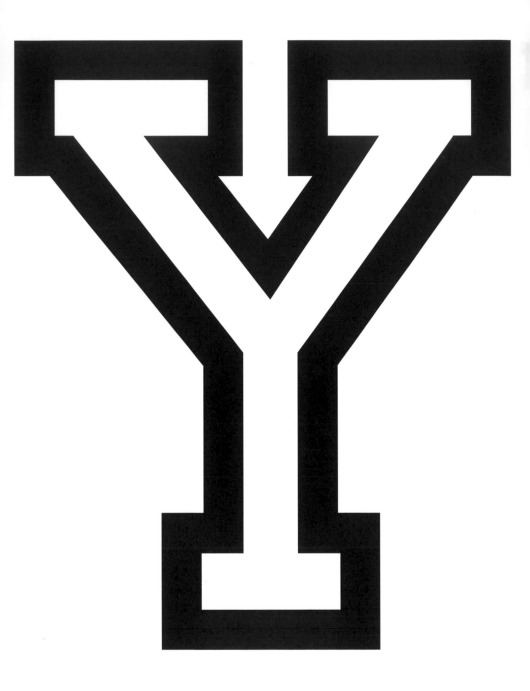

# YES!

A word used to express an affirmative reply to a question, statement, command, etc.
—OED

A waiter approaches a table of gnarled regular diners at a Jewish delicatessen and hopefully asks, "Is *anything* all right?" Of all the words in any language none is more desired than "yes," even if, as in the waiter's case, the chances are slim to none. Learning to ask for, attain, recognize, and hear *yes* to serve our unique needs and desires is a fundamental driver of thought and action. We all aspire to be loved, to belong, to achieve, to succeed, to be accepted, to be recognized, and to be rewarded. *Yes* is always part of attaining these goals. Every wish and endeavor undertaken has *yes* in some guise as its objective. At each fork in the road (Y) when a decision awaits, or query is to be answered, I hope for yes.

There are people who prefer to say "Yes," and there are people who prefer to say "No." Those who say "Yes" are rewarded by the adventures they have, and those who say "No" are rewarded by the safety they attain. There are far more "No" sayers around than "Yes" sayers.
—*Impro: Improvisation and the Theatre*, Keith Johnstone

As X is the letter of the unknown and mystery, Y has long been thought of as the symbol of moral decision. Known as the philosophical letter its shape has traditionally been attributed to Pythagoras.

Pythagoras invented the Y to represent the age of adolescence, when youth is drawn toward pleasure or toward virtue: the allegory being that Hercules, that is to say man. . . . was walking one day through the fields alone, and lost in thought, came to a broad road which forked and divided into two roads, one of which was very broad and the other very narrow. On the broad road was a dame named Pleasure, who held out her hand to him and bid him come, and on the narrow road was another named Virtue, who likewise wished him enter upon her road. The letter of Pythagoras, divided by its fork into two horns, seems to proclaim the meaning of human life.
—Geofroy Tory and Felice Feliciano quoted in *The Alphabet Abecedarium: Some Notes on Letters*, Richard Firmage

Who would have thought that Y, such a simple letterform, would represent the essence of the human condition as well as one of the most vexing of philosophical questions. To formulate, analyze, decide, and strike a balance between one road and another, between right and wrong, yes and no, go or no-go, uniquely differentiates our species. Our ability to choose enables us to manifest that most singular human trait: the ability to make mistakes. It is our constant monitoring and correction of misunderstanding that provides the path to enlightenment and learning.

Mistakes are at the base of human thought. If we were not provided with the knack of being wrong, we could never get anything useful done. We think our way along by choosing right and wrong alternatives, and the wrong choices have to be made as frequently as the right ones. We get along in life this way. We are built to make mistakes, coded for error.

We learn as we say by "trial and error." Why do we always say that? Why not "trial and rightness" or "trial and triumph"? The old phrase puts it that way because in real life that is the way it is done. . . . With two sides debating in the same mind, haranguing, there is amiable understanding that one is right and one is wrong. Sooner or later the

thing is settled, but there can be no action at all if there are not the two
sides, and the argument.
—*The Medusa and the Snail*, Lewis Thomas

To err **is** human! How we acknowledge and cope with that
truth greatly determines how we live our lives. If we try to avoid
error at all cost, and berate ourselves when mistakes are made,
our options and sense of fulfillment will be extremely limited.
By recognizing that missteps will naturally occur, accepting
their consequences, and positively acting on the newly derived
insights, we enable expanded understanding and alternative
possibilities to emerge. It is the difference in response between,
yes (*Isn't that interesting?*) and no (*I screwed up.*). Of course no
one is fully at one end of the spectrum or the other. We all make
choices that we feel are best for us, guided by our history, our
nature, and the information we have at hand. But there are
inherent limitations to our discretion.

Since the beginning of recorded time there has been a question of the extent of that power to choose, and the human capacity to exercise meaningful decision-making. The idea that we
possess free will to determine our destiny, rather than leading a
predetermined fated existence, commands attention as a central
philosophical issue from earliest times.

The idea of Fate is older than philosophy itself, and since the dawn of
the discipline philosophers have been trying to show what is wrong
with the idea that our fates are sealed before we are born. It has
seemed very important to demonstrate that we are not just acting out
destinies but somehow choosing our own courses, making decisions—
not just having "decisions" occur in us.
—*Elbow Room*, Daniel Dennett

In every human society there is an ongoing effort to balance
the needs of the society at large against the perceived rights
of individuals to determine their own fate. With the ability to
decide my destiny and exercise my will freely I become responsible for my actions and ultimately for my lot in life. Without
free will my actions are predetermined wholly by my genetic
makeup, or by an outside force (perhaps divine). If true, my
"human condition" might be alleviated of a great deal of angst,

but my life would most certainly be diminished and far less interesting. Dennett rightly points out that more than 99 percent of the population is much more concerned with daily survival, and couldn't care less about issues of free will. Although it is important to flag that my ability to choose may be an illusion, I am happy to leave the dialogue regarding its validity to the philosophers and metaphysicians (wherever they are), and go about my daily routine under the assumption that I am master of my destiny.

As a result of our species' extraordinary cognitive development, memory, and the capability to recollect experiences, each of us believes we have the individual capability to control our thoughts and determine our actions. Our uniqueness lies in this discretionary ability to shape our view of the world, individually model our behavior, and make our own decision by evaluating the stimuli we perceive, applying the lessons we have learned, and choosing among the alternatives we create. Our sensory experience has been greatly enhanced with the discovery of the telescope, microscope, electrical/nuclear power, x-rays, and a host of other useful tools. Properly deployed these capabilities enable remarkable transformations of our landscape, a broader appreciation of our environs, and a perceived capacity to better control our destiny.

Conversely, if used indiscriminately they imbue us with the power to destroy our habitat and the systems that support our existence. In reality they afford us little or no power to influence the overarching natural universal forces that provide the context of our existence—the orbit and spin of the Earth, the temperature of the Sun, tectonic plate shifts, etc. In our democracy the right to vote does give us the ability to choose our leaders, but we have limited direct influence to shape the governing philosophy, cultural beliefs, explicit laws, and implicit environment rules that largely determine our actions. At best, we exercise our individual discretion to influence our interactive behaviors with others, our lifestyle, and our immediate living conditions.

The idea of individual rights stems from the instinctive belief that each of us is unique in a manner that can truly be known only by ourselves. At the same time it is our nature to associate and socialize with each other in communal settings to assure security, manage the environment, and to satisfy our fundamental psychological need to belong.

The struggle for individual rights juxtaposed against the need for communal belonging has been ongoing since the recorded history of mankind. From the broadest perspective the degree of freedom granted to an individual helps shape the culture and defines the architecture of their society. In every organized setting, especially in the United States, there is an ongoing tension to maintain the balance of individual rights against the laws, rules, regulations, moral dictates, and social pressures that are deemed necessary to manage, govern, and satisfy the populace's needs for "safety and happiness." The fundamental assumptions underlying the establishment of the democratic governing principles of the United States speak directly to these "unalienable rights" of individuals.

We hold these truths to be self-evident, that all men are created equal, that they are endowed by their Creator with certain unalienable Rights, that among these are Life, Liberty and the pursuit of Happiness.— That to secure these rights, Governments are instituted among Men, deriving their just powers from the consent of the governed.—That whenever any Form of Government becomes destructive of these ends, it is the Right of the People to alter or to abolish it, and to institute new Government, laying its foundation on such principles and organizing its powers in such form, as to them shall seem most likely to effect their Safety and Happiness.

Like free will for most of us preoccupation with individual rights is rarely front and center in daily life. Unless I feel they have been grievously restricted or an extraordinary event occurs (war, natural disaster, terrorism), I accept the status quo as the reality I must endure. That certainly is not the case for others within the U.S., and around the globe. Suppression of individual rights is at the root of a majority of the current upheavals we are witnessing worldwide. In many cases these are struggles to win greater autonomy and broaden participation in the determination of individual destinies. In other instances, like Afghanistan, there is a backlash against modernity and the struggle attempts to impose traditional restrictions on individual rights that have previously been granted. In most of the world, freedom to choose has been highly restricted to a small segment of society. And even within that privileged set, discretion of action has been highly prescribed by social convention. The status of women throughout the world is a stark example of the exercise of restrictions on individual decision-making and inherent rights. Even within the "liberal democracies" equal status for women is a recent achievement that is an ongoing incomplete work in process.

In more traditional and/or authoritarian societies expressions of individuality are highly restricted and the forms of belonging strictly dictated. In cultures that honor individuality the range and diversity of paths open to individuals are greater and varied, enabling a wide spectrum of expressive opportunities, beliefs, occupations, recreations, and lifestyles. But even in the most open societies the desire for conformity and acceptance of social norms inhibit the possibilities for true self-expression. Rather than despair over the fact that we affect so little of the natural world, in the context of the entire universe, we should revel in our belief that we can exercise discretion to explore alternatives and create possibilities for ourselves that are not open to any other known beings. For me the two operative words to drive these explorations are *Why* and *Yes!* (after all this is an essay on Y). Our ability to make decisions lies at the heart of our humanity; *why* and *yes* are key components of every thoughtful decision. *Why:* to thoughtfully choose among alternatives we must understand the motivation, the reason, the risks and the possible consequences of our decision. *Yes:* to ensure an outcome that will improve and benefit our group, our surroundings, and us.

A friend takes the comedian Henny Youngman to the ballet. After a minute of watching the dancers perform on their toes (*en pointe*) he turns and asks his companion, Why don't they just get taller girls? *Why* is the spark that underlies our understanding of our environment, our history, and our actions. Whenever we ask *why*, it is an attempt to explain phenomena we presently observe, can recall from accounts of the past (either historical or our own), or contemplate in the future. *Why* assumes that it is possible to deconstruct what has happened, is happening, or is about to happen. My ability to choose between yes and no, as the fork in Y illustrates, lies at the heart of these explanations. At each junction the decisions I make are hopefully rooted in the assessment of the best course of action for the stated goal. Most of the time I can come to a conclusion without a great deal of fuss. Either the decision is self evident or the outcome is not important enough to me to require much thought. At those rare times when the choices are important I may undertake some analysis and data gathering. In our scientific age gathering, assessing, and then using data to support the comprehension of events is given great weight. Yet my judgment relies on a host of factors. My experience, emotions, and perception all are contributors to each of my *whys* often in inexplicable ways.

The work of Freud and his disciples introduced the key role of the unconscious and the emotions in influencing choices. Advances in PET scans and studies of cognitive brain function have illuminated the complexity and limitations of neurological mechanisms on decision-making. Beyond these biological restrictions are the belief structures that are the foundation of "rational thought." Recent advances in science—relativity, quantum mechanics, big bangs, dark matter—are stark examples of how our conception of *why* can be radically altered. Behavioral assumptions as well as cultural differences are equally important in determining our course of action. On the fiftieth anniversary of the Cuban missile crisis a quote from Graham Allison and Philip Zelikow's seminal book about the decision processes that shaped that event, *Essence of Decision,* dramatically illustrates the nuance required to understand complex decisions. To begin he quotes President Kennedy:

The essence of ultimate decision remains impenetrable to the observer —often, indeed to the decider himself. . . . There will always be the dark and tangled stretches in the decision-making process—mysterious even to those who may be most intimately involved.

Allison and Zelikow brilliantly analyze the influence of unrecognized assumptions upon Kennedy and his advisers as the sought the *why* of the crisis:

I explore the influence of unrecognized assumptions upon our thinking about events like the missile crisis. Answers to questions like why the Soviet Union tried to sneak strategic offensive missiles into Cuba must be affected by basic assumptions we make, categories we use, and our angles of vision. But what kind of assumptions do we tend to make? How do these assumptions channel our thinking? What alternative perspectives are available? This study identifies the basic frame of reference used by most people when thinking about foreign affairs.

Furthermore, it outlines two alternative frameworks. Each frame of reference is, in effect, a "conceptual lens." By comparing and contrasting the three frameworks, we see each magnifies, highlights, and reveals as well as what each blurs and neglects.

In our post-modern culture we are ever-increasingly dependent on the "conceptual lenses" *du jour*—the scientific method, technology, and the internet. We have developed highly quantitative methods related to decision analysis. By assigning probabilities to particular outcomes associated with alternative actions taken under uncertain conditions, it is mathematically possible to compute the optimal behaviors that will increase the likelihood of making the right alternative. These are indeed powerful tools, but rarely of use in our daily lives. In most of our choices there are a myriad of behavioral issues that come into play alongside any logic we employ. As Allison and Zelikow so clearly illustrate, even in almost every circumstance understanding the assumptions that underlie these "lenses" is equally as important, if not more so, than the results they produce.

As an example, a Google search most often yields the sought results, but they are presented in accordance with Google's priorities, which are imbedded in their search engine's algorithms. Understanding these underlying rules becomes increasingly difficult, if they can be found at all. As we are progressively driven by consumerism, technology, and the multiple messages that bombard us, our ability to truly comprehend the fragmented world we live in may in fact be diminished. We are increasingly "in touch" with each other through enhanced communication —social networks, television, e-mail—and yet paradoxically that touch is most often at a distance and in isolation. Rather than exploring and celebrating our diversity and complexity we are all too often restricting our interactions.

Online we easily find "company" but are exhausted by the pressures of performance. We enjoy continual connection but rarely have each other's full attention. We can have instant audiences but flatten out what we say to each other in new reductive genres of abbreviation. We like that the Web knows us, but this is only possible because we compromise our privacy by leaving electronic breadcrumbs that can easily be exploited. . . . The ties we form on the Internet are not, in the end, the ties that bind. They are the ties that preoccupy.
—*Alone Together*, Sherry Turkle

Turkle goes on to remind us that the Web is in its infancy and as it matures so, she hopes, will our abilities to use it more wisely. Like most technology it reinforces the trend to understand the world through the conceptual lens of function. Our preoccupation is with the underlying mechanisms, how they function, what corrections we can make when they go awry, and their predictability. We want to know how something works and that it can be relied upon. As a result we also increasingly think of ourselves as a conglomeration of machines that carry out certain functions that we constantly understand better and that we can ultimately control. Although our understanding of function is ever increasing, as pointed out earlier, our power to understand the underlying drivers, and influence and/or direct the overriding functions of our world are exceedingly limited. As a result we have little tolerance and patience with the unevenness and unpredictability of the inevitable unforeseen events in our lives, as well as natural cataclysmic events such as earthquakes, hurricanes, and drought. We are prone to act as if the world is understandable, explainable, measurable, and therefore predictable.

We are just an advanced set of monkeys on a minor planet. But we can understand the Universe. That makes us something special. . . . The usual approach of science to construct mathematical models cannot answer the questions of why there should be a universe for the model to describe. Why does the universe go to all the trouble of existing. . . . My goal is simple. It is a complete understanding of the universe, why it is as it is and why it exists at all.
—Stephen Hawking

Our capacity for introspection coupled with the overarching belief that we can solve the riddles before us, including why we exist, defines "humanity."—If *why* is at the heart of our questioning, *yes* exemplifies our optimism and our ability to project, imagine, shape and believe in a future that goes beyond what we have known in the past, or what we experience in the present.

*Yes* can play a pivotal role in all aspects of our lives, yet few of us fully utilize its power. *Yes* is the door to positive energy, to imagination, to possibility, to fulfillment. Each of us produces our unique map of reality, and in turn, each of us is the primary author of our script of life that we make up and play out as we go along. But the play is not set in stone (if we have free will), because it must interact with and accommodate the performances of others we encounter. It is an improvisation. And what is the first rule of improvisation? Say yes!

The world of *yes* may be the single most powerful secret of improvising. It allows players who have no history with one another to create a scene effortlessly, telepathically. Safety lies in knowing that your partner will go along with whatever you present. . . . Saying yes is an act of courage and optimism; it allows you to share control; it is a way to make your partner happy. *Yes* expands your world. . . . Saying yes (and following through with support) prevents you from committing a cardinal sin—blocking. Blocking comes in many forms; it is a way to control the situation instead of accepting it. We block when we say no, when we have a better idea, when we change the subject, when we correct the speaker, when we fail to listen, when we simply ignore the situation. The critic in us wakes up and runs the show.
—*Improv Wisdom: Don't Prepare, Just Show Up*, Patricia Ryan Madson

Saying yes to pleasurable invitations is easy. It is at major crossroads that we need to make more deliberate decisions.—Do we enter unknown territory by saying *yes* or play it safe by saying *no*? The reality we construct is our choice.—Are we willing to risk the unknown, and experience possibilities that at first blush seem crazy and unworkable, or do we take the safer path of comfort and the road most traveled.—Learning to say *yes* constructively to face difficult dilemmas or to solve tough problems takes practice, even for the most optimistic.—Becoming comfortable with the inherent risks of yes and adapting to "out of the box" thinking requires the deliberate use of wishing, speculating, guessing, absurdity, and approximation.

To support imaginative *yes* thinking, Synectics, a firm specializing in creativity employs the aphorisms cited below when working with individuals or groups. Their underlying assumption is that "the ultimate solutions to problems are rational; the process for thinking them is not."

**Join**, don't judge, **Probe**, don't assume, **Hunt** for objectives, don't get bogged down in problems, **Stay loose** until rigour counts, Don't justify pessimism: **be an optimist with concerns, Don't reject a weak idea,** use its faults to better it, **Fight problems, not people, Assume valuable**

**implications, Pretend the idea works, Jump to favorable conclusions**
whenever possible.
—*Imagine,* Synectics brochure

Engaging in these types of activities to seek *yes* broadens
our universe. It also enhances our ability to better answer our
*why* questions. The more perspectives we absorb, the richer
our appreciation of the world becomes. Aside from our direct
experiences, watching movies, playing video games, and reading
books are a few of the other powerful modalities that open up
additional windows for us to broaden our horizons. Fiction and
especially the use of interior monologues in modern novels gives
us a direct opportunity to vicariously witness the constructed
world, motivations, and actions of the imagined characters. In
*The Art of Fiction,* David Lodge explores 50 aspects of practicing
the art—beginning, suspense, time-shift, allegory, ending—
using quotes from select novels to illustrate his points.

I have always regarded fiction as an essentially rhetorical art
—that is to say, the novelist or short story writer persuades us to
share a certain view of the world for the duration of the reading
experience, effecting, when successful that rapt immersion in
an imagined reality that Van Gogh caught so well in the painting "The Novel Reader."

Lodge goes on to say that as in life "the novel has always
been centrally concerned with erotic attraction and desire,"
pinpointing the most fundamental, universal, and overriding
reason for getting to **yes!**

Yes when I put the rose in my hair like the Andalusian girls used or
shall I wear a red yes and how he kissed me under the Moorish wall
and I thought well as well him as another and then I asked him with
my eyes to ask again yes and then he asked me would I yes to say yes
my mountain flower and first I put my arms around him yes and drew
him down to me so he could feel my breasts all perfume yes and his
heart was going like mad and yes I said yes I will yes.
—*Ulysses,* James Joyce

*Yes indeed!*

# z

**zabaglione and**

## ze

**Zabaglione**  A dessert consisting of egg yolks, sugar, and wine whipped to a frothy texture
—OED

**Zero**  Much Ado About Nothing

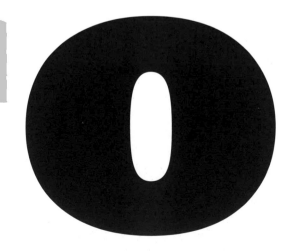

Choosing between zabaglione and zero as the subject of this "Z" essay has been a constant struggle. In many ways these "Z's" are representative of two of my lifelong interests—cooking and scientific thought. On the one hand—how fitting to finish with zabaglione, a sensual, delicious, and elegant way to end a meal, and by extension my set of muses. A riff on these sweet rewards as a celebration for the hard work and struggle that marks much of our existence seems natural. It is not a coincidence that *stressed* spelled backward is *desserts*. It would also serve as an homage to M.F.K. Fisher, whose series of alphabetical essays in *Gourmet* was an early source of inspiration for this series.

On the other hand, zero is such an intriguing and critical mathematical/scientific concept. Exploring its pivotal role in shaping our concept of the modern world is equally attractive. An essay on zero would represent the last "standing bottle of beer on the wall," having started with 26. It could also tip its hat to the other inspirational writer whom I have striven to emulate —Lewis Thomas.

In previous essays I have written about food (Karola's Kitchen) and the importance of zero (Number). After much vacillation I have decided that my best solution would be to briefly revisit different aspects of both subjects, liberally quoting both M.F.K. Fisher and Lewis Thomas. Thomas primarily expounds on the interaction of man and nature, while Fisher, using food and hunger as a springboard, explores the nuances of human relationships. Their acumen, clarity, and facility with words supply an inexhaustible quantity of insights and wisdom. I try not to read them in a crowded place but save them for a quiet corner where I can just stop, stare off into space, and think about the implications of what they have written.

It seems to me that our three basic needs, for food and security and love, are so mixed and mingled and entwined that we cannot straightly think of one without the others. So it happens that when I write of hunger, I am really writing about love and the hunger for it, and warmth and the love of it and the hunger for it. . . . and then the warmth and richness and fine reality of hunger satisfied. . . . and it is all one.
—*The Art of Eating*, M.F.K. Fisher

There in a nutshell have we Mary Frances's worldview. Although her subject invariably revolves around food and its consumption, it is just a trigger for her to display her acute observations on the human condition and her prodigious learning. Her erudite perceptions are delivered with passion, prejudice, charm, and wit. She can hold her own with any philosopher or raconteur. She raises the enjoyment of food and the reflection on it pleasures to the heights of critical analyses found in music, art, or any scientific endeavor.

But for all her astute observation she never loses sight of the primary importance of food and eating as the basis of forming and maintaining the essential bond that weaves our lives together.

Sharing food with another human being is an intimate act that should not be indulged in lightly.
—*The Art of Eating*, M.F.K. Fisher

Whether it is Easter dinner, Seder, Communion, or a simple family dinner, the ritual of eating and drinking creates a set of experiences, and in turn memories, that are uniquely poignant.

Every cuisine tells a story. Jewish food tells the story of an uprooted, migrating people and their vanished worlds. It lives in people's minds and has been kept alive because of what it evokes and represents. My own world disappeared forty years ago, but it has remained powerful in my imagination. When you are cut off from your past, the past takes a stronger hold on your emotions. . . . Every family has its own special dishes for festive occasions. Although in my day the community had become relatively homogenized and many delicacies had become obligatory on every party table, those dishes which reflected the origins of families were also there, and you could trace the family's ancestry by looking at the table. . . . Behind every recipe is a story of local tradition and daily life in far off towns and villages. It is a romantic and nostalgic subject. . . . It is about ancestral memories and looking back and holding on to old cultures, and it is about identity. It has been like that since Biblical times.
—*The Book of Jewish Food*, Claudia Roden

Many of my happiest memories are sparked by these recollections of a shared meal or the introduction to a new taste sensation. The settings range from the simplest kitchen, to a greasy spoon, to the most elegant of three-star restaurants in Paris. The food may have played a starring role at the time, but as the years pass the more powerful memories converge on the shared experience and the forged emotional bonds with those who were there at the time.

When a man is small, he loves and hates food with a ferocity which soon dims. At six years old his very bowels will heave when such a dish as creamed carrots or cold tapioca appears before him. His throat will close and spots of nausea and rage swim in his vision. . . . In the same way, some foods are delicious, and he thinks of them and tastes them with a sensuous passion which too often disappears completely with the years.

Perhaps there are little chocolate cookies as a special treat, two apiece. He eats his, all two, with an intense but delicate avidity. His small sister, Judy puts one of hers in her pocket, the smug thing. But Aunt Gwen takes a bite from each of her cookies and gives what is left of one to Judy, what is left of the other to him. She is quite calm about it.

He looks with dreadful wonder. How can she bear to do it? He could not, could not have given more than a crumb of his cookie to anyone. Perhaps even a crumb would be too big. Aunt Gwen is wonderful; she is brave and superhuman. He feels a little dizzy as he looks at the bitten cookie in his hand. How could she do it?
—*Serve It Forth*, M.F.K. Fisher

One "sensuous passion" which does not seem to abate for most of us is the desire for something sweet. Preserved fruits were introduced in the middle ages, followed by marzipan, caramels, and ice cream in the seventeenth century. The noun *dessert* originates from the French verb *desservir,* to unserve. It is literally that which is served after the others are taken away. It did not become firmly established as a course until around 1900 when Russian style service of one dish at a time, *service a la russe,* took precedence over French service, *service a la française,* where all dishes—savory and sweet—were served simultaneously. Many of the dishes we now recognize as dessert, puddings and pies, were originally meat-based and only evolved to full-fledged sweets in the nineteenth century. Much of Europe is still in the habit of ending a meal with a bit of cheese and/or fruit rather than a fanciful confection. The origin of many an elaborate dessert comes from commemorating a celebratory occasion and/or feast day of which the Italians are past masters.

Although the craving remains forever, much as for a reformed smoker, many deny themselves the satisfaction of partaking in a gratifying culinary finale for reasons dietary, ascetic, or whatever.

I prefer to regard a dessert as I would imagine the perfect woman: subtle, a little bittersweet, not blowsy and extroverted. Delicately made up, not highly rouged. Holding back, not exposing everything and, of course, with a flavor that lasts.
—Graham Kerr

Seize the moment. Remember all those women on the Titanic who waved off the dessert cart.
—Erma Bombeck

Chocolate seems to be the odds-on favorite ingredient.

If any man has drunk a little too deeply from the cup of physical pleasure; if he has spent too much time at his desk that should have been spent asleep; if his fine spirits have become temporarily dulled; if he finds the air too damp, the minutes too slow, and the atmosphere too heavy to withstand; if he is obsessed by a fixed idea which bars him from any freedom of thought: if he is any of these poor creatures, we say, let him be given a good pint of amber-flavored chocolate . . . and marvels will be performed.
—Jean Anthelme Brillat-Savarin, translated by M.F.K. Fisher

Great desserts, more than any other part of the meal, are remembered for their texture as much as their taste. Describing a dessert without a consistency report—light as a feather, moist, dense, smooth as silk, heavenly—is invariably incomplete. "Hau-gum," or mouth feel, is as essential in Chinese and other Asian cooking as is flavor. The science of mouth feel has become an essential part of all aspects of Western food technology, especially within the molecular gastronomy movement (Ferran Adrià at El Bulli (now closed), Grant Achatz at Alinea, and Thomas Keller at The French Laundry). It has essentially turned the kitchen into a chemistry lab. Coupled with an ever-deeper understanding of the science of cooking (for example, see Harold McGee, *On Food and Cooking: The Science and Lore of the Kitchen*) these new culinary geniuses can literally make a dish explode in your mouth. (This exquisite combination of kitchen art and science is not to be confused with the industrial version, which seeks a "bliss point" for junk food—that perfect combination of sugar, salt, fat, crunch, and mouth feel to keep convenience store and supermarket cash registers ringing.)

But the culinary alchemy that produces transcendental results has long been intuitively known by the great chefs of the past, especially when it comes to dessert. Unlike a majority of recipes where ad libs and variations are often tolerated without consequence, expert baking and dessert-making requires strict adherence to proportion, measurement, and technique to produce the desired results. Note the fine demarcations between soft ball, hard ball, soft crack, and hard crack on a candy thermometer. The slightest variation can make a soufflé fall, pastry cream turn to glop, or a cake become leaden. Producing remarkable results is an art.

A great dessert can also be simply a piece of fruit. M.F.K. Fisher devotes an entire essay to her endless pleasure of preparing and eating a tangerine:

Almost every person has something secret he likes to eat. He is downright furtive about it usually, or mentions it only in a kind of conscious self-amusement, as one who admits too quickly. . . . I discovered how to eat little dried sections of tangerine. My pleasure in them is subtle and voluptuous and quite inexplicable. . . . I cannot tell you why they are so magical. Perhaps it is the little shell, thin as the layer of enamel on a Chinese bowl that crackles so tinily, so ultimately under your teeth. Or the rush of cold pulp just after it. Or the perfume. I cannot tell.
—*Serve It Forth*

And that finally brings me to my secret pleasure, ethereal zabaglione. Known in France as *sabayon*, it is one of the simplest, lightest, tastiest, and satisfying of all desserts I know. Consisting of only three ordinary ingredients (eggs, sugar, and spirits), when combined under the proper heat and flick of the wrist, a magical transformation occurs in no time.

**Zabaglione**

4 egg yolks

4 teaspoons sugar

4 tablespoons Marsala, Grand Marnier, or Cointreau

Carefully whisk all ingredients over simmering water in a double boiler until thickened like pudding. Take on and off the heat while cooking so as not to scramble the eggs. Serve warm in wine glasses or over your favorite berries. Enjoy!

TRY IT. If you have made it before, all the better. If you have not, it is one of the wonders of the dessert world.

Zabaglione is also compelling to me because it is primarily made with eggs, objects that some call perfect. Using eggs as a bridge I will now attempt to perform an expositional tap dance to my reflections on zero. The easiest way to effect that transition would be to point out that zeros are often referred to as goose eggs, especially in the context of baseball scorekeeping. But eggs are much more fascinating. Their function, nutritional value, and shape make them one of the most mysterious and remarkable of universal symbols. Birth, renewal, fragility, spring, potential, and the Earth are among the multitude of meanings associated with eggs. The beautiful aesthetic outer shape of an intact egg gives no clue to what is happening inside. They are sealed units in which magical transformations occur hidden from view. With their quiet tranquility, eggs do not reveal their secrets unless or until their shells are cracked.

Probably one of the most private things in the world is an egg until it is broken
—*Serve It Forth*, M.F.K. Fisher

The same principles of encapsulation can be extended to how little we know about the cosmos, nature, corporations, individuals, and ourselves. Lewis Thomas understands our attempt to explain our surroundings as unique to our species. He is in awe of the process and yet constantly reminds us of how narrow and incomplete our penetration and understanding of nature's shell, and the infinitesimal probability of our existence.

We are, perhaps, uniquely among the earth's creatures, the worrying animal. We worry away our lives, fearing the future, discontent with the present, unable to take in the idea of dying, unable to sit still. . . . It is in our genes to understand the universe if we can, to keep trying even if we cannot, and to be enchanted by the act of learning all the way. . . . The body of science is not, as it is sometimes thought, a huge coherent mass of facts, neatly arranged in sequence, each one attached to the next by a logical string. In truth, whenever we discover a new fact it involves the elimination of old ones. We are always, as it turns out, fundamentally in error.

   Science, especially twentieth-century science, has provided us with a glimpse of something we never really knew before, the revelation of human ignorance. We have been used to the belief, down one century after another, that we more or less comprehend everything, bar one or two mysteries, like the mental processes of our gods. Every age, not just the eighteenth century, regarded itself as the Age of Reason, and we have never lacked for explanations of the world and its ways. Now, we are being brought up short, and this has been the work of science. . . . Statistically the probability of any one of us being here is so small that you would think the mere fact of existence would keep us all in a contented dazzlement of surprise. We are alive against the stupendous odds of genetics, infinitely outnumbered by all the alternates who might, except for luck, be in our places.
—*Late Night Thoughts on Listening to Mahler's Ninth Symphony*, Lewis Thomas


   The paradox in Thomas's observations is that the more we are able to penetrate the workings of nature, the more we become aware of our profound lack of importance in the greater scheme of things and our woeful understanding of its mechanisms.
   So it was with the acceptance of zero. If you are like me, you have given almost zero thought to the significance of zero. Why waste time thinking about nothing when there is so much else of importance to take up my precious mental energy and time? Zero is valueless. In fact just the opposite is true. This humble symbol ranks among the most necessary, powerful, and useful of all existing concepts. As X gets my vote for the most interesting letter, o—representing nothing, naught, zilch—gets my nod as the most interesting and influential of all numbers and symbols. Conceived in all probability as the symbol for an empty column on a

counting board, the Indian sunya was destined to become the turning point in a development without which the progress of modern science, industry, and commerce is inconceivable. And the influence of this great discovery was by no means confined to arithmetic. By paving the way to a generalized number concept, it played a fundamental role in practically every branch of mathematics. In the history of culture the discovery of zero will always stand out as one of the greatest single achievements of the human race.

—*Number: The Language of Science*, Tobias Dantzig

In its quiet way zero has played an essential role in all aspects of human endeavor. It is a critical character in shaping the conception of our world. Philosophers have long wrestled with the origins of existence. How the universe and life came to exist has been a perplexing concern from ancient times to the present. Is it possible that it all emerged from a void? The egg plays a whimsical role in posing this classical causality dilemma about "the mere fact of our existence." Which came first: the chicken or the egg? The chosen answer to the quandary has a dramatic effect on one's beliefs and worldview. Contemporary evolutionists think that Darwin put the answer to rest, while Creationists keep the battle ever alive. Aristotle's resolution, which played a dominant role in shaping and controlling western thought on the matter until late into the seventeenth century, was to conclude that you couldn't create something out of nothing. Therefore birds, eggs, and an encapsulated universe always existed. The existence of a void was inconceivable. This Aristotelian nutshell worldview, which rejected the concept of a time and a place when and where nothing existed, as well as an infinite universe, dramatically affected the incorporation of the concept of zero and its counterpart—infinity—in European thinking.

The scientific achievements that finally overwhelmed the dogmatic Aristotelian views of the church were due in large part to technological breakthroughs like printing and the telescope. Of equal and perhaps even greater importance were the constant advancements made in mathematics. The ancient Greeks were enthralled with numbers and shapes. The mathematical proofs of Pythagoras, and myriad of others, are still key in shaping the western conception of the world. The Babylonians were highly skilled in computation and were among the first to utilize a marker for zero in their numerical notation. Vestiges of the Babylonian's base 60 system are still extant in the way we measure time. Perhaps, because they were unhindered by the strictures of Western thought/theology, the most sophisticated and oldest evidence of advanced mathematical thinking is to be found in the East, notably in Persia and India. The Indian Bakhshali Manuscript, which may date back to AD 350, is thought to contain the first documented use of zero. By the ninth and tenth centuries, Persian and Hindi treatises on algebra and the decimal system, most notably by Al-Khwarizmi and Al-Uqlidisi, abounded. The introduction into western Europe of the concept of zero along with the modern Hindi-Arabic decimal system is attributed to the 1202 publication of Fibonacci's *Liber Abaci*—(The Book of the Abacus). Although counting boards that implicitly utilized zero were widely used in Medieval times, it would still take almost four more centuries for the positional decimal system with its all-important zero to replace the cumbersome Roman numerals in daily commerce.

Through the ages, mathematics has provided the language and framework that enables scientists to explore, predict, and discover the nature of reality. Galileo once stated that, "Nature's great book is written in mathematical symbols," and Einstein wondered, "How is it possible that mathematics, a product of human thought that is independent of experience, fits so excellently the objects of physical reality?" The history of mathematics is fascinating (at least to me), and is replete with conceptual breakthroughs. Among the most important and impactful is the work of the seventeenth century geniuses. Descartes's analytic geometry and Newton and/or Leibnitz's (depending who you believe got there first) calculus, completely revolutionized the way we look at and interact with nature. With their advent the processes of the real world could be quantifiably described by real numbers and their functional relationships.

In both developments zero played a fundamental role. Analytic geometry enabled algebra to be applied to geometric problems. By mapping functions using 0,0 as their origin and reference point, Cartesian coordinates unified two classic fields of mathematics and greatly fortified each of them. Calculus emerged as a measure of the instantaneous rate of change (distance/time) of a moving object. To accurately solve the problem required grappling with the one exception to arithmetic operations: the inability to divide by zero. Addition, subtraction, multiplication, and division apply uniformly to all numbers with one exception—the indeterminacy of dividing by zero. Since instantaneous essentially means that the value of time is set to zero, the use of ordinary then known methods to calculate the ratio of distance/time were *verboten*. With calculus, both Newton and Leibnitz successfully provided solutions to the problem. Both actually finessed the anomaly of zero division in their formulations. Thirty years later L'Hospital finally came up with the concept of limits to resolve the issue. Calculus allowed the accurate description and measurement of the laws of motion, including the celestial bodies. Today calculus is universally used in every field of scientific endeavor—biology, physics, economics, sociology, etc. It guides spacecraft, predicts population growth, and analyzes the spread of disease. The modern world could not function without it.

For me, the Information Age is one of the most striking examples of how a theoretical mathematical conception (involving the concept of zero) was transformed and applied to the practical workings of the world. In 1854, the English mathematician George Boole published *An Investigation of the Laws of Thought, on Which Are Founded the Mathematical Theories of Logic and Probabilities.* Although Boole himself looked upon his treatise as "the most valuable contribution that I have made or am likely to make to [s]cience," he had no idea of its ultimate value. "Boolean Algebra" involves only two quantities, 0 and 1, and only three operations—and, or, and not. Boole's breakthrough was to assign logical, not numerical values, to 0 and 1. By having them symbolize "on" or "off " or "true" or "false" Boole ingeniously employed the rigor of algebra to provide a systemic grammatical framework for solving logic problems. An interesting piece of work, but rather arcane. And then, almost a century later, Claude Shannon demonstrated in his master's thesis that Boole's algebra could be used to design and optimize telephone switching circuits. The rest is history.

Along with the work of Turing, Weiner, von Neumann, and others, Shannon's insights, as well as his subsequent work on Information Theory, a discipline that provides the theoretical framework for the codification, storage, transmission, and processing of data/messages, laid the foundation for the digital age. The reduction of circuits and their operation to the simplicity of switching between two states (off and on) enabled the development of ever faster and extremely reliable machines. Buildings filled with mechanical relay switches have been transformed and replaced by fingernail-size chips that contain billions of switches that can be turned on and off at speeds approaching a trillion times a second. For my first job out of college I programmed an IBM computer that contained 58,000 vacuum tubes and filled a four-story building with its mainframe, tape drives, and massive drum memories. These monsters have morphed into the infinitesimal integrated circuits that enable, underpin, and increasingly magnify the capability of our current technological environment—digital computers wedded to a web of high-speed communications. Whether it is a massive data center, a desktop computer, or a smartphone, the internal workings—instructions, data, and circuitry—in "digital computers" are all reliant on codes consisting of zeros and ones, binary numbers represented in switching circuits that toggle between off (0) and on (1). Wireless transmission we now so easily take for granted also consists of a never-ending stream of zeros and ones. At this very moment you are surrounded by billions upon billions of zeros and ones invisibly floating in the air all around you. Turning on a device—television, smart phone, radio—allows you to intercept and transform them so you can instantly view, listen, and interact with their message. Zero represents half the reality of this digital domain. A miraculous achievement.

Every aspect of our lives and human endeavor has been transformed. Art, music, photography, woodworking, and architecture all rely on the digital encoding and transmission of data. Zero, as the basis for coding, sending, and deciphering signals has also taken on a pivotal role in almost every aspect of science. Neurophysiology studies how nerve cells switch on and off and is urgently trying to solve the memory codification system of the human brain. The decoding and the mapping of the human genome, and the mechanisms that turn genes on and off in a DNA molecule have transformed biology. Most notably physics has been revolutionized by the theory of relativity and quantum mechanics. Black holes, dark matter, and the energy of a vacuum all involve phenomena related to the existence of a zero state. Like Lewis Thomas, I leave these paradoxes and mysteries to those who can comprehend and understand them.

Starting from nothing, zero has become an inescapable part of our language and our everyday experience and description of the world. Mega, micro, milli, million, billion, infinity, light year, centigrade, Fahrenheit, abyss, void, vacuum, zero in on, zero tolerance, ground zero, zero-zero visibility, vanishing point, and interval are but a few of the prefixes and descriptors that relate to some aspect or value of zero. Phrases about nothing are also in constant use—it has nothing to do with me, there is nothing new in this world, nothing's changed, nothing ventured nothing gained, he was nothing to me. Zero also plays a dual role in signaling the Alpha and/or the Omega— the beginning or the end of an endeavor. Presently it represents the Omega of my odyssey through the alphabet. I have counted down from 26 to zero. It has been an incredible journey. I have renewed old friendships, have strengthened the relationships I hold dear, and have made a host of new friends. I cannot thank you all enough for your interest, encouragement, feedback, criticisms, and suggestions.

I leave you with a morsel of Wallace Stevens to savor, and one of my favorite stories about René Descartes, the brilliant seventeenth-century philosopher and mathematician.

I do not know which to prefer,
The beauty of inflections
Or the beauty of innuendoes,
The blackbird whistling
Or just after.

Descartes was invited to a sumptuous dinner that ended with his favorite dessert, Zabaglione (what a coincidence!). His hostess, noting his enjoyment and empty plate, inquired if he would like a second helping. After much thought René replied, "I think not," and instantly vanished.

Adieu

## About the typefaces

This book was set in FF Scala, an old style, humanist, serif typeface designed by Dutch typeface designer Martin Majoor in 1990 for the Muziekcentrum Vredenburg in Utrecht, the Netherlands. The FF Scala font family was named for the Teatro alla Scala (1776–78) in Milan, Italy. Like many contemporary Dutch serif faces, FF Scala is not an academic revival of a single historic typeface but shows influences of several historic models. Similarities can be seen with William Addison Dwiggins' 1935 design for the typeface Electra in its clarity of form, and rhythmic, highly calligraphic italics. Eric Gill's 1931 typeface Joanna (released by Monotype Corporation in 1937), with its old style armature but nearly square serifs is also similar in its nearly mono-weighted stroke width.

Section heads, quotations, and folios are set in FF Scala Sans, a humanist sans-serif typeface designed by Dutch designer Martin Majoor in 1993 for the Vredenburg Music Center in Utrecht, the Netherlands. It was designed as a companion to Majoor's earlier serif old style typeface FF Scala, designed in 1990.

The introductory typeface for each chapter was chosen for its aesthetic as well as its name; each font begins with the letter of the alphabet it represents—Akzidenz-Grotesk for "A," Bodoni for "B" and so on.

**ABCDEFGHIJKLMNOPQRSTUVWXYZ**
**abcdefghijklmnopqrstuvwxyz**

**Akzidenz-Grotesk is a grotesque (early sans-serif) typeface originally released by the Berthold Type Foundry in 1896 under the name Accidenz-Grotesk. It influenced many later neo-grotesque typefaces after 1950.**

ABCDEFGHIJKLMNOPQRSTUVWXYZ
abcdefghijklmnopqrstuvwxyz

Bodoni is a series of serif typefaces first designed by Giambattista Bodoni (1740–1813) in 1798. The typeface is classified as Didone modern. Bodoni followed the ideas of John Baskerville, as found in the printing type Baskerville: increased stroke contrast and a more vertical, slightly condensed, upper case; but took them to a more extreme conclusion. Bodoni had a long career and his designs evolved and varied, ending with a typeface of narrower underlying structure with flat, unbracketed serifs, extreme contrast between thick and thin strokes, and an overall geometric construction.

ABCDEFGHIJKLMNOPQRSTUVWXYZ
abcdefghijklmnopqrstuvwxyz

Cochin is a transitional serif typeface. It was originally produced in 1912 by Georges Peignot for the Paris foundry Deberny & Peignot and was based on the copperplate engravings of French artist Nicolas Cochin, from which the typeface also takes its name. In 1977 Cochin was adapted and expanded by Matthew Carter for Linotype. The font has a small x-height with long ascenders.

ABCDEFGHIJKLMNOPQRSTUVWXYZ
abcdefghijklmnopqrstuvwxyz

DIN 1451 is a realist sans-serif typeface that is widely used for traffic, administrative and technical applications. It was defined by the German standards body DIN-Deutsches Institut für Normung (German Institute for Standardization) in the standard sheet DIN 1451-Schriften (typefaces) in 1931.

ABCDEFGHIJKLMNOPQRSTUVWXYZ
abcdefghijklmnopqrstuvwxyz

Ehrhardt is an old-style serif typeface that is believed to have been
designed by Miklós (Nicholas) Tótfalusi Kis, who was eventually
credited with the design of the Janson typeface. From 1937 to 1938,
the Monotype corporation recut the type for modern-day usage.
Usage includes the Penguin 60s series of books that were published
to commemorate that company's 60th anniversary.

**ABCDEFGHIJKLMNOPQRSTUVWXYZ**
**abcdefghijklmnopqrstuvwxyz**

Futura is a geometric sans-serif typeface designed in 1927
by Paul Renner. It was designed as a contribution on the
New Frankfurt project. It is based on geometric shapes that
became representative of visual elements of the Bauhaus
design style of 1919–1933

ABCDEFGHIJKLMNOPQRSTUVWXYZ
abcdefghijklmnopqrstuvwxyz

Georgia is a transitional serif typeface designed in 1993 by
Matthew Carter and hinted by Tom Rickner for the Microsoft
Corporation, as the serif companion to the first Microsoft sans-
serif screen font, Verdana. Microsoft released the initial version
of the font on November 1, 1996, as part of the core fonts for the
Web collection. Georgia is designed for clarity on a computer
monitor even at small sizes, partially effective due to a large
x-height. The typeface is named after a tabloid headline titled
"Alien heads found in Georgia."

ABCDEFGHIJKLMNOPQRSTUVWXYZ
abcdefghijklmnopqrstuvwxyz

Helvetica was developed in 1957 by Max Miedinger with Eduard
Hoffmann at the Haas'sche Schriftgiesserei (Haas Type Foundry) of
Münchenstein, Switzerland. Haas set out to design a new sans-serif
typeface that could compete with the successful Akzidenz-Grotesk
in the Swiss market. Originally called Neue Haas Grotesk, its design

was based on Schelter-Grotesk and Haas Normal Grotesk. The aim of the new design was to create a neutral typeface that had great clarity, no intrinsic meaning in its form, and could be used on a wide variety of signage.

ABCDEFGHIJKLMNOPQRSTUVWXYZ
abcdefghijklmnopqrstuvwxyz

Industrial 736 was designed by Bitstream and is very similar to the font Torino.

ABCDEFGHIJKLMNOPQRSTUVWXYZ
abcdefghijklmnopqrstuvwxyz

Joanna is a transitional serif typeface designed by Eric Gill (1882–1940) in the period 1930–31, and named for one of his daughters. The typeface was originally designed for proprietary use by Gill's printing shop Hague & Gill. The type was first produced in a small quantity by the Caslon Foundry for hand composition. It was eventually licensed for public release by the Monotype foundry in 1937.

ABCDEFGHIJKLMNOPQRSTUVWXYZ
abcdefghijklmnopqrstuvwxyz

Kabel is a geometric sans-serif typeface designed by German typeface designer Rudolf Koch, and released by the Klingspor foundry in 1927. Like its contemporary Futura it bears influence of two earlier geometric sans-serif typefaces; the 1919 Feder Schrift, drawn by Jakob Erbar, and moreso his 1922 design called Erbar.

ABCDEFGHIJKLMNOPQRSTUVWXYZ
abcdefghijklmnopqrstuvwxyz

Lucida Grande is a humanist sans-serif typeface. It is a member of the Lucida family of typefaces designed by Charles Bigelow and Kris Holmes. It has been used throughout Mac OS X user interface since 1999, as well as in Safari for Windows up to the browser's version 3.2.3 released on 12 May 2009.

ABCDEFGHIJKLMNOPQRSTUVWXYZ
abcdefghijklmnopqrstuvwxyz

Myriad is a humanist sans-serif typeface designed by Robert Slimbach and Carol Twombly for Adobe Systems. The typeface is best known for its usage by Apple Inc., replacing Apple Garamond as Apple's corporate font since 2002. Myriad is easily distinguished from other sans-serif fonts due to its special "y" descender (tail) and slanting "e" cut. Myriad is similar to Frutiger.

ABCDEFGHIJKLMNOPQRSTUVWXYZ
abcdefghijklmnopqrstuvwxyz

News Gothic is a realist sans-serif typeface designed by Morris Fuller Benton, and released by the American Type Founders (ATF) in 1908. The typeface was originally drawn in two lighter weights, a medium text weight using the title News Gothic, and a closely related light weight marketed under the name Lightline Gothic. The typeface family was enlarged in 1958 with the addition of two bold weights. News Gothic is similar in proportion and structure to Franklin Gothic also designed by Benton.

ABCDEFGHIJKLMNOPQRSTUVWXYZ
abcdefghijklmnopqrstuvwxyz

Optima is a humanist sans-serif typeface designed by Hermann Zapf between 1952 and 1955 for the D. Stempel AG foundry, Frankfurt, Germany.

ABCDEFGHIJKLMNOPQRSTUVWXYZ

PIONEER WAS DESIGNED BY RONNE BONDER AND TOM CARNASE IN 1970.

ABCDEFGHIJKLMNOPQRSTUVWXYZ
abcdefghijklmnopqrstuvwxyz

Quorum is hybrid between serif and sans-serif styles.
Designed by Ray Baker in 1977.

**ABCDEFGHIJKLMNOPQRSTUVWXYZ**
**abcdefghijklmnopqrstuvwxyz**

Rockwell is a serif typeface belonging to the classification slab serif, or Egyptian, where the serifs are unbracketed and similar in weight to the horizontal strokes of the letters. The typeface was designed at the Monotype foundry's in-house design studio in 1934.

ABCDEFGHIJKLMNOPQRSTUVWXYZ
abcdefghijklmnopqrstuvwxyz

Sabon is an old style serif typeface designed by the German-born typographer and designer Jan Tschichold (1902–1974) in the period 1964–1967. The typeface was released jointly by the Linotype, Monotype, and Stempel type foundries in 1967.

ABCDEFGHIJKLMNOPQRSTUVWXYZ

TRAJAN IS AN OLD STYLE SERIF TYPEFACE DESIGNED IN 1989 BY CAROL TWOMBLY FOR ADOBE. THE DESIGN IS BASED ON THE LETTERFORMS OF CAPITALIS MONUMENTALIS OR ROMAN SQUARE CAPITALS, AS USED FOR THE INSCRIPTION AT THE BASE OF TRAJAN'S COLUMN FROM WHICH THE TYPEFACE TAKES ITS NAME.

# ABCDEFGHIJKLMNOPQRSTUVWXYZ
## abcdefghijklmnopqrstuvwxyz

Univers is the name of a realist sans-serif typeface designed by Adrian Frutiger in 1954. It is one of a group of neo-grotesque sans-serif typefaces, all released in 1957, that includes Folio and Neue Haas Grotesk (later renamed Helvetica). These three faces are sometimes confused with each other because each is based on the 1898 typeface Akzidenz-Grotesk. These typefaces figure prominently in the Swiss Style of graphic design.

# ABCDEFGHIJKLMNOPQRSTUVWXYZ
## abcdefghijklmnopqrstuvwxyz

Vista Slab was designed in 2008 by Xavier Dupré. It belongs to the Vista sans family, The designer's intention was to create a typeface family for text and display that would combine the humanist appeal of calligraphic forms with the pragmatic simplicity of the sans.

# ABCDEFGHIJKLMNOPQRSTUVWXYZ
## abcdefghijklmnopqrstuvwxyz

Weidemann font's original name was Biblica, as it was designed for the collaboration of the Catholic and Protestant churches in the publication of a bible. The mass of text for which the font was intended meant that many characters needed to fit onto one line but without rendering the words illegible. Thus, narrow spaces do not compromise the legibility or the elegance of Weidemann.

## ABCDEFGHIJKLMNOPQRSTUVWXYZ
## abcdefghijklmnopqrstuvwxyz

Xenia was designed for ParaType in 1990 by Lyubov Kuznetsova. A bold square-serif style used in advertising and display typography. The decorative style was added in 1993 by Lyubov Kuznetsova and Alexander Tarbeev.

## ABCDEFGHIJKLMNOPQRSTUVWXYZ

YEARBOOK WAS DESIGNED BY MONOTYPE DESIGN STUDIO IN 1994.

## ABCDEFGHIJKLMNOPQRSTUVWXYZ
## abcdefghijklmnopqrstuvwxyz

Zurich was designed by Bitstream and is very similar to Helvetica.

## About the author

Stephen Lorch has been an Independent Management Consultant to industry, government/military, foundations, museums, and universities for over 35 years. Associated for over 40 years with Harvard University, and its affiliated institutions, as a project director, researcher and clinician, he has extensive experience as a lecturer at the university and post-graduate level on management strategy, organizational development, information systems, and executive coaching. He currently lives with his wife Jane in Little Compton, Rhode Island. Visit www.offthetopofmyheadessays.com.

## About the book designer

Jean Wilcox has been designing books for over 25 years, from university publications to major museum exhibition catalogs. She was the assistant manager in the renowned graphic design department of The MIT Press before launching Wilcox Design in 2000. Jean's design work has been recognized with awards and citations from leading graphic arts organizations and design publications. Visit www.wilcoxinc.com.